# VOLUME II: THE WAY OF THE SEEDED EARTH

## PART 1

## THE SACRIFICE

# JOSEPH CAMPBELL

## HISTORICAL ATLAS OF WORLD MYTHOLOGY

# VOLUME II

# THE WAY
# OF THE SEEDED
# EARTH

## PART 1

# THE SACRIFICE

HARPER & ROW, PUBLISHERS   NEW YORK

CAMBRIDGE, PHILADELPHIA, SAN FRANCISCO, LONDON
MEXICO CITY, SAO PAULO, SINGAPORE, SYDNEY

FRONTISPIECE

**1.** Yamunā Devī, goddess of the river Jumna. Elūrā, Kailāsanātha compound, A.D. 750–850. Standing among lotuses, supported by a great tortoise, the goddess of the river Jumna appears within the frame of a *makara toraṇa*. The makaras (crocodilelike monsters symbolic of the sources of the flowing waters of life) are ridden by dwarf *yakshas* (earth spirits of fertility and wealth), while pouring into their open mouths from the mouths of two back-to-back makara heads above, streams of the waters of her life-supporting river shape the gateway (*toraṇa*) of the deity's beneficent apparition

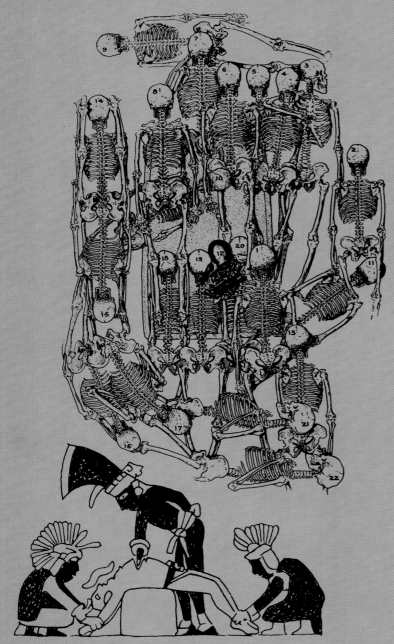

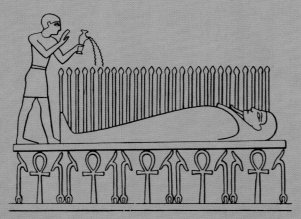

Library of Congress Cataloging-in-Publication Data: Campbell, Joseph, 1904–1987. Historical atlas of world mythology. Includes bibliographical references and indexes. Contents: v.1. The way of the animal powers. pt.1. Mythologies of the primitive hunters and gatherers. pt.2. Mythologies of the great hunt—v.2. The way of the seeded earth. pt.1. The sacrifice. I. Mythology. I. Title. BL311.C26 1988 291.1'3 87-40007
ISBN 0-06-055150-X (v.2, pt.1)        88 89 90 91 92 10 9 8 7 6 5 4 3 2 1
ISBN 0-06-096350-6 (v.2, pt.1) (pbk.) 88 89 90 91 92 10 9 8 7 6 5 4 3 2 1

# TABLE OF CONTENTS

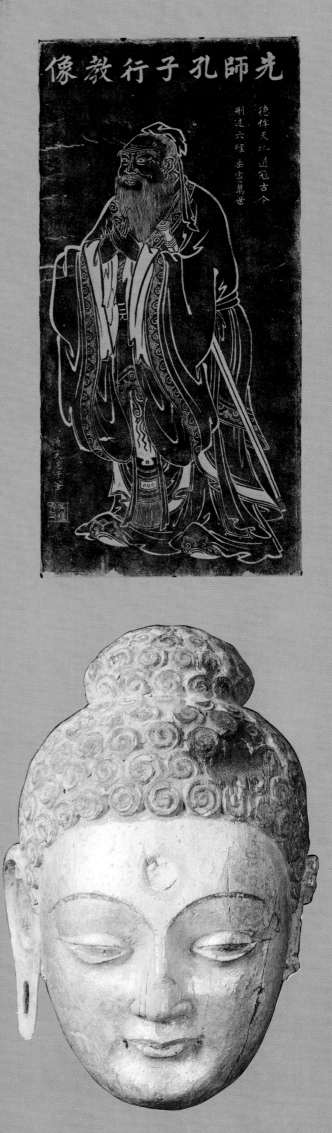

# PROLOGUE

"What descends to the earth as the breath of passion returns to heaven in the spirit of contemplation."[1]

*(Edgar Wind)*

**2.** "Primavera," by Sandro Botticelli, tempera on wood, 2.1 × 3.2 m. (7 ft. × 10 ft. 6 in.), 1477–78, Uffizi, Florence.

At the touch of Zephyr, the spring breeze (right), the earth-nymph Chloris breathes flowers and at the touch of her hands Flora's garment bursts into bloom. Cupid, though blindfolded, aims accurately at the Grace "Chastity," into whose eyes "Delight" with heaving bosom gazes, while "Beauty," taking their hands, holds the two in balance. These three, in their round, reveal aspects of the play through human feeling of the will of Venus (center); as do Flora, Chloris and Zephyr, the force of her will in nature. Mercury (left), moved likewise by her influence, elevates his gaze and wand to the heavens.

3.

## OF THE WILL IN NATURE

"The seeds of a flowering plant show under the microscope two sheath leaves, which are to form and protect the young sprout growing with its organs of life-support and -reproduction toward the light. And there is in addition a third sheath, containing the future root, which tells us that the plant is destined irrevocably to become once again part of a landscape. In higher animals we observe, in contrast, that the fertilized egg forms in the first hours of its individualized existence an outer sheath by which the living substance of its future organs of support and reproduction (the plant element in the animal) is enclosed and shut off from the mother body and *all the rest of the world.* This outer sheath establishes the essential character of animal existence and distinguishes," states Spengler in conclusion of this observation, "the second way in which life has evolved upon this earth."[1]

In human consciousness the contrasting claims of these separated ways of the one living tide that moves within us all are experienced as conflicting urges, and in the myths and rites of the greatly differing tribes and nations of this now fully inhabited planet, the irreducible conflict between the plant element and the animal of our biology has been resolved generally in terms favoring either one or the other of these two manners of life.

"Consider," Spengler writes, "the flowers at nightfall as with the setting sun they close, one after another. There is about the moment something uncanny that sinks into one: a disturbing sense of mystery before this blind, dreamlike, earthbound manner of being. The mute forest, the silent meadow, that thicket and this twining vine, do not stir of themselves. It is the wind that plays with them. Only the little gnat is free. It dances still in the evening light. It moves whither it will.

"A plant is nothing of itself. It forms a part of the landscape in which chance made it take root. The twilight, the chill, and the closing of every flower: this is not cause and effect, not danger and willed response, but a single process of nature that is taking place around, with, and within the plant. The individual is not free to look out for itself, to will for itself, or to choose.

"But an animal can choose. It is released from the bondage of all the rest of the world. That swarm of gnats there dancing still on our walkway; a solitary bird still flying through the evening; a fox approaching stealthily a nest: these are *little worlds for themselves within another, larger world.* In a drop of water, an infusorian invisible to the human eye, though it lives but a second, with but a tiny corner of this little drop as its theater, is *free and independent in the face of the universe.* The gigantic oak upon one of whose leaves the droplet hangs—is not.

"Bondage and independence: that finally is the deepest differentiating feature of all vegetable and animal existence. And yet only the plant is wholly what it is. In the being of an animal there is something dual. A plant is nothing but a plant; an animal is a plant and yet something more. The herd huddling together trembling in the knowledge of some danger; a weeping child clinging to its mother; the individual in despair striving to find a way to his God: all such are seeking to return from life in freedom to that vegetal bondage out of which they had been emancipated into solitude."[2]

Throughout those timeless Paleolithic ages of *Homo sapiens'* first appearances among the animals of the continents of this earth (the millennia of what Jamake Highwater has called the "primal mind"),[3] the principal determinant of the recently evolved human brain's interpretation of life—which had formerly been lived simply on impulse—was the ungainsayable ordeal of the hunt: immediate confrontation with another dangerous animal in the life-supporting task of delivering death. Leo Frobenius, in his fundamental publication *Paideuma* (1921),[4] employed the Greek term from which our own word "pedagogy" is derived (παιδἄγωγια, "education"; παιδευμα, "that which is reared up or educated, nursling, pupil, scholar") to characterize the pedagogical effect of environmental factors on the structuring of human life and thought, whether (1) upon those open animal plains of the Paleolithic Great Hunt, where the lessons for human life were derived from the observation of animals, or (2) in the enclosing jungles of the torrid equatorial zone, where the model for life was of the earthborn, teeming plant world (see I.1: 40–41).

No consistent, clearly separating line between the natures of man and beast, such as we find, for example, in Genesis 1:26–30, was ever drawn in these mythologies; for the two were experienced as of the one life which informs all things: the earth; the mountains; the winds, sun, moon, and stars; the rivers, the forests, and the sea. Moreover, in any such so-called animistic view there is no such thing as absolute death, only a passing of individuals back and forth, as it were, through a veil or screen of visibility, until—for one reason or another—they dissolve into an undifferentiated ground that is not of death, but of potential life, out of which new individuals appear. In such early mythologies the mythic figures that most closely resemble the creator-gods of the later mythological orders are not properly *creators*, but *world shapers*, experimenting and often blundering, who make their appearances in landscapes already present but incomplete, composed of a substance rather soft that can be manipulated and, in one shape or another, brought to life. Death comes into the world of these animated shapes as a consequence, either of a deliberate choice or act on someone's part, or in consequence of a blunder; but it is never quite extinction. For the so-called dead inhabit villages of their own and may return either as newborn infants or as ghosts.

Invisibles of a second sort are thought to inhabit (or, indeed, to be) the sun, the moon, the earth, the sky, certain mountain peaks and bodies of water, particular stones, or even spearpoints well made. These are experienced as felt presences, but may also be envisioned, whether in human or in some animal form, either of waking life or of dream. All animals in their species are experienced as powers of this kind, more immediately in accord with the will in nature than are human beings. For as told to Natalie Curtis (about 1904) by the Pawnee chieftain Letakots-Lesa (see I.1: 8): "In the beginning of all things, wisdom and knowledge were with the animals, for Tirawa, the One Above, did not speak directly to man. He sent certain animals to tell man that he showed himself through the beasts, and that from them, and from the stars and the sun and the moon man should learn."[5]

"Animals," states Goethe in his last letter to Wilhelm von Humboldt, March 13, 1832, "are instructed by their organs. So remarked the ancients. But likewise, I should add, are human beings, who, however, have the advantage of being able, in return, to instruct their organs."[6]

"And how wonderful the instructions are which animals receive from their organs may be judged," states Walter F. Otto in comment on this observation, "from their so-called instinctual actions, which are frequently so ingenious that one might impute to animals detailed knowledge and forethought, whereas no such knowing or thinking, in our sense, can possibly have been present. The knowledge which to us is inconceivable resides in the organs themselves, which are qualified by their very structure to execute actions which, if they had been of conscious human intention, should have called for the most thoroughgoing schooling and reflection. We watch a female bird that has been rendered fertile for the first time building the nest in which her young are to be raised. And we are even more amazed when her male partner joins her in the mysterious performance. But there are many even more astonishing feats of instinctive animal behavior, which surpass by far anything that our human consciousness and learning can achieve."[7]

Like the sun, the moon, and the stars, animals are aspects of the natural order, every species endowed with a power of its own, which is manifest in its individuals. Any given eagle, buffalo, salmon, or raven, may be regarded and experienced, therefore, either in the secular way, as *this* eagle, *this* buffalo, *this* fish, *this* raven, or in a sacred way, as *the* eagle, *the* buffalo, and so on. In myths, folktales, and fables, certain animals usually appear in the character of their species: Raven, Jaguar, and Monitor Lizard, for example. In the context, however, of the necessities of the hunt, animals are slaughtered in the practical, secular way, for food. A psychology of tension is thereby established on many levels, which it is the function of hunting rituals and their mythologies to resolve; the model in nature being the analogy of the carnivore (the lion, the eagle, the serpent, the wolf) killing and eating its prey. "The lion dwelling together with the lamb," that is to say, not unnaturally, as idealized in Isaiah 11:6, but naturally, in the way of the will in nature, with the lion eating the lamb and the lamb cooperating as a willing victim: itself having spent all of its own brief lifetime eating grass, which had likewise cooperated by continuing to grow inexhaustibly from that bountiful invisible source which is the mystery-vessel of life. Likewise, animals dwell in hidden villages of their own from which they continue to appear seasonally to be slaughtered by their hunters.

The underlying mythic theme—which occasionally becomes explicit, as in the Blackfoot legend of the *Buffalo's Wife* (see I.2: 234)—*is of a covenant between the animal and human villages* whereby in recognition of the necessities of the way of the will in nature, the animals are given as individuals willingly to the nourishment of the human tribes, with an understanding that through appropriate rites recognition will be rendered in a sacred way to their transtemporal species, and the given lives thus returned in spirit to their living ground.

There can be little doubt that the Late Paleolithic temple caves (Lascaux, Altamira, El Castillo, and others) were in some way sanctuaries for such rites (see I.1:58–66.). As likenesses of the cosmic womb out of which the daylight appearances of the herds of game annually issued, they held in timeless images the everlasting forms of which those animal appearances were the manifestations in time. Indeed, one has only to enter into any one of those caves to become convinced (at least while down there, enclosed underground in a womb of eternal darkness, removed from all sense of extended space, yet among visions of herds that once did annually appear upon what then were the grazing plains of what now is Europe) that here in the dark of the womb of the pregnant earth is actuality, while above, in the extended light world—which here seems remote and alien—are the appearances only of insubstantial phantoms.

The numerous female figurines of that same high

4.

period of the Paleolithic Great Hunt were surely personifications in human form of the indwelling power of that same mother womb. What their actual uses were can be only surmised: whether as fetishes to aid childbirth, as protectresses of the family hearths, or as personifications of the mystery already symbolized in the caves, to be implored in some way for the fecundity of the necessary herds. The noble little example of *The Woman with the Horn*, from the rock shelter at Laussel (see I.1:46, 67)—which might have served as illustration to some legend akin to that of the Blackfoot *Buffalo's Wife*—suggests that a myth of some kind must have justified the cult of these Paleolithic "Venus" figurines, whereby the necessary slaughter of the hunt became transformed into a ritual enactment, in the way of the animal powers, of the will in nature.

# AGRICULTURAL ORIGINS AND DISPERSALS

Whether the *idea* of plant and animal domestication originated at one time and place or in several hearths independently is a question still debated. Leo Frobenius early suggested Southeast Asia as the likely matrix, not only of both plant and animal domestication, but also of ocean voyaging,[8] and Carl Sauer, in *Agricultural Origins and Dispersals* (1952), supported this view with botanical and zoological, as well as geographical, evidence.[9]

"As the cradle of earliest agriculture," Sauer states, "I have proposed Southeastern Asia. It meets the requirements of high physical and organic diversity, of mild climate with reversed monsoons giving abundant rainy and dry periods, of many waters inviting to fishing, of location at the hub of the Old World for communication by water or by land. No other area is equally well situated or equally well furnished for the rise of a fishing-farming culture."[10] The earliest plants there domesticated were monocotyledons (yams, bananas, ginger, taro, turmeric, the sago palm, pandans, bamboos and sugar cane) which are propagated by clones or cuttings; while the animals (dog, pig, fowl, duck and goose) are all, as Sauer points out, "animals of the household, in contrast to the herd animals originating in Southwest Asia."[11] In his view, both types of domestication originated, not with the men, whose work was fishing, but with the women at home. "In this culture," he declares, "the women had domain over the tilled land and the homes. Women were cooks and cultivators, domestics and domesticators. These societies were largely developed and organized by their women. It was through them, it is inferred, that descent was reckoned and membership in the household determined. Matrilineal and matriarchal societies arose."[12]

In the Southwest Asian matrix, in contrast, the plants domesticated were chiefly grains, propagated by seed, and the animals (besides those known to the Southeast) were sheep, goats, and cattle. Extensive as well as intensive archeological researches throughout this part of the world have revealed a critical period, c. 9000 to 7000 B.C., for the beginnings there of plant and animal domestication;[13] whereas in Sauer's view the Southeast Asian beginnings "may well lie several times seven thousand years in the past": in the period, that is to say, of the last Ice

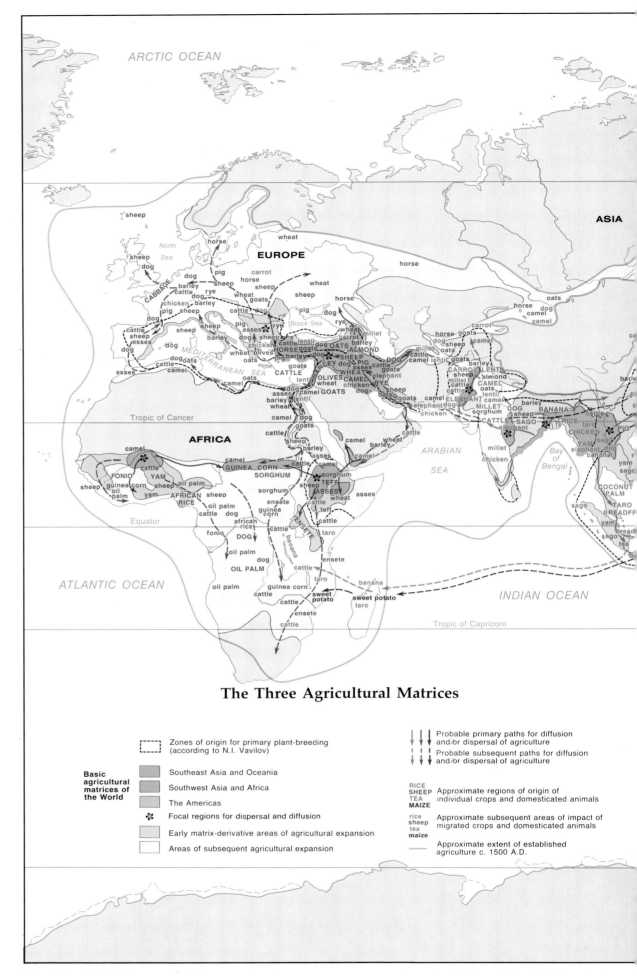

## The Three Agricultural Matrices

**Basic agricultural matrices of the World**

- - - - Zones of origin for primary plant-breeding (according to N.I. Vavilov)

Southeast Asia and Oceania

Southwest Asia and Africa

The Americas

✷ Focal regions for dispersal and diffusion

Early matrix-derivative areas of agricultural expansion

Areas of subsequent agricultural expansion

↓↓↓ Probable primary paths for diffusion and/or dispersal of agriculture

↓↓↓ Probable subsequent paths for diffusion and/or dispersal of agriculture

RICE
SHEEP
TEA     Approximate regions of origin of
MAIZE   individual crops and domesticated animals

rice
sheep   Approximate subsequent areas of impact of
tea     migrated crops and domesticated animals
maize

——— Approximate extent of established agriculture c. 1500 A.D.

**Map 1** About 11,000 years ago (the exact date is a matter of some dispute), the attentions of our earliest hunting and gathering forebears turned from the transient mysteries of the Animal Powers to the regenerative potential of the Seeded Earth. Throughout the tropical and temperate regions, as planting techniques improved and became more efficient, primitive agricultural communities began to flourish, a new social order arose to supercede the old that centered around mobile bands of hunter-gatherers, and a new mythology was born.

Three dominant agricultural centers arose (virtually simultaneously from an aeonian perspective), each cultivating its own particular plants and domesticat-

ing its distinctive animals. In a relatively brief period of time, each of these core agricultural hearths expanded its sphere of influence over an ever-widening territory. Eventually three discrete "matrices" of early agriculturalists were discernible, each definable by a common dependency on its own plants and animals, by a similar worldview and social order, and, perhaps most importantly, by a shared mythological perspective. Over time, but arguably early in their cultural development, these matrices began to interact and to trade, so that by A.D. 1500, a worldwide, intercommunicating agricultural complex had been formed.

The three principle agricultural matrices are color-

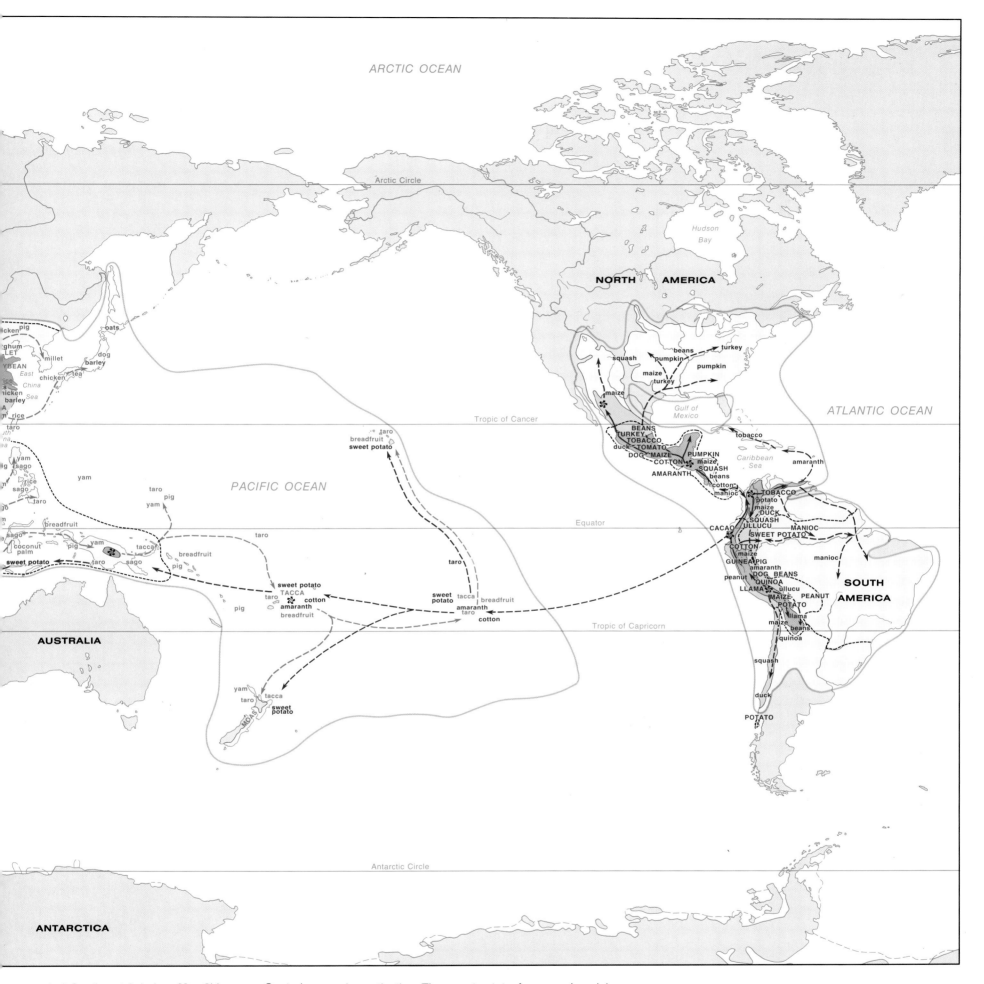

coded: Southeast Asia (see **Map 2**) in green, Central and South America (see **Map 3**) in mauve, and Southwest Asia and Northeast Africa (see **Map 4**) in deep orange. Shown in light orange are the areas which these matrices first affected; yellow denotes the regions into which they subsequently extended their influences. Maps 2, 3, and 4 detail and amplify the information rendered in this map.

Each crop and domesticated animal (indicated by its common name) is color-keyed to the matrix of its origin; so too, are the arrows that indicate probable paths of dispersal and diffusion. Names in capital letters denote places of origin, while those in lower-case letters mark areas of subsequent cultivation or

domestication. The sweet potato, for example, originated near Peru, was dispersed throughout the islands of the Pacific, passed through Indonesia, and was finally carried across the Indian Ocean to Madagascar and southern Africa. Similarly, the chicken, originally domesticated in the jungles of present-day Thailand (the Southeast Asian matrix, colored green), was widely dispersed and can be found, for example, in green print in western Europe. Such wide diffusion of plant and animal species is often cited as some of the strongest evidence supporting those who argue for significant contacts at a very early date between agricultural societies widely scattered across the globe.

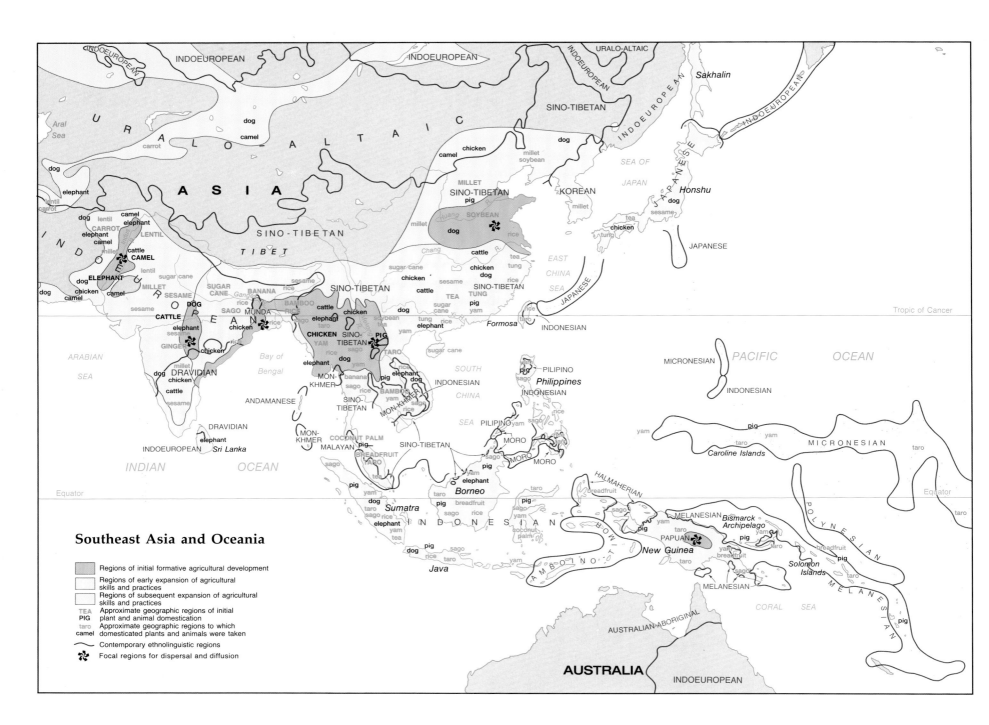

**Southeast Asia and Oceania**

Regions of initial formative agricultural development

Regions of early expansion of agricultural skills and practices

Regions of subsequent expansion of agricultural skills and practices

TEA
PIG — Approximate geographic regions of initial plant and animal domestication

taro — Approximate geographic regions to which domesticated plants and animals were taken
camel

—— Contemporary ethnolinguistic regions

✿ Focal regions for dispersal and diffusion

Age deglaciation and the rising of the oceans to their present level.[14] For the New World the period of transition from hunting and gathering to settled village life has recently been estimated to have extended (in Middle America) from c. 7200 to 1500 B.C.[15] These dates, however, are for seed planting (maize, beans, squash and gourds, chili-peppers, amaranths, etc.), whereas Sauer has identified two distinct zones of plant cultivation in the Americas, a northern (Middle and North American) of seed planting, and a southern (Caribbean and South American) of vegetative clones and cuttings (yuca, for example, and the sweet potato). Moreover, Sauer believes the vegetative to have been the earlier of these two orders, pointing for its source of inspiration across the Pacific to Southeast Asia.[16] Gordon R. Willey, Richard S. MacNeish, and Paul C. Mangelsdorf, on the other hand, not only argue for the Middle American seeding center as the earlier, but also reject any suggestion of a motivating influence from abroad.[17]

In any case, the number of food plants cultivated in Precolumbian America was

enormous and included, besides those already named, the potato, pineapple, avocado and peanut, papaya, guava, tomato, pumpkin, various beans, vanilla, cacao, coca, the coconut and the banana. Tobacco, rubber, and three species of cotton were also known. Whereas, in contrast, the only animals domesticated were the turkey and dog in the seed-planting zone and, in the vegetative, the Muscovy duck, llama and alpaca, guinea pig and a breed of low slung dog that was fattened for food. Chickens, also, are reported, of a breed that lays blue and olive-green eggs, and the meat and bones of which are black.[18] For the argument of an absolutely independent New World development, these chickens are, of course, inconvenient; so too, the bottle gourd, coconut and banana, which are also known on both sides of the Pacific. One of the South American cottons — of an exceptional 26-chromosome (instead of the usual 13-chromosome) variety — has been found distributed throughout the Pacific, from the Galapagos to Fiji, having arisen, as Professor Sauer states, "by the combination of a 13-chromosome Asiatic with a 13-

**Map 2** The agricultural matrix of Southeast Asia. Divisions between ethnolinguistic groups are rendered in red ink; domesticated animals are noted in black, crops in green. Again, capital and lower-case letters are used to distinguish probable centers of origin from areas of subsequent diffusion. The Southeast Asian agricultural matrix is thought to be the oldest of the three principal centers, arguably because of its extremely favorable climate, the diversity of its indigenous food crops, and the variety of resident wildlife suitable for domestication (see above, p. 12).

**Map 3** The agricultural matrix of the Americas. Color codings in this map are the same as those used in Map 2, as are the usages of capital and lower case letters. As in the Old World agricultural centers, a large number of plants were cultivated in the Americas. Several of these—particularly beans, maize, and the sweet potato—were especially well suited to providing nutrients essential to the human diet and quickly became established as staples. In contrast to the Old World matrices, however, few animals were domesticated in the Americas. The dotted line cutting through present-day Honduras and Nicaragua marks the division between planters of seed crops, such as maize, and cultivators of plants propagated by means of cuttings and runners, such as the sweet potato.

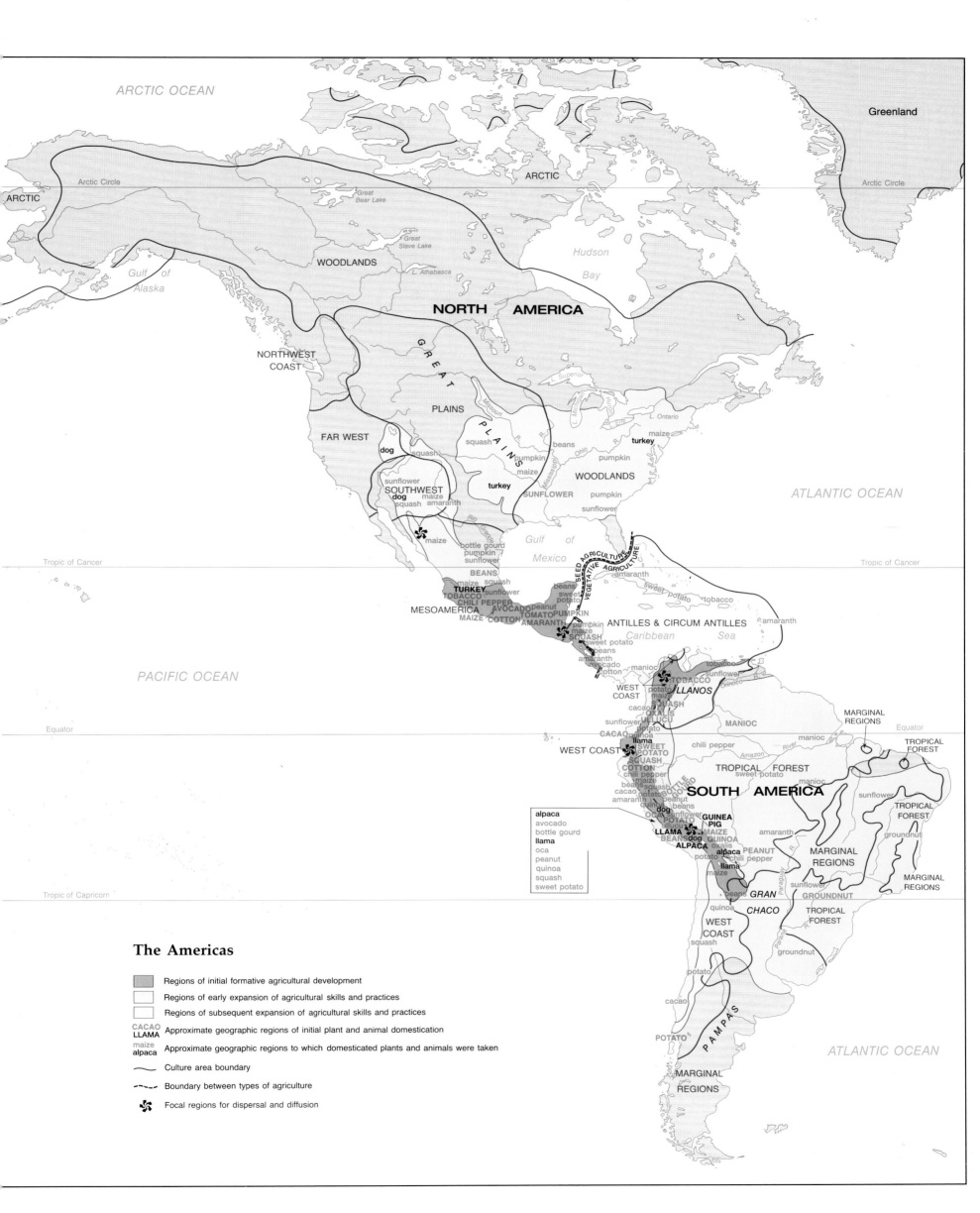

ARCTIC OCEAN

Greenland

Arctic Circle

ARCTIC

ARCTIC

Gulf of
Alaska

*Great
Bear Lake*

*Hudson*

*Bay*

WOODLANDS

*L. Athabasca*

*Great
Slave Lake*

Arctic Circle

NORTH   AMERICA

NORTHWEST
COAST

G
R
E
A
T

*L. Superior*

FAR WEST

PLAINS

P
L
A
I
N
S

*Missouri*

squash

squash

*L. Michigan*

*L. Ontario*

*L. Erie*

maize

ATLANTIC OCEAN

dog

beans

*Ohio*

turkey

*Mississippi*

pumpkin

SOUTHWEST

sunflower

dog

turkey

maize

pumpkin

maize

SUNFLOWER

WOODLANDS

pumpkin

*Rio*

squash

amaranth

sunflower

*Grande*

maize

bottle gourd
pumpkin
sunflower

Gulf   of

Mexico

SEED AGRICULTURE

VEGETATIVE AGRICULTURE

amaranth

Tropic of Cancer

BEANS

squash

Tropic of Cancer

maize

squash

TURKEY

sunflower

beans

*sweet potato*

tobacco

TOBACCO
CHILI PEPPER

AVOCADO

peanut

ANTILLES & CIRCUM ANTILLES

*Caribbean*

amaranth

MESOAMERICA

TOMATO

PUMPKIN

*Sea*

MAIZE

COTTON

AMARANTH

pumpkin

maize

SQUASH

*sweet potato*

PACIFIC OCEAN

beans

amaranth

avocado

cotton

manioc

tobacco

sunflower

*Orinoco*

TOBACCO

WEST
COAST

SQUASH

*LLANOS*

potato

maize

OXALIS

MARGINAL
REGIONS

Equator

cacao

ULLUCU

MANIOC

chili pepper

manioc

Equator

TROPICAL
FOREST

sunflower

quinoa

potato

CACAO

llama

WEST COAST

SWEET
POTATO

SQUASH

*Amazon*

*River*

manioc

*sweet potato*

TROPICAL   FOREST

manioc

sunflower

TROPICAL
FOREST

COTTON

chili pepper

BOTTLE GOURD

beans

squash

cacao

potato

peanut

amaranth

cacao

SOUTH   AMERICA

alpaca
avocado
bottle gourd
**llama**
oca
peanut
quinoa
squash
sweet potato

quinoa

sunflower

OCA

dog

beans

POTATO

GUINEA
PIG

amaranth

MARGINAL
REGIONS

MARGINAL
REGIONS

LLAMA

MAIZE

BEANS

dog

QUINOA

BOTTLE
GOURD

oxalis

PEANUT

MARGINAL
REGIONS

ALPACA

alpaca

chili pepper

potato

llama

maize

quinoa

*GRAN*

beans

GROUNDNUT

Tropic of Capricorn

*CHACO*

sunflower

TROPICAL
FOREST

WEST
COAST

squash

groundnut

*Paraguay*

*Paraná*

potato

cacao

P
A
M
P
A
S

POTATO

ATLANTIC OCEAN

# The Americas

- Regions of initial formative agricultural development
- Regions of early expansion of agricultural skills and practices
- Regions of subsequent expansion of agricultural skills and practices
- **CACAO**
  **LLAMA**  Approximate geographic regions of initial plant and animal domestication
- maize
  alpaca  Approximate geographic regions to which domesticated plants and animals were taken
- Culture area boundary
- Boundary between types of agriculture
- Focal regions for dispersal and diffusion

MARGINAL
REGIONS

15

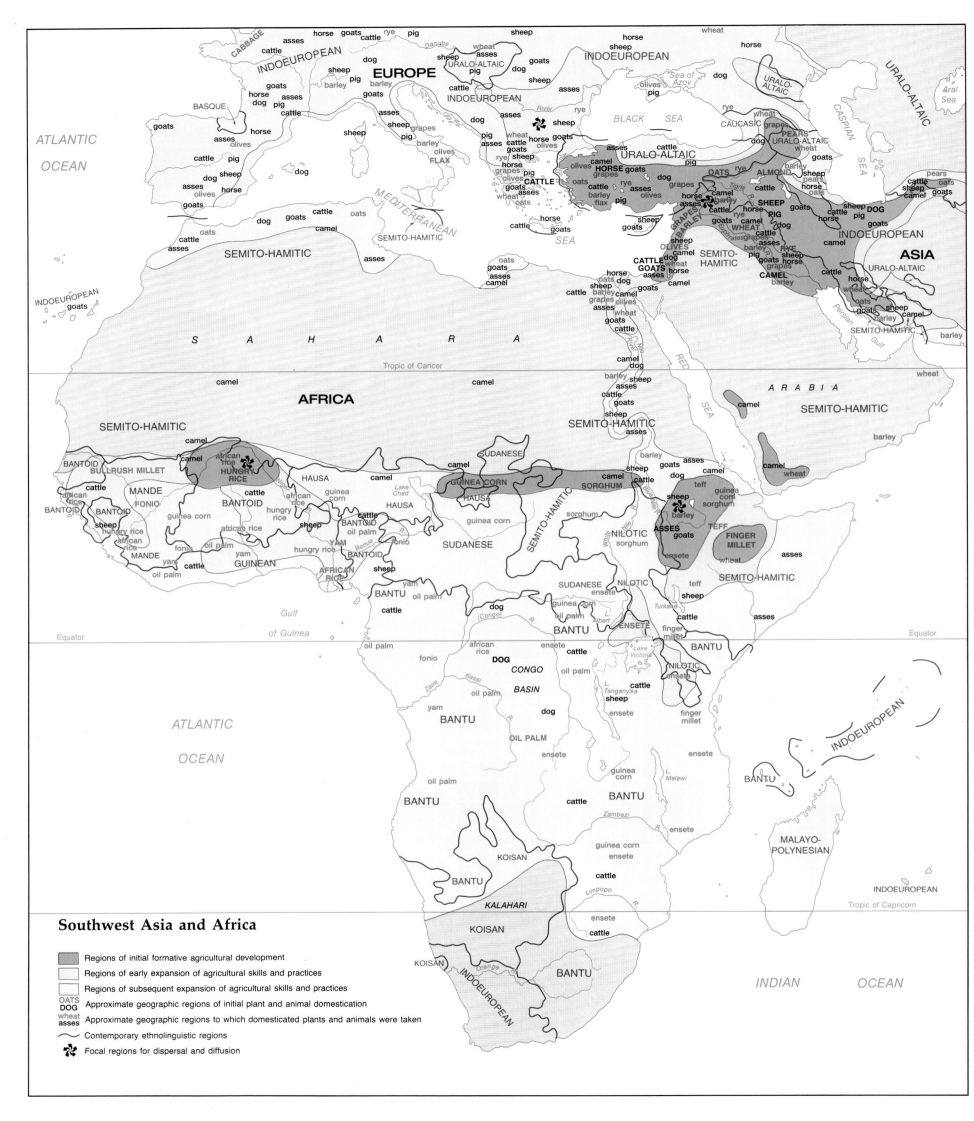

## Southwest Asia and Africa

- ▓ Regions of initial formative agricultural development
- ▒ Regions of early expansion of agricultural skills and practices
- □ Regions of subsequent expansion of agricultural skills and practices
- **OATS DOG** Approximate geographic regions of initial plant and animal domestication
- wheat asses Approximate geographic regions to which domesticated plants and animals were taken
- ⌒ Contemporary ethnolinguistic regions
- ✺ Focal regions for dispersal and diffusion

**Map 4** The agricultural complex of Southwest Asia and Africa. Again, in this map the use of color codings, as well as of capital and lower case letters, is consistent with that of Maps 2 and 3. The Nile River valley provided a secure and navigable route through the Sahara. Along this concourse the herd animals first domesticated in the Middle East easily passed into Abyssinia and the rest of Africa. The many grains and other crops indigenous to Mesopotamia, on the other hand, although later cultivated all over Europe, never found their way south of the Sahara. Apart from the ass, which was widely favored throughout the Mediterranean region as a beast of burden, those plants and animals that were vital to the sub-Sahara were not dispersed into Southwest Asia and Europe.

chromasome American ancestor."[19] And this indication of a commerce, not only from Asia to America, but also the other way, is corroborated by the testimony of the American sweet potato, which was carried from Peru, together with its Peruvian name, *kumara,* across the Pacific to Melanesia, and then on, but without the name (according to at least one distinguished authority), into Africa.[20] No botanist would allow for a theory of the independent evolution on two sides of an ocean of, say, the single species, sweet potato *(Ipomoea batatas),* coconut palm *(Cocos nucifera),* or bottle gourd *(Lagenaria vulgaris).* If the social scientist can do so for such a catalogue of identical traits as that here reviewed, then surely, he must have somewhere in his theorizing imagination a psychological explanation that seems to him more plausible than the obvious navigational one, of transportation across a pacific sea by some South or East Asian fishing folk, who knew perfectly well how to cross water.

As Frobenius noted half a century ago in a chapter on the relationship of geography to culture provinces, whereas the winds and currents of the Atlantic Ocean course chiefly along the coasts and in but one direction across latitudinal lines, those of the Pacific favor intercontinental voyaging. "The Pacific Ocean," as he saw it, "has all the characteristics of an immensely expanded inland sea. Coastal shipping is possible from the southern tip of Africa, along the South and East Asian coasts, to the northwestern tip of America, and then southeastward to the southern tip, without crossing anywhere more open water than the 100 kilometers of Bering Strait. Moreover, the central part of the Pacific Ocean is rich in islands, which, like a chainlike continuation of Indonesia, lead out into a region of regular monsoons that provides what amounts to a training range for seafaring."[21]

"That the Asiatic planting and fishing culture was expansive is shown," states Sauer, "by its spread across the islands of the Pacific and its penetration of tropical Africa, of the Mediterranean, and of western Europe. A diffusion about the northern margin of the Pacific should have presented no greater difficulties. Beyond Japan lie coasts and streams gently inviting to skilled boatmen and fishermen. Here are the finest waters of the world for anadromous fish, such as salmon and sturgeon, the best crabbing grounds, and here were large numbers of sea-inhabiting mammals readily taken along shore, such as the Stellar sea cow and the walrus. Inland seas and island chains provided sheltered harbors and facilitated water travel. Over most of the route growing timber or driftwood was available in abundance for boats and gear, for fuel and houses. It would seem strange that peo-

**5.** The bottle gourd, *Lagenaria vulgaris,* also known as the calabash. The bottle gourd is the only plant to have been indisputably cultivated in both the Old and New Worlds prior to Columbus's voyages, and provides convincing evidence of worldwide cultural exchange long before the era of European exploration.

**6 a–b.** The sweet potato, *Ipomoea batatas,* and the coconut palm, *Cocos nucifera.* Although there is an ongoing dispute about the geographical origins and means of dissemination of both the sweet potato and the coconut palm, they were widely distributed in antiquity throughout the southern hemisphere and in the tropics north of the equator, where today they often serve as a dietary staple.

ple who were adept boatmen and skilled fishermen and hunters on and by the water, should have held back from entering such coasts. They may well have continued to colonize northward from Japan, but have given up planting in the coasts of low summer warmth.

"Numerous resemblances in customs between the Indians of our Northwest coast and peoples of Indonesia are familiar," he continues. "In Kamchatka, the Alaskan Peninsula, Kodiak, and on the coast of British Columbia, there were matrilineal societies, living in multifamily houses with notions of property, prestige, and art forms which are about what might be left of Southeast Asiatic culture from which an adverse environment had eliminated certain possibilities, in particular agriculture...

"The burden of denying passage to boat people having the skills mentioned would seem to me to rest," Sauer concludes, "on those who object to such diffusion into the New World. The passage may have been made at great leisure or it may have been made rapidly, by groups that leapfrogged from one fishing cove or stream mouth to another, to see what lay beyond. A few generations may have sufficed for a passage about the northern margin of the Pacific Ocean, during the spread of Mesolithic cultures."[22]

# DIFFUSION, CONVERGENCE, AND PARALLELISM IN THE FORMATION OF CULTURES

**Map 5** Distribution in South America of the noun, *hualpa*, "chicken." "The general distribution of these names," states George F. Carter, "is suggestive of an introduction at some point on the Pacific coast somewhere in Ecuador or northern Peru."[2]

The concurrent appearances in three parts of the world greatly distant from each other—Middle America (from Mexico to Peru), Southeast, and Southwest Asia—c. 10,000 B.C., of signs, not only of incipient agriculture, but also of matching mythological innovations, cannot be readily explained.

One proposal (*diffusionism*) has been of a dispersal, one way or another, of the *idea* of plant and animal domestication, whether by trade, by chance, or by folk migration; and where tangible evidences of such contact can be adduced there is little ground for disputation. For example, we are told in Plato's *Phaedo* that when Socrates had drunk the death potion to which he had been condemned in the year 399 B.C. by a court of Athenian citizens, he asked one of his compassionating friends to pay for him a cock that he still owed to the god of healing, Asklepios.[23] Now, since it is known that the part of the world from which barnyard fowl originally derived is Southeast Asia[24], it is evident that there must have arrived in Greece, some time before c. 400 B.C., at least one vessel of some kind bearing oriental barnyard fowl. That it may have brought ideas as well may be open to question. But that there is only one way for a chicken to get from the Bay of Bengal to Athens is manifest, and that way is by what is known to anthropology as *diffusion*.

At the time of the Spanish conquest of Peru, chickens were already known throughout western South America, where they were called *hualpa*[25] (see Map 5). Indeed, the name of the Inca murdered by Pizarro on August 29, 1533, was Atahualpa, which suggests for the fowl that crows at sunrise a noble context of associations. For the Inca was revered as a descendant of the Sun whereas, coincidentally, the beautiful chickens honored in Japan at the imperial shrines at Ise are associated there with the royal cult of the sun-goddess Amaterasu. Moreover, Asklepios, to whom Socrates had intended to offer a cock, was an heir and successor in the art of healing of the Greek sun-god, Apollo. Consistent associations of this kind suggest a broad distribution, not only of a tangible chanticleer, but also of an associated mythology of the sun.

Where real or imagined geographical obstacles to such a vast diffusion are recognized, however (as where, for example, a prehistoric crossing of the Pacific by sailing raft or canoe from Southeast Asia to America would have to be acknowledged), anthropologists now commonly hypothesize an alternative explanation covered by the mystical term *convergence*, denoting *an independent, apparently acci-*

**7.** Greek black-figure kylix with chicken design and inscribed ΗΕΡΜΟΛΕΝΕΣ ΕΠΟΙΕΣΕΝ (Hermogenes made [this]). Gela, Sicily, sixth century B.C.

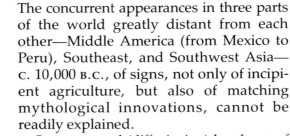

**8.** Two chickens and their young. Painting attributed to Hui Tsung (A.D. 1101–1125), last emperor of the Northern Sung dynasty.

**9.** Cattle fording a river, detail of a wall-painting from Dahshur, Egypt. Old Kingdom, Fourth Dynasty, c. 2500 B.C.

**10.** Contemporary Egyptian farmer and his cattle. From the Old Kingdom to the present day, even introduced breeds of cattle have quickly developed a distinctive Egyptian form.

*dental development of similarities between separate cultures.* To the problem of the widespread occurrence of the chicken in South America such an explanation cannot, of course, be applied, since, according to the findings of the natural sciences, identical biological species do not evolve independently by convergence on separated continents. Diffusion in this case, therefore, is the only possible explanation, whether by prehistoric sailing raft or (as some would have it) by the Spanish, c. A.D. 1500 (too late, however, for the naming of Atahualpa; moreover, the Spanish birds were of a European breed, with another name, *pollo,* and had been delivered to the wrong coast.[26] There are, nevertheless, other instances of identical particulars appearing in separated cultures where explanations by convergence *can* be reasonably supported; especially when (as in both Southeast Asia and South America) similar geographical (rain forest) conditions prevail in the environments.

The educative (*paideumatic*) influence of an inhabited space upon its population has here to be recognized. This is a force that can be formative, not only of cultural, but even of biological particulars. Similarities have been noted, for example, between the body forms of Amazonian Indians and the Dayak of Borneo. Must these be attributed to a transpacific migration of Indonesians to Brazil? Or may we here have an example of the convergent shaping by the environment of two distinct Mongolian populations?

Writing of the mysterious paideumatic influence of a local region on the physical form of its inhabitants (whether human, animal, or plant), Frobenius cites an observation of the botanist and explorer George Schweinfurth (1836–1925), following his years of research in the upper Nile valley and southeastern Sudan:

"'The native [Egyptian] breed of cattle has been repeatedly wiped out by epidemics in the course of a single century and replaced by breeds of differing kinds from the north, east, and south. Nevertheless, after but a few generations cattle showing the distinctive features of the earlier breed have again appeared, so that, for the most part, Egyptian cattle today correspond in form exactly to those de-

picted in artworks of the Old Kingdom.'

"To every game warden," Frobenius adds in comment to this observation, "this tendency is familiar. By the distinctive form of a wild stag's antlers, the river, indeed the very stream valley, of its habitat can be identified. And if a new stock be introduced from some distant quarter, stags of the new lineage— even where the earlier will have completely disappeared before introduction of the new—will soon be exhibiting antlers of the same forms as those of the earlier, native breed. But this, finally," Frobenius continues, "is no more than a special instance of what is a common occurrence in the plant world. Dandelions grown on mountain heights of one to two thousand meters from seeds brought up from the valley acquire a form distinctly different in type from that of the plants below."[27] "Such a paideumatic transformation," he concludes, "neither chemistry, physics, nor meteorology can explain."[28]

In comparative studies of the numerous likenesses that might seem to connect the rain-forest cultures of South America and Southeast Asia, it has become customary (in North American anthropological circles, at least) to invoke the principle of convergence as an unimpeachable argument against every appeal to the material as evidence of diffusion. The number of manifest likenesses between the Old and New World Cultures, however, is enormous.

As appears on the next ten pages, they include: the dwelling of whole communities in a single longhouse; an architecture on piles; masked apparitions of mythic beings; the headhunt with its ceremonial preservation of the taken heads; slit-log gongs and a considerable battery of other characteristic musical instruments; the panpipe; tattooing; the blowgun, with its poisoned darts; certain types of fish weir and animal trap; fish poisons and the pounding of bark cloth (tapa); and so on.

**11**

11. Gallery of a Tribal Longhouse at Long Pelaban, Kayan River, Northern Borneo.

12. Interior of an Apinayé Great House. North Central Brazil (between the Tocantins lower Araguaia rivers, to about 6° 30′ S.) after Francis De Castelnau, 1852.

13. Dayak Totems between two Sections of a Tribal Longhouse. Upper Mahakam River (above Longiram), Central Borneo, 1925.

"The Dyak villagers, as a rule, live under one roof in a communal house, rather than in separate dwellings. In this respect they resemble the Iroquois Indians of North America . . . Each long house, or *lamin* as it is also called, may accommodate forty or fifty families . . . It is really a long straight shed on stilts, and is divided into one-room apartments. Each of these single-room apartments accommodates one Dyak family . . . The longest *lamin* that I visited was about six hundred feet in length."[3]

14. Traditional Iroquois longhouse, sheltering many families, built of poles lashed to construct a frame some 23 feet wide and from 40 to 300 or more feet long, then covered with bark. At one end was the men's door, at the other, the women's. Partitions jutting from the side walls left a long center aisle from end to end, each family (it is supposed) with a stall of its own.

15. Telok Djulo, a Dayak settlement on piles. Upper Barito River, Central Borneo, about 1915.

16. A riverbank dwelling built on piles in the Colombian lowlands. The fact that such structures may be found today even on dry, hilly lands suggest that this architectural style may be a survival from a time when their builders inhabited swampy terrain.

**12**

17. Mask at the annual Purification Rites. Bobo, Upper Volta, Western Sudan.

18. *Amnangib*, age-grade of the married male adult, here in full ceremonial attire. Photos: Paul Wirz, c. 1916, at Domandeh.

19. Dayak Masked Dancer. Upper Mahakam River (above Longiram), Central Borneo, 1925.

20. The male initiation rites of the Ona were conducted in a special lodge of the men's society, the *klóketen*, from which women were excluded; and associated with the mystifications of this institution were a number of such Hallowe'en spooks as we see here. These apparitions would appear from time to time, ranging through the bush of areas about the men's house, and any woman or child seeing one or more of them was to suppose that they were the inhabitants of the *klóketen* with whom the men held converse in their meetings. An important moment in the initiations of a boy took place when he was compelled to get up and wrestle with one of these char-

**13**

**15**

**14**

**16**

acters, who would let the youngster put him down, after which the masquerade was uncovered, and the boy turned into a man. There was a legend of the *klóketen* having been originally of the women, who abused their power, when it then was taken and kept from them by the men.

**21.** Sherente Great Anteater Masqueraders. North-Central Brazil.

**22.** The Hopi kachina Hahiwuqti, from an 1893 photograph taken during the Sokoyo rites of Powamu, the Bean-Planting Ceremony of February-March. "Kachina" means "the charge of the energy of life," which, during a six-month ceremonial season, is represented by both actors in costume (as here), and by finely-wrought dolls. The start of the season is heralded by the appearance of a few kachinas soon after the winter solstice, and by the time of Powamu, the first major festival of the year, they are a common sight in Hopi villages. During Powamu, Hahiwuqti and the other Sokoyo kachinas arrive and terrorize the children of the village by threatening to devour them unless their parents ransom them back with gifts of food and promises of good behavior. As the ceremonial season progresses, the number and variety of kachinas gradually increase until the summer solstice, when they leave this world and return to the spiritual realm.

21

**23.** Headhunter in full regalia, from Buria in West-Ceram Indonesia.

**24.** Panare Hunter with Blowgun. Central Venezuela, at the sources of the Cuchivero river.

**27.** Scene witnessed by Captain Cook, of the offering of a human sacrifice at the great *morai* of Tahiti, September 1st and 2nd, 1777. Drawing by John Webber, artist to Captain Cook's fourth and last voyage.

No less than 49 skulls of earlier victims were counted by Captain Cook along the altar in the background. The bodies on the scaffold were of sacrificed dogs and pigs. A high moment of the ceremony occurred when a presiding priest plucked out the left eye of the victim and, presenting it to the high chief Otoo, in whose name the rite was being conducted, held it to his open mouth; then took it away. "This," wrote Captain Cook in his account of the occasion, "they call 'eating the man,' or 'food for the chief,' and we may observe here some traces of former times, when the dead body was really feasted upon."[5]

There are Egyptian "Pyramid Texts," from c. 2500–2200 B.C., which may also be of relevance here as indications of a shared myth:

*Take to thyself the Eye of Horus, he brings it to thee; put it in thy mouth.*

*Behold, we bring thee the great left eye as healer.*

*I have brought thee the Eye of Horus, that thou mayest equip with it thy face, that it may purify thee, that its odor may come to thee . . . It defends thee against the violence of the arm of Seth.*[6]

The sacrifice at the Tahitian *morai* was to have gained the favor and support of the god of the shrine for Chief Otoo (here standing by Captain Cook) in a war that was in prospect with the high chief of Moorea, a neighboring island.

**25.** Punan Hunter with Blowgun. Jungle nomad from the lower Kayan river, Borneo. About 1915.

**26.** A shrunken head from a Jivaro headhunting expedition. According to an authoritative recipe for the shrinking of a taken head: "The skin is cut and removed from the skull, the lips are everted and pinned or sewed together, and the whole head skin is boiled with a plant which somewhat shrinks it and fixes the hair. It is further reduced by placing hot stones and sand inside it; then it is smoked, polished, and kept in a jar."[4]

The Jivaro are a tribe of headhunting horticulturalists inhabiting the Montaña of southern Ecuador, a rainforest tract north of the Marañon river.

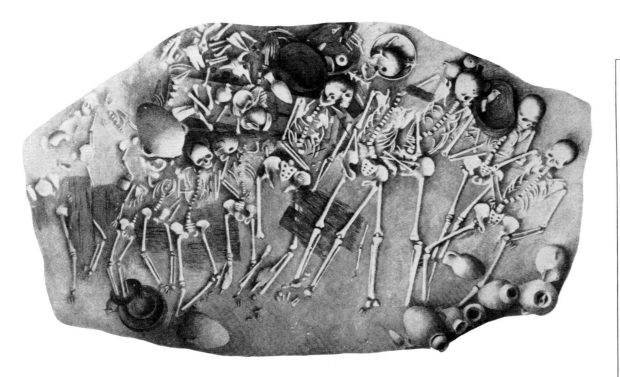

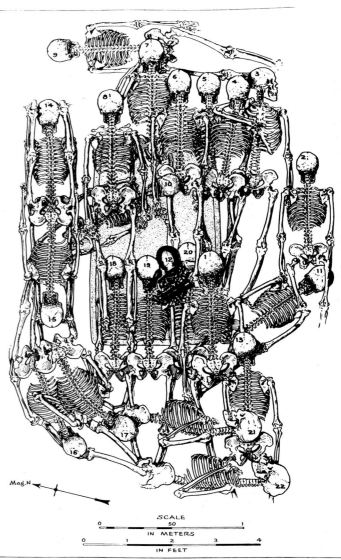

**28.** Mass simultaneous burials in rock-cut tomb. Jericho. Middle Bronze Age, early second millenium B.C.

"Exceptionally such tombs might contain about 40 burials. The average was about 20. Most of the dead lay, side by side, on rush mats. Only one in the center of the tomb, lay on a bed: probably a man of importance, with the members of his family, adults, adolescents, and children. The supply of food is liberal, with jars of liquid, drinking vessels and platters, ranged around the edge of the burial; also meat usually in the form of roasted sheep, either jointed or entire."[7]

**29.** Precolumbian grave containing mass simultaneous burial. Panama, southwest of the Canal, from a cemetery known today as Sitio Conte, on the Rio Grande de Coclé.

The main occupant (No. 12), surrounded by the extended bodies of his retainers, was seated on a stone slab, on which his body seemed to have been desiccated by fire. Above and around the bodies funeral offerings and jewelry were piled in great abundance. In several of the graves there were found over 200 pottery vessels. Tools and implements include metates, sharpening and grinding stones, polishing stones, crudely chipped stone blades, bone points, stingray points, bone spear throwers, stone shaft straighteners, drills, mirrors, and chisels of gold or stone. Burial was a rite reserved for the nobility, and for wives, retainers, and captives selected to accompany their lords to another world.[8]

23

**30.** In Botswana, southern Africa, this young Kung Bushman wife has set up the cat's cradle known in Ireland as the "Ladder" and the "Fence," in Nigeria as the "Calabash," and in Hawaii as *Ma-ha-lii-lii* and *Pu-kau-la*. (See I.1:**181**.)

**31.** At Yirrkala, an aboriginal township in north-eastern Arnhem Land, Australia, this young woman's string figure is supposed to represent a canoe. (See I.2:**244**.)

**32.** In the Tuamotus, Central Polynesia, Tukua of Napuka demonstrates the figure there known as "Overflowing Springs." The upper and lower diamonds represent two springs, and the interior lines, flowing water.

**36.** Slit-log Gong. Equatorial Africa. Banda, Central African Empire.

**37.** Youth playing panpipes. Malaita, Solomon Islands.

**38.** Alune woman, weaving. West Ceram, Indonesia.

Also known to both the Old World and the New were cat's cradle games (string-labyrinth figures, comprising many transformations, each with a name); and loom weaving; mythologies featuring the killing of a divine, semidivine, or (in folktales) outstanding individual, out of whose buried (sometimes dismembered) body the basic food plants grow and, associated with this mythology, human sacrifice and cannibalism involving elaborate, masked ceremonials mimetic of the essential mythic event.

Moreover, with the passage of time and development in both hemispheres of higher forms of civilization, the multiplication of shared features progressed beyond enumeration, including, for example, wool for weaving, sheared from flocks of domesticated sheep in the Old World or from llamas and alpacas in the New; pottery utensils, both coarse and refined (incised and painted platters, bowls, cups, and saucers); pottery figurines (nude female statuettes and, later, highly developed ceramic sculptural arts); knowledge of the wheel (used in America only for toys, see below: Figures 47, 48); metallurgy in copper, silver, and gold, with alloys; figures cast by the lost-wax process; copper repoussé; tiny metal bells; pendants of carved jade; conch-shell trumpets; sailing rafts and canoes; elabo-

**33.** Kini Ainaiha, of Koloa, Hawaii, exhibits the figure known as the "Originating House," *Halekumukuakia.*

**34.** A Cudavero, in the Gran Chaco, northern Argentina, extends a figure widely known throughout the South Pacific as well (in the Tuamotus, the Marquesas, Society Islands, Austral Islands, Tonga, Fiji, and North Queensland, Australia), where it is used to illustrate the legend of a character, Mageogeo, trapped in the net of Tukutukurahonui, the Spider, who, when refused release, tore the net and broke free.

**35.** An Eskimo grandfather teaches cat's cradle games to his granddaughter. (See I.2:**311**.)

**39.** Wapishana women at an upright loom, British Guiana, South America. "True loom weaving," states Robert H. Lowie, writing of the South American tropical forest tribes, "has a high, though incomplete, correlation with cotton. Probably the distinctive type, called 'cincture,' or vertical loom, is one consisting of two uprights perforated top and bottom to permit the insertion of cross beams around which the parallel warp threads are looped, the anterior and posterior ones being separated by a movable rod, while a thinner stick divides the even and odd threads (during the process of manufacture) . . . This loom is found in the Guianas, west to the Rio Negro, and south to the Yuracare of Bolivia . . . Bordering the Andes, many tribes use a horizontal loom, the 'belt loom' being the most common. One end of the loom is attached to a tree or house post, the other to the weaver's belt."[9]

**40.** A Yaguy panpipe player from the Amazon basin. Panpipes are made from bamboo, wood, or stone, and are found worldwide, most notably in central Europe and in many areas bordering the Pacific Ocean.

Panpipes have had a variety of religious and social uses. The earliest known examples are double-winged versions from China, the wings representing the female and male principles of the *yin* and the *yang.* The instruments made their first appearance in Europe in the sixth century B.C. on bronze from the Illyrian Hallstatt culture of northeastern Italy, where they figured prominently in offertory processions and festive meals. In the Solomon Islands (see above: **37**), they are used in initiation ceremonies. In pagan Greece panpipes were associated with the nature god Pan, who was thought to be able to tame

wild animals simply by playing them, and which represented his function of harmonizing the nonrational qualities of men and beasts.

**41.** Witoto slit-log gongs. Southeastern Colombia, between the Piraparaná and upper Caguetá rivers.

Played in pairs of "male" and "female" and beaten with rubber-headed sticks, the gongs are capable together of four notes, two to each. "By prearranged codes," states Julian H. Steward, "the Witoto, Bora, and Okaina can send fairly complicated messages 6 to 8 miles . . . Other instruments are three-tube and many-tube panpipes, bamboo and human- or animal-bone flutes, longitudinal flutes with a hole in the center played in pairs at festivals, rattles affixed to the legs or to sticks, castanets, and sacred bark trumpets."[10]

rate ceremonial centers oriented to the quarters, including pyramids and temple towers, some containing royal burials; divine kings and queens, bearing royal scepters, seated upon thrones, flanked by attendant fan bearers, carried about on royal litters, and dwelling in magnificent palaces; stone architecture incorporating ventilation systems, spiral stairways, corbeled roof vaulting, colonnades, and sculptured images of deities in the round and in bas-relief; painted murals; mosaics; figured tapestries; stelae and memorial monuments; causeways and canals; terracotta; lime concrete; mythologies of divine incarnations, sacrificed gods, deaths and resurrections, heavenly ascensions and returns; stratified heavens above and stratified hells below, with populations of gods, demons, and souls of the dead; consecrated priesthoods; nuns and nunneries; rituals of fasting, abstinence, confession and penance, matrimony, holy orders, and extreme unction; symbolic crosses; swastikas; incense used in the veneration of gods represented in sculptured images; and intoxicants associated with religious ceremonials.

Finally, in later Mexico are found books in a hieroglyphic script; positional (duodecimal) mathematics; astronomical observatories; association of each of the visible planets with a diety; birth horoscopes; a calendar of accurately measured cycles of time within greater cycles of cosmic eons, past and to come; formulae for the prediction of both solar and lunar eclipses; association of each of the four quarters of space and quarters of the cycles of time, not only with a color and a god, but also with one of the classic four elements, Fire, Air, Earth, and Water.

**42.** Borobudur, a richly ornamented Buddhist temple. Java, A.D. eighth–ninth century.

**43.** "El Castillo," Temple of Kukulcan (Quetzalcoatl). A.D. eleventh–fifteenth century (Mayan Post-Classic Period). Chichén Itzá, Yucatán.

**44.** Pope Alexander VI, Rodrigo Borgia, in a litter carried by six monks. Rome, 1492–1503.

**45.** The Timucuan Queen Elect is brought to the King. Florida, c. 1550. Engraving by Theodore de Bry, 1591, from a watercolor by Jacques Le Moyne de Morgues, 1564. (See I. 2:**387**.)

Examples of wheeled clay toys: **46.** Clay dog and wheeled clay bullock cart, child's toys. Indus Valley Civilization, c. 2300–1750 B.C. **47.** Clay dog on wheels. Painted redware, Tlaxcala, Mexico, A.D. 800–1250. All varieties of domesticated dog, whether of the Old World or the New, are considered as originating from a single wild dog species native to Southeast Asia.[11]

**48.** Clay caiman or alligator. Buffware, Veracruz, Mexico. And as to the wheel: Was it invented but once, in the Near East, c. 3500 B.C?

**49.** The Buddha Sākyamuni, hands in the postures, "Fear not" (*abhaya-mudrā*) and "Boon bestowing" (*varada-mudrā*). Altarpiece of gilt bronze (detail). Hopei, China, A.D. early sixth century.

**50.** The Mayan Maize god. Stone carving. Copan, Honduras. Mayan late Classic Period, A.D. seventh–eighth century.

27

Besides *diffusion* and *convergence*, there is a third factor to be reckoned with in comparative cultural studies—particularly, studies of mythology—namely, *parallelism*, which is a term denoting *the independent development of similar elements or traits in several cultures from a common element*. (Compare *convergence*, as defined above, page 18.)

The "common element" in mythology is, of course, the human psyche, which is a function of the human body (male or female; in childhood, adolescence, maturity, and old age); every organ of the body having an impulse of its own to action; the organs and their intentions coming frequently into conflict, as announced for example in dream, nightmare, neurotic and psychotic breakdown, or in visionary intuitions of possible harmony and fulfillment.

Myth, like dream, is an expression of the human imagination thus grounded in realities of the psyche and, like dream,

reflecting equally the influences and necessities of a specific social environment (nomadic hunting-and-gathering tribe; settled agricultural sib, city state, or nation; vagrant desert horde; or militarist empire), which, in turn, is linked to a landscape. The common ground, or element, of all mythology is consequently the biology of *Homo sapiens sapiens*, whereas the differentiating factors are (1) geography and (2) the cultural stage. For it is a fact that every mythological system has taken shape within a given geographical horizon, conditioned not only by the landscape from which its imagery is derived, but also by the limits of the body of information according to which all appearances in that only known world are interpreted.

At the opening of Volume I.1 of the present work the observation is cited of the nineteenth-century ethnologist, Adolf Bastian (1826–1905), to the effect (1) that there is a general psychic unity of man-

kind which is responsible for certain "elementary ideas" (*Elementargedanken*) that are common to all peoples, and (2) that these elementary ideas substantially inform all of the various "folk traditions" and local "folk ideas" (*Völkergedanken*), which in the various provinces of the globe and periods of history have significantly differed in response to (3) the conditioning controls of geographical environment and the laws of cultural evolution.

In India a like distinction between universal and local values, especially in relation to the imagery of artworks, has been recognized and defined. As noticed and discussed by Ananda K. Coomaraswamy in one of his numerous articles on the subject,[29] works of art depicting "anything and everything," "colored by worldly passion," and "dependent on moods" are qualified as "provincial, local, popular" (*deśi*), and regarded as aesthetically insignificant. Such images are not "liberating" (*vimuktida*) and do not,

**51.** Crested-bird swastika with sun-swastika at center. From an engraved shell gorget. Spiro Mound, LeFlore County, Oklahoma. c. A.D. 700–1200 Mississippian Civilization.

**52.** Winged-rattlesnake swastika with sun-cross at center. From an engraved shell gorget. Spiro Mound, LeFlore County, Oklahoma. c. A.D. 700–1200 Mississippian Civilization.

**55.** Cuna basket. Panama (west and south of Canal), Height 8⅝ inches.

**53.** Swastika of antelopes, Sammana ware, Iraq, c. 4000 B.C.

**54.** Swastika, with birds and fish. Sammana ware, Iraq, c. 4000 B.C.

**56.** Priest cutting out the heart of a sacrificial victim. Line drawing from a bas-relief at the temple ruins at Chichén Itzá, Yucatan. Mayan post-classic period, A.D. eleventh–fifteenth century.

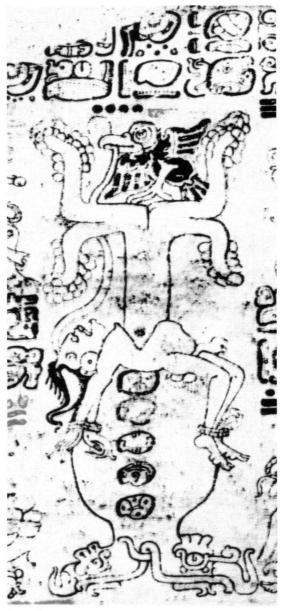

**57.** Sacrifice scene from the Dresden Codex. Rising from the victim's body is the Tree of the Middle Place. Due to the deterioration of many Mayan codices, most images taken from them are illegible without the aid of a carefully prepared line drawing. This is one of the few exceptions (compare line drawing below: **78**).

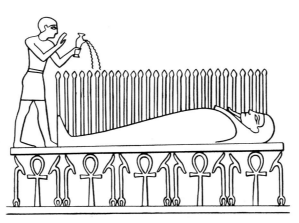

**58.** Osiris Germinante. Mummy with growing grain. Bas-relief. Philae, Egypt.

**59.** Sacrifice victim with corn growing out of his belly, illustrating the mythic sense of the sacrifice: life itself arising from the open body of the victim. Piedras Negras, Guatemala, A.D. eighth century.

therefore, appear in temples, where the mind, through contemplation, is to be released from attachment to the merely historical (temporal and local) aspects of phenomenality and opened to a recognition of that informing ground *(brahman)* which animates all things and is at once our own "being" *(sat)*, our "consciousness" *(cit)*, and our "bliss" *(ānanda)*. The Indian gods are envisioned personifications of modes of this everlasting source; not things in themselves, not facts, but, as it were, transparencies reflecting the will in nature and, as such, their images are appropriate to temples. In contrast to the figures in works of art of the secular genre *(deśī)*, they open the mind to *brahman* and are known, therefore, as the "path," or the "way" *(mārga)*. The noun *mārga* is derived from the Sanskrit verbal root *mṛg*, to hunt (by following the track of an animal through the forest to its lair); the animal to be found through contemplation of the image of a god being, of course, that indwelling golden "person" *(purusha)* which is one's own eternal portion.

Thus the dieties of India are to be recognized as visionary personifications of states of consciousness and blissful being *(saccidānanda)* to be discovered within oneself. They are instances of what C. G. Jung termed "archetypes of the unconscious" and Bastian, "elementary ideas." But all dieties—no matter of what people—are of this nature, sprung from the common ground of the human imagination, though turned to the local aims and needs of a given folk, in a given place, at a given time. So that discovered likenesses between the gods, myths, and rites, say, of fifth-century Greece and Inca Peru, may reasonably be accounted for by a theory of *parallelism*—unless, of course, they relate to some such symbolic figure as the rooster, which can have arrived in its various sanctuaries only by *diffusion*.

In sum, whereas through the long history of the Way of the Animal Powers an uninterrupted course of diffusion of associated symbolic forms can be readily traced from Africa and Europe across Asia to Australia and through Beringland to America (see I.2: Map 31), in the case of the Way of the Seeded Earth the fairly simultaneous appearances in three distinct parts of the world—after some four

million years of Paleolithic hunting, gathering, and fishing—of signs, not only of Stone Age peoples beginning to cultivate the soil, but also of identical mythologies arising in association with this work, has not yet been explained. European scholars have generally favored the probability of a broad sharing both of culture goods and of ideas *(diffusion)*; Americans have almost unanimously rejected every suggestion of a transpacific commerce, attributing as much as they think possible to what Frobenius has termed the "paideumatic" influence of the landscape *(convergence)* and the rest to carriage by the Portuguese and Spanish in the late fifteenth and early sixteenth centuries A.D.; whereas Bastian, Jung, and, among British scholars, Frazer, have acknowledged the force of what Frazer in *The Golden Bough* has described as "the effect of similar causes acting alike on the similar constitution of the human mind in different countries and under different skies,"[30] which is to say *parallelism*.

In the main, I should think that for most of the earth it can be assumed that all three of these argued forces will have operated in the formation of those widespread cultural continuities which it is my purpose in the present work to lay before the reader's eye; while, with regard to that very special mystery of an American order of civilizations so like in form to those of the opposite hemisphere that over a hundred obvious correspondences could be catalogued (including cat's cradle games and the four classical elements) in the course of a couple of morning hours' recollection, each of us must decide for himself, whether to believe it possible that the human mind might be programmed in such detail that through the interfacing simply of the psyche and a landscape such a multitude of correspondences could have evolved.

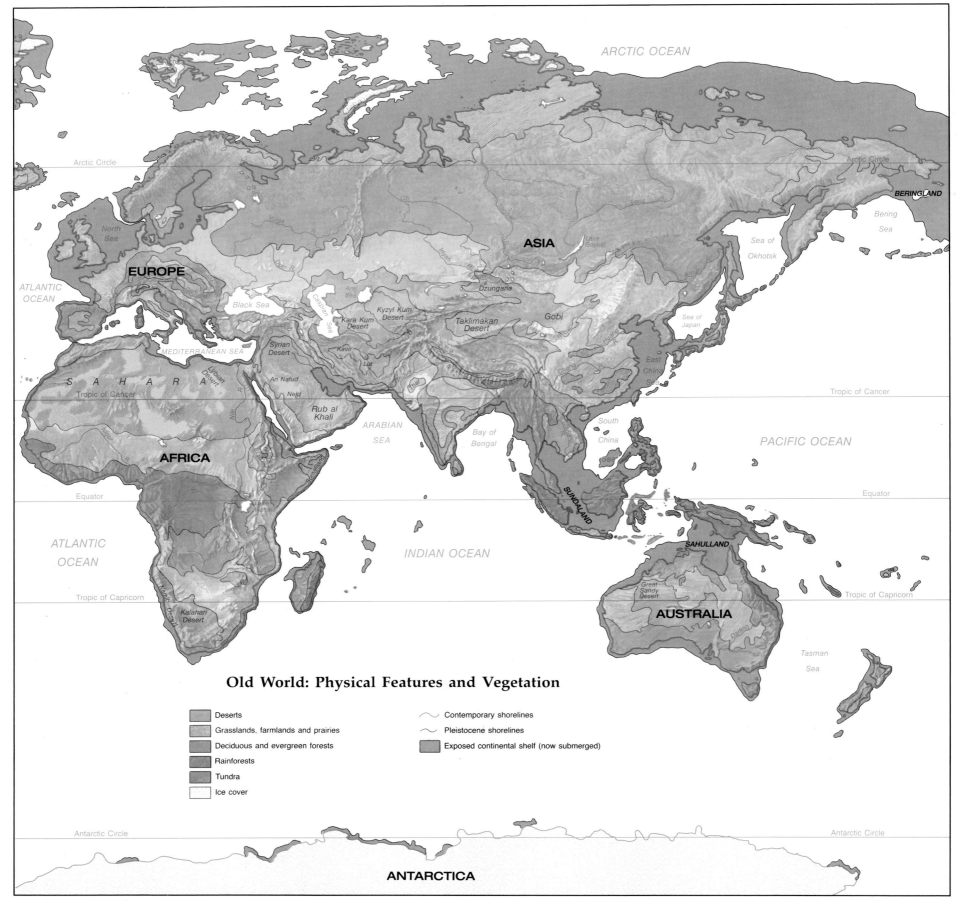

## Old World: Physical Features and Vegetation

Deserts
Grasslands, farmlands and prairies
Deciduous and evergreen forests
Rainforests
Tundra
Ice cover

Contemporary shorelines
Pleistocene shorelines
Exposed continental shelf (now submerged)

ARCTIC OCEAN

Arctic Circle

BERINGLAND

Bering Sea

North Sea

Sea of Okhotsk

ATLANTIC OCEAN

EUROPE

ASIA

Lake Baykal

Volga

Ob

Irtysh

Lena

Amur

Don R.

Dnie

Black Sea

Aral Sea

Caspian Sea

Dzungaria

Kara Kum Desert

Kyzyl Kum Desert

Taklimakan Desert

Gobi

Sea of Japan

MEDITERRANEAN SEA

Syrian Desert

Libyan Desert

Kavir

Lut

Huang

East China Sea

Tropic of Cancer

S A H A R A

An Nafud

Nejd

Thar

Chang

Tropic of Cancer

Nile

Rub al Khali

ARABIAN SEA

Bay of Bengal

South China Sea

PACIFIC OCEAN

AFRICA

Shebelli

SUNDALAND

Equator

Equator

ATLANTIC OCEAN

INDIAN OCEAN

SAHULLAND

Zambezi

Kalahari Desert

Great Sandy Desert

AUSTRALIA

Tropic of Capricorn

Tropic of Capricorn

Darling

Tasman Sea

Antarctic Circle

Antarctic Circle

ANTARCTICA

**Map 6**

30

# TWO WAYS TO RAPTURE

The sovereign role of geography in determining the destinies of races becomes evident when such a physical map as that of the Old World here shown is thoughtfully considered. Immediately notable is the chain of deserts reaching from Africa into China: the Sahara, Syro-Arabian desert, Persian deserts, Taklimakan, and Gobi. In the centuries following c.4000 B.C. these five became the homelands of five expansive language groups: the Hamites, Semites, Indo-Europeans, Uralo-Altaics, and Mongols; each of which in time became dominant in a distinct historic domain: the Hamites in Egypt, Semites in the later Near East, Indo-Europeans in Europe and northern India, Uralo-Altaics in the earlier Near East, and the Mongols in both China and Southeast Asia. As interpreted by Frobenius:

"Deserts are the landscapes of stern physical discipline and requirements of strong will. Endurance of the extreme or else disaster is here the message, but with an eye also to the opulence of the riverlands, their luxuries, their comforts, and their peace. So that when the valley dwellers in their lassitude mellow to a certain point, the hard-weathered, trial-tested sons of the desert descend upon them and claim mastery. Whereupon there ensues an interchange. The conquered take on the language of the victors, who appropriate the earlier inhabitants' civilization. And since in every one of the areas in which this interchange has occurred the native culture was rooted either in well-watered valleys, along coastlands, or on river courses (landscapes in which water is of the greatest influence), the geographical sense of this cultural conflict, finally, is of an adjustment of the effects of the planet's two extreme types of terrain."[31]

Northward of the desert belt extend those vast areas of grassland, forest, and then tundra which during the all but endless millennia of the Middle and Late Paleolithic Great Hunt were the Happy Hunting Grounds of races inured to the cold of the impending glaciers, who, in pursuit of the game that was both the physical support and mythic inspiration of their lives, were led across Beringland into and down the length of the Americas.

"When a man sought to know how he should live," said the Pawnee chieftain Letakots-Lesa, "he went into solitude and cried until in vision some animal brought wisdom to him."[32] The solitary vision quest of the adventuring individual was the type mystery of those rugged races. In its extreme form it is to be recognized in the psychological transformation of the shaman overtaken by spiritual familiars; and in Volume I.2 we have traced the evidences of a prehistoric diffusion of this order of rapture all the way from the Late Paleolithic temple caves of Europe, across Siberia and into America, as far south as to Tierra del Fuego (see I.2: Map 31 ).

Africa, we now know, was the cradle of the human race. It was thus from Africa that the earliest hunting populations of Europe were derived, and from Africa, as well, that the regions eastward, along the Tropic of Cancer, were first entered and explored. During the final glacial age (the Würm, c. 50,000–8,000 B.C., when there was so much of the earth's water locked in glacial ice that the oceans were 300 to 400 feet lower than today; so that both Beringland in the north and, in the south, Sahulland and Sundaland, lay exposed) the migrating tribes entering what are now Australia and New Guinea (as well as those then entering America) were without exception hunters—as are the aboriginal Australians to this day.

Shamanic raptures culminating in trance states have been recorded of (and described by) the native holy men, not only of Siberia and the great northern tract, but also of Australia and Tierra del Fuego (see I.2: 169–170 and 160–164). Among the Bushmen of the South African Kalahari desert, furthermore, trance dancing is practiced as a communal exercise out of which visions of a spirit world are brought and healing powers derived (see I.1: 94–99). In short: the visionary quest and experience have been consistently associated with the ritual lore of hunting-and-gathering peoples over the whole earth, the earliest evidences being already represented in the Late Paleolithic caves.

The epochal turn from hunting and gathering to plant and animal domestication, which seems to have occurred in Southeast Asia, roughly (very gradually, of course, through a long series of progressive changes) around 10,000 B.C., resulted in a fundamental shift of human interest and concern throughout those areas between the Gobi desert and Australia that on our map are colored dark green. The paideumatic influence of the animal powers, which through millennia

**60.** In Lapland (note the reindeer sleigh) a shaman lies in trance with his drum on his back and his female associate, brush in hand, watching to keep flies away. For it is thought that flies on his body while a shaman's spirit is in flight might hinder, even prevent, the spirit's return. Seventeenth century engraving. (See I.2:156–179 and **302**.)

**61.** Rock painting from the "crypt" of the great temple cave Lascaux, in the Dordogne, France, c. 15,000–9,000 B.C. Wearing a bird mask, a shaman lies on his back, phallus erect, evidently in trance, before a bison mysteriously wounded; for there is no one behind the bull who might have hurled the envisioned lance. (See I.1:58–66 and **105**.)

**62.** A Kung Bushman visionary dancer, entering into or returning from trance, is assisted by a fellow dancer. Botswana, Africa. c. A.D. 1960. (See I.1:90–97 and **162**.)

**63.** Bushman hunting scene on the Kalahari desert. A poisoned javelin is being skillfully aimed at a solitary grazing eland. (See I.1:**160/161, 168/169.**)

had supported and inspired human life and thought, gave place then and there to that of the tropical forest and very different model of the plant world, where out of death and rot young sprouts appear.

Already in Volume I, pages 103–112, a radical contrast has been noted between the ways of thought and action of the African Bushmen, hunters on the open plain, and the Pygmies, hunters also, but in the rain forest of the Congo (which on our map, page 30, is also dark green). The perspectives of an open plain extending into distance, showing separate things; both near and far, distinct in space, are unknown in the enclosing forest, where there is no perception of distance, no visible horizon, and all is enveloped in immediate life. There is no separating out

**64.** Pygmies gathering a harvest of small game. Through a section of their wilderness a long net had been laid, into which the animals had then been driven by the noise of the whole community of men, women and children closing in on them through the forest. (See I.1:**188** and **189.**)

and away of individuals alone; only the group, where all is well. Colin Turnbull, in his charming book *The Forest People, A Study of the Pygmies of the Congo,* describes in a memorable passage the utter bewilderment and then panic of one of his Pygmy friends whom he had conducted to the forest's edge to view from a height the prospect of an extensive plain where to the unpracticed eye distant herds appeared as ants. In terror the Pygmy turned and fled into his forest.[33]

The Pygmies have no trance dancing and no traditions (apparently) of the individual vision quest. All their rituals are communal. Even their music is of a number of pipes, each sounding only one note, blown, one by one at random by a cluster of seated pipers, in celebration, as it were, of the random soundings of the forest by night. The tension of the Bushman stalking an eland into which he is about to send a poisoned projectile, and his sympathetic identification, then, with the animal during its day or two of agony as the poison does its work, have no counterpart in the hunting ways of the forest-dwelling Pygmy tribes. At ease and at home in the protection of their jungle, they accept without especial ceremony, as fallen fruit, the relatively easily trapped or captured and killed game that fall to them. Nor do we find among them anything like the stern separation of male and female domains of concern that prevails among the Bushman tribes. The tutorial effects, evidently, of the plant-dominated forest and animal-dominated plain, even on the primal level of the simplest hunting-and-gathering peoples known, are thus in every sense contrary. And where plant cultivation then became the pursuit of highest concern—as it did after c. 10,000 B.C. in each of the chief geographical centers of agricultural origins—divergences in the social ways, rites, and myths, on the one hand, of the *animal* taught and, on the other, of the *plant*-cultivating societies, were increased.

Frobenius's recognition in the interactions on the hard stage of world history of the reciprocal virtues of these two orders of human life points to the inevitability of their operation. They are as apparent today on that hard stage as they were when the walls of Jericho fell to the sound of Joshua's trumpets. And in their bearing, moreover, on the spiritual, no less than on the historical, exercise of man's faculties, they are again evident today, as ever, in what have been called (to quote William James), "the varieties of religious experience," which are also, finally, of but two orders: those of the individual in solitude and those of any community as a whole.

In Japan, the first has been described as *ji-riki,* "one's own power; self-reliance," and the second as *ta-riki,* "outside power; another's power; salvation from without." In India they are called, respec-

**65.** Preparatory to entering trance an East Siberian (Yakut) shaman, beating his single-headed drum, invokes his familiar spirits. (See I.2:171–172.)

tively, "the way of the monkey" and "the way of the kitten"; for when a kitten is in trouble it calls "meow!" and its mother carries it to safety, but the little monkey, when carried by its mother, has to ride clinging with its own strength to her body. The type of the "monkey way" in India is of the yogi; in Buddhism, it is the way of Zen. Among the types in India of the "way of the kitten carried by its savior," the best-known today and most popular is of Vishnu in his incarnation as Krishna, encircled by and at the same time participating in the rapturous round dance of the Gopīs; while in Buddhism, the Savior most widely celebrated and revered is the inexhaustibly compassionate Buddha Amitābha (Amida in Japan), to whose paradisial lotus pond all those are carried who earnestly call upon his name.

Returning to the discussion by Spengler of the animal way (of release to freedom), and the plant way (of bondage, rootedness to the earth), we read: "There are appropriate names for these two orders: the plant is something *cosmic;* the animal, in addition, is a *microcosm in relation to a macrocosm.* Only insofar as a living unit can distinguish itself from the All and determine its position with respect to it, can it be said to be a microcosm. Even the planets in their great cycling courses are in bondage. . . .

"All that is cosmic is distinguished by *periodicity,* it has a pulse, a rhythm. All that is microcosmic is distinguished by *polarity*: the word 'against' epitomizes its whole character. It possesses tension. We speak of tense alertness, intense thought. But *all* awake relationships are by nature tensions: sense organ and perceived object, I and Thou, cause and effect, subject

**66.** Seated Buddha from one of the six temples surrounding the grand sanctuary of Mi'son. Vietnam, A.D. tenth century. Now in the Museum of Danang.

**67.** The priest Ganjin. Painted dry lacquer. Height 2 feet 8½ inches. Tōshōdai-ji, Nara, Japan, A.D. eighth century. The figure is of linen saturated in lacquer and modeled over a core that was subsequently removed.

Ganjin (Chinese Chien Chen) was a Chinese monk who arrived in Japan 754 A.D., on invitation of the imperial family, to supervise the establishment there of an austere Chinese monastic school of Buddhist thought and practice known in Japan as Ritsu ("regulation," "law"). Concerned principally with *vinaya*, the founding rules of Buddhist monastic life, its main temple is Tōshōdai-ji, where this magnificent portrait of its founder is preserved, who then was blind.

and predicate. Each of these implies a distinction in space and thereby a 'tension' [*Spannung*], and where the state that is significantly called *détente* [*Abspannung*, 'relaxation'] appears, fatigue immediately sets in and finally, in the microcosmic system, sleep. A human being asleep, relieved of every tension, is in a plantlike state."[34]

The two classic ways, then, to "release" (*moksha*) from the fatiguing animal/human state of tension as a microcosm in a macrocosm are, on the one hand, surrender to the authority of some endowed group or charismatic individual and, on the other hand, the realization, in full tension, of one's metaphysical identity as a microcosm with the macrocosm: "thou art that" (*tat tvam asi*).[35] In the high domain of the great "world religions," these two ways are represented in the founding ideals and disciplines, respectively, of the Christian and the Buddhist traditions. "I am the vine," the sacrificed Savior states, "you are the branches" (John 15:5); "no one comes to the Father but by me" (John 14:7). In contrast to which were the last words reported of the Buddha to his following of monks: "And now, O priests, I take my leave of you; all the constituents of being are transitory; work out your salvation with diligence."[36]

The geographical backgrounds of these complementary ways were, finally, the animal plains of the temperate and arctic North, of the vision quest and shamanic visionary voyages that have been viewed and reviewed in Volume I, and now, in contrast, the tropical equatorial belt of dionysian group ceremonials, to which are to be devoted the following chapters.

**68.** Krishna's "dancing ring" (*rāsamaṇḍala*). Painted cloth. 7 feet 8 inches by 8 feet 4 inches. Rajasthan, c. 1800.

In the timeless forest of Vrindavan, by the sacred Jumna, the gopīs (wives of a seminomadic cattle-herding band) nightly waking to the sound of Krishna's flute, slipped quietly (in dream?) from their husbands' beds and scattered to the moonlit wood, to join there in ever-circling dance the dark Lord who is the life and being of all beings. And he, replicating himself in as many forms as there were gopīs to be satisfied, so gratified all with the ardor of his love that each conceived herself to be with him alone.

# THE SACRIFICE:
## THE PRIME
## SYMBOL

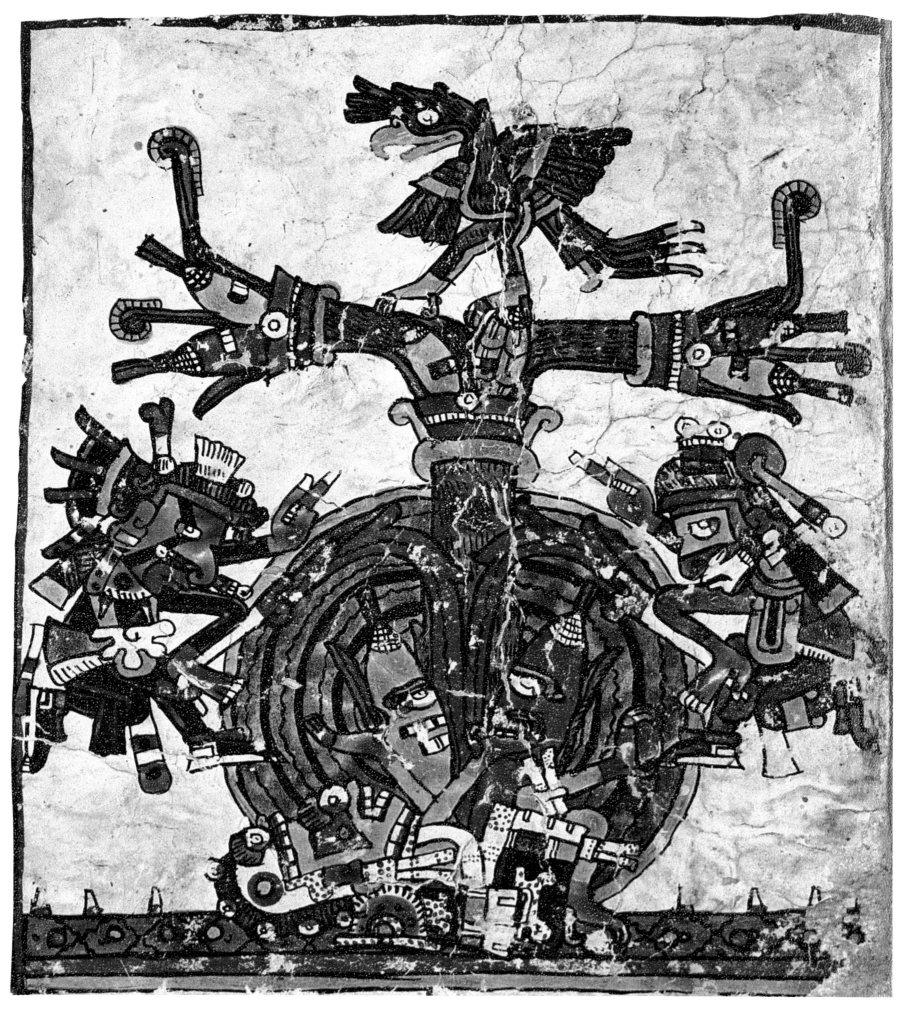

**69.** Tree of the Middle Place. Painting from *Codex Borgia,* Mexico, c. A.D. 1500. Rising from the body of an earth goddess recumbent on the spines of the caiman, or alligator, of the abyss, the Tree, encircled by the World Sea, is surmounted by a quetzal bird of bright plumage. Two streams of blood pour into the goddess, and from her body rise two ears of maize, a yellow and a red. The gods in attendance are Quetzalcoatl, the Feathered Serpent, god of the breath of life (of whom the quetzal bird is an attribute), and Macuil-xochitl, known also as 5 Flowers, lord of the dance and music, and of play.

Personifying the fertile earth, this goddess of life out of death is normally identified by a skull or skeletal jaw, which may be represented either as her head or as a kind of crown. She is known as the Maize Stalk Drinking Blood; also as 9 Grass. She is the mother of the gods and is in legend associated with a place called Skull[12] (that is, Place of the Skull). Compare Calvary (Latin *calvaria,* "skull"), also Golgotha (Aramaic *gūlgūlthā,* "skull"), i.e. *Place of the Skull.* In Mesoamerican art generally, skulls, skeletal jaws, and skeletonization appear as symbols not simply of death, but of generation and fertility out of death. As

noticed by Jill Leslie Furst, treating this goddess in a monograph entitled *The Skull as Fertility Symbol*: "The apparent contradiction between fertility, generation and rebirth on the one hand and bones on the other is in fact perfectly comprehensible in the context of general Native Mesoamerican ideology, in which the skeletal remains were—and in fact, here and there continue to be—regarded as the seat of the essential life force and the metaphorical seed from which the individual, whether human, animal, or plant, is reborn. . . ."[13] (See below: **97**).

# THE MYTH

"She was alone, the goddess Tlalteutli, walking on the primordial waters—a great and wonderful maiden, with eyes and jaws at every joint that could see and bite like animals. She was observed by the two great gods, Quetzalcoatl, the Plumed Serpent, and Tezcatlipoca, the Smoking Mirror. Deciding to fashion the world of her, they transformed themselves into serpents and came at her from either side. One seized her from the right hand to the left foot, the other from the left hand to the right foot, and together they ripped her asunder. From the parts they fashioned, not only earth and heavens, but also all the gods. And then to comfort the maiden for what had happened to her, all those gods came down and, paying her obeisance, commanded that there should come from her all the fruits that men require for life. From her hair they made trees, flowers and grass; from her eyes, springs, fountains, and the little caves; from her mouth, rivers and the great caves; from her nose, valleys; and from her shoulders, mountains. But the goddess wept all night, for she had a craving to consume human hearts. And she would not be quiet until they were brought to her. Nor would she bear fruit until she had been drenched with human blood."[37]

Throughout the ranges, not only of the early planting cultures, but also of all those archaic high civilizations whose mythologies were inspired by the idea of the earth and its biosphere as a self-sustained living entity, two complementary themes are outstanding. One is of death as the generator of life; the other, of self-offering as the way to self-validation. In the symbolism of the sacrifice both are comprehended, and in this Aztec image of the fantastic nymph Tlalteutli, they are represented as *together* fundamental to the constitution of temporality. For here, not only has an immortal been sacrificed to produce the living temporal world, but this world's life itself now exacts an unceasing immolation of temporal lives: *life lives on lives*. The image is metaphoric of the first condition of phenomenality. Its proper reference, therefore, is not to an event in the mythological past, "once upon a time," *in illo tempore*, "in the Beginning," but metaphorically, through that imagined form, to an actuality that is of now and forever, as are the connotations of all myth. The reference, that is to say, is transcendent of the illustrations. Mythological space and time being transtemporal and universal, the mythological moment is *NOW*. Its dwelling, moreover, is *HERE*, as an implicit dimension of this world as known. So that when any mythologized figure either is represented in a work of art or becomes personified in a rite, the intended reference, again, is to an imme-

**70.** The Dream of the Virgin. By Christoforo Simone dei Crocefissi, c. A.D. 1350. The bird here shown at the top of the Tree of Redemption is the pelican, which, according to the nature lore of the European Middle Ages, nourishes its young on blood drawn from its own breast—as Christ through the giving of his Holy Blood has nourished mankind to Salvation. The pelican, therefore, is in medieval Christian art emblematic of the saving grace of Christ's blood in the holy sacrifice of the mass. Compare **69** (opposite), on top of the Tree of the Middle Place, the quetzal bird as an attribute of the dead and resurrected Mesoamerican savior Quetzalcoatl, the Feathered Serpent, who, following a universal flood, created a new human race by descending to the Underworld and recovering there from the Lord of the Dead a collection of ancestral bones, to which he then gave life by pouring upon them blood drawn from his own sexual member.

diate here and now. The mind of the beholder is carried to the metaphorically connoted insight. Time collapses, past and present are as one, the mythic Immortal and its local representation are in connotation the same; so that in worship the two are to be experienced as identical: "This is my body. . . . This is the chalice of my blood." Those words of consecration of the Roman Catholic mass (according to a pious belief confirmed as dogma at the Fourth Lateran Council, A.D. 1215) are to be understood as transubstantiating the bread and wine of the sacrament of the altar literally into the body and blood of Christ Jesus; so that in the sacred space and time of the sacrifice of holy mass, past and present are undifferentiated, and the two sacrifices, of the altar and of Calvary, are the same.

A greatly gentled humanization of the archetype of the reciprocal dual sacrifice appears, therefore, in the medieval European "Dream of the Virgin," where in

contrast to the stark Mesoamerican symbolization of the creative ferocity of the will in nature, an order of values transcendent of the biological is recognized. The Aztec event is situated in a mythological age antecedent to the beginning of time, which is yet to be understood as enduring behind the veil of time as the creative ground of phenomenal life. Rites of physical blood sacrifice replicating the original incident are required to bring the social order to accord and thereby to refresh, according to this elementary philosophy, the force of the play throughout the social body of the energies of the tide of life. In contrast, the occasion of the Virgin's dream was of a realization in the course of historic time, and the primal sacrifice here was of a human, not of a supernatural, virgin; one, furthermore, not taken violently, but who in response to an angelic summons, offered herself willingly: "Be it done unto me according to thy word" (Luke 1:38); to which self-offering the supernatural response was that of which we read in Paul to the Philippians—of that one, "who, though he was in the form of God, did not count equality with God a thing to be grasped [or clung to], but emptied himself, taking the form of a servant, being born in the likeness of man. And being found in human form he humbled himself and became obedient unto death, even death on a cross" (Philippians 2:6–8).[38]

In the Christian figure of the crucified Christ Jesus, who was at once "true God" and "true Man," the two primal sacrifices are conjoined, as (1) of a God (Second Person of the Trinity) who "emptied himself" to participate as Man in the sorrows of this world, and (2) of a heroic historical personage (the Nazarene, son of Mary), who offered his life to the representation here, in this vale of tears, of a transcendent end, "not of this world" (John 18:36). The *imitatio Christi* of the founding Christian ideal is, therefore, as in Paul's instruction (Philippians 2:1–5): self-offering in humility and love "to the interests of others."

**71/72.** Memorial stelae on a former widow-burning ground at Kiken, near Mysore, South India.

In India living survivals and broken remnants can be identified from every period of the spiritual history of mankind. The symbolic rosette and lifted hand of these widow-burning memorials to four immolated women carry into the modern period archaic iconographic motifs that were originally associated with the Sumerian goddess Inanna, who descended to the Netherworld to witness there the funeral rites of her beloved, the "Bull of Heaven" (who was identified astrologically with the constellation Taurus, as was she with the planet Venus, as the evening and then the morning star). In the Underworld Inanna was slain and hung on a stake to rot, but at the time of the vernal equinox, when the constellation Taurus reappears in the evening sky and the local Near Eastern agricultural cycle is resumed, she, together with the Heavenly Bull whom her undaunted loyalty had rescued, arose from the Land of No Return to their life eternal.

In India the two terms of the dual sacrifice have been long symbolized in (1) the mythic image of Purusha (*puruṣa*: the transcendent "Person"; "Being of all beings"), which in itself is one, yet as the indwelling Reality of each is broken up, as it were, into many (see I.1: Figure 5 and text); and (2) the founding social ideal of *dharma* (from the verbal root *dhṛi*, "to hold, to preserve"), that categorical order of established duties through the performance of which the virtuous individual supports and preserves, not only his society, but thereby the order of the universe. Widow burning (*satī*, "suttee"), which in India was continued until forbidden by British law in 1829, was but an extreme statement of this structuring, first principle of Indian life. Through the complete giving over of herself to her *dharma* as a wife at one with her spouse, the good woman has disengaged herself from the mere appearance of separateness and in spirit identified both her spouse and herself with the nondual Being of all beings. The word *satī* is the present participle, feminine, of the Sanskrit verb "to be"; for such a wife has

Evidence in the Near East of something very like a suttee burial has been dated c. 60,000 B.C. (in northern Iraq: see I.1:52–53, and **76**). Entire courts in earliest Egypt, Sumer, and China were normally interred alive in the great tombs of deceased monarchs. And as already shown (see above: **28, 29**), mass burials around the remains of what appear to have been high personages have been uncovered in Neolithic Jericho and in America, in Panama, on the Pacific coast.

**73.** Goddess on a lion throne, into whose presence a votary bearing an offering is being conducted. Babylonian cylinder seal (greatly enlarged), c. 1750 B.C. The goddess enthroned is Ishtar, Babylonian counterpart of Sumerian Inanna. There is a lion beneath her feet and on the altar before her lies the head of a sacrificed ram. A rosette with eight petals, standard symbol in this culture for the planet Venus (= Ishtar), appears before her in conjunction with a crescent moon. Three figures approach in worship, the middle one (perhaps masculine) carries a young goat for sacrifice, and behind these three is a dog.

Examining in detail this scene, we note that the votary (who would represent the owner of the seal) is being introduced to the enthroned goddess by a lesser female divinity (wearing a low horned head-dress) whose raised right hand by the rosette sug-

gests the Indian emblem of a suttee sacrifice. The third female (wearing a high horned headdress, like that of the goddess enthroned) is the fertility goddess Gula, whose attendant animal is a dog. The symbolic plant elevated in her hand is then a branch of the tree of eternal life, the same that in Buddhist thinking is the Bo-tree, and in Christian, the Cross, Holy Rood.

In Classical iconography the dog is the animal of Hermes, guide to the knowledge of immortality. With its nose to the ground it follows an invisible trail, and such a trail, by analogy, would be that of the Mystic Way (Sanskrit, *márga*, from the verbal root *mrg*, to hunt by trailing an animal to its lair: see above: 29). The valuable animal thus to be found is here the lion lying at Ishtar's feet and reflected on her throne. The lion is symbolic of the sun. Vanishing into the sphere

of the sun to become in three days resurrected, the moon is recognized as in counterpart the sacrifice offered in the altar fire; whereas Venus — following as evening star the sun into the netherworld, then heralding as morning star the promise of its rising — is the model celestial of the Way itself of spiritual transformation through self-immolation.

So that in sum, the message pictured on this ancient seal is of its owner's faith in his chosen guardian divinity, by whom he has been brought to the altar of that Savior whose celestial sign — first as evening, then as morning star — marks the way to self-transcendence. An interesting detail of this scene is the swastika posture of the guiding figure's arms, one hand drawing her devotee to the altar, the other pointing to the symbolic star. This posture in later Classical art is a characteristic of the Gorgon.

identified herself truly with that which (in terms of Hindu belief) she has always been.

In Middle America, both in Mayaland and in the Toltec and Aztec north, a veritable frenzy of sacrifice provided human hearts and blood enough, not only for the earth-goddess beneath, but also for the no less ravenous sun-god above. The modern tourist in Yucatan viewing at Chichén Itzá the large ceremonial ball court is amazed to learn that at the end of each festival game the captain of the *winning* team knelt in midfield to be there beheaded. Wars were conducted for the gaining of captives to be sacrificed on the summits of great temple towers, the broad stairways of which they would mount as gods ascending in triumph to their moment of transfiguration. St. Augustine wrote that the savior went to the cross as a bridegroom to his bride, and this was very much the attitude, apparently, of many of those sacrificed on the Middle American ball courts and on the summits of the temple towers.

Moreover, among many of the North American warrior tribes to whom the arts and associated rites of Middle American maize agriculture had been carried, there

**74.** Repoussé gold plaque, A.D. twelfth–thirteenth century, found in the Sacred Cenote, or Well of Sacrifice, at Chichén Itzá. In c. 1566, describing the function of the Sacred Cenote, the Spanish Bishop Fray Diego de Landa wrote: "Into this well they have had, and then had, the custom of throwing men alive as a sacrifice to the gods, in times of drought, and they believed they did not die though they never saw them again. They also threw into it a great many other things, like precious stones and things which they prized."[14]

are distinct signs of a sharing of this understanding. The methodical torture of captives reported of the Iroquois and their neighbors, for example, was almost certainly a distant reflex of the Middle American sacrifice; and the battle cry "It's a good day to die!" reported of the Sioux braves riding into the rain of bullets of General Custer's cavalry at the battle of the Little Bighorn was an expression of the same mentality, untouched by fear.

There is a telling report, from the year 1637, by the French Jesuit missionary François Le Mercier (1604–1690), where the behavior described, not only of a young Iroquois captive about to be tortured to death, but also of his Huron captors, clearly reveals (it seems to me) that the youth was going, and indeed was being conducted, to his exceedingly painful death as a bridegroom to his bride.

"On the 2nd of September, we learned that an Iroquois prisoner had been brought to the village of Onnentisati, and that they [the Huron] were preparing to put him to death. This Savage was one of the eight captured by them at the lake of the Iroquois; the rest had saved themselves by flight. At first we were horrified at the thought of being present at this spectacle,

**75.** Temple No. 1, called Temple of the Great Jaguar, at the eastern end of the Great Plaza at Tikal, Petén, Guatemala. Height to top of the roof comb: 170 feet. Mayan Late Classic Period, c. A.D. 700.

As one of five such towers marking the ceremonial center of what formerly was a Mayan urban area of some 222 square miles, it has been observed that in the course of the hour of sunset during the equinoc-

tial seasons (late March and late September) a broad shadow cast from Temple No. 2, at the western end of the Plaza, climbs slowly the tall stairway of sacrifice to enter the chapel door.

but, having well considered all, we judged it wise to be there, not despairing of being able to win his soul for God.

"Accordingly we departed, the Father Superior, Father Garnier, and I together. We reached Arontaen a little while before the prisoner, and saw this poor wretch coming in the distance, singing in the midst of 30 or 40 Savages who were escorting him. He was dressed in a beautiful beaver robe and wore a string of porcelain beads around his neck, and another in the form of a crown around his head. I will say here that, up to the hour of his torment, we saw only acts of humanity exercised toward him, but he had already been quite roughly handled since his capture.

"We approached to look at him more closely; he raised his eyes and regarded us very attentively. The Father Superior was invited to make him sing; but he explained that it was not that which had brought him there. He approached him

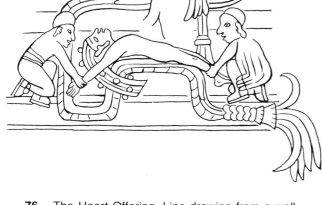

**76.** The Heart Offering. Line drawing from a wall panel, Temple of the Warriors, Chichén Itzá, Yucatán. Mayan Postclassic Period, A.D. eleventh–fifteenth centuries.

The victim, painted blue (the sacrificial color), is stretched across an upward-curving altar (to elevate the breast) by four old men called *chacs*, one to each arm and leg, who are also painted blue. The altar is here pictorially identified with the dragonlike "Feathered Serpent" emblematic of Quetzalcoatl (Mayan, Kukulcan), whose very name (*quetzal* = "quetzal bird"; *coatl* = "serpent") declares that in him are conjoined the antithetic powers mythologically connoted in the bird and the serpent (see below: **78**).

Astrologically, Quetzalcoatl is identified with the planet Venus, both as evening and as morning star, and is thus, like Babylonian Ishtar (see above: **73**), a model celestial of the Way to spiritual transformation through sacrifice. In this scene the victim, stretched across the god's altar, is identified with him by analogy. The *nacom*, the executioner, approaches, plunges into the victim's breast the sacrificial knife, thrusts a hand into the opening and rips out the heart, which he sets, still throbbing, on a salver that he hands to the *chilan*, the presiding priest.[15]

**77.** Stela from Santa Lucia Cotzumalhuapa, Guatemala. Mayan Late Classic Period, c. A.D. 700.

The *chilan*, presiding priest of the occasion, having received from the *nacom* the pulsing heart, swiftly smears with blood the face of the image of the god to whom the sacrifice is being made and elevates the offering, which the god descends to receive.[16] The little figure facing the officiating priest and pointing likewise upward is the ghost or spirit of the victim (note the opened belly) participating in the offering. The head before which the heart is held represents the image of the god.

and told him that we all felt a great deal of compassion for him. Meanwhile, they brought him food from all sides,—some bringing sagamité, some squashes and fruits,—and treated him only as a brother and a friend. From time to time he was commanded to sing, which he did with so much vigor and strength of voice that we wondered how he could be equal to it,— especially as he had done hardly anything else day and night since his capture. A Captain [chieftain], raising his voice, addressed to him these words: 'My nephew, thou hast good reason to sing, for no one is doing thee any harm; behold thyself now among thy kindred and friends.' Good God, what a compliment! All those who surrounded him, with their affected kindness and their fine words, were so many butchers who showed him a smiling face only to treat him afterwards with more cruelty.

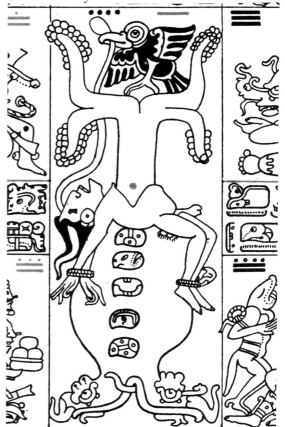

**78.** Line drawing, page 3a, the Dresden Codex. Precolumbian Mexico, c. A.D. fourteenth century.

Revealed here is a mythic reading of the sacrifice. The glyph *Ahau*, just beneath the victim, denotes the last day of a *katun* (a Mayan calendric cycle of 7,200 days), while rising from the victim's opened belly is the Tree of the Middle Place, which in the Beginning sprang from the body of the sacrificed cosmic goddess (above: **69**). Hers was the primal sacrifice, of which every other is a likeness, and was of world creation; this is of world renewal at the end of an age.

At the top of the tree is a quetzal bird (or perhaps vulture) consuming a snake that has emerged from the victim's head. Serpents shed their skins to be as it were reborn and are accordingly metaphorical of the power of earthbound life to throw off death; whereas birds (which fly and are the only creatures besides man that sing) are associated universally with the raptures of the spirit released from bondage to the earth. The evident sense of a bird consuming a serpent emerging, as here, from the body of a sacrifice should then be, of the entering or transformation of a serpent soul into a bird; which is to say, the dedication through this sacrifice of the next secular age and its life to a life in the spirit.

**79.** A 1723 copperplate engraving by the French artist Bernard Picart (1673–1733), from an eighteenth-century survey entitled *The Religious Ceremonies and Customs of the Several Nations of the World* published in London in 1731, showing a man being bound for sacrifice by the Antis, a tribe that inhabited the foothills of the Andes before the Incas drove them out. In the background, under a small hilltop hut, hangs a corpse, the victim of a previous ceremony. The text accompanying Picart's numerous illustrations, although exaggeratedly gruesome in order to titillate and to pique the curiosity of the book-buying public, correctly notes the transfiguration of the victim into a god: "They put all their captives to death without the least mercy, but with this difference, that a prisoner of no distinction was immediately put to death, whereas a man who was thought worthy of that fatal honour, was sacrificed with great solemnity; for which purpose he was stript naked, then they tied him to a great stake....They did not immediately tear him to pieces, but first cut the flesh from the most brawny parts...after which their men, women, and children smear'd themselves with his blood of these unhappy wretches, and devour'd them before they were dead....[They] call'd this bloody execution a religious ceremony, and rank'd all such as had suffer'd death with courage...in the number of their gods, and lodg'd 'em under hutts [sic] on the tops of their mountains...."

"In all the places through which he had passed he had been given something with which to make a feast; they did not fail here in this act of courtesy, for a dog was immediately put into a kettle, and he was brought into the cabin where the people were to gather for the banquet. He had someone tell the Father Superior to follow him. So we entered and placed ourselves near him; the Father Superior took occasion to tell him to be of good cheer; that he would in truth be miserable during the little life that remained to him, but that, if he would listen to him and believe what he had to tell him, he would assure him of an eternal happiness in Heaven after his death.

"Seeing that the hour of the feast was drawing near, we withdrew into the cabin where we had taken lodgings, not expecting to find an opportunity to speak further with him until the next day. But we were greatly astonished and much rejoiced when we were told that he was coming to lodge with us. And still more so afterwards, when the Father Superior had all the leisure necessary to instruct him in our mysteries,—in a word, to prepare him for Holy Baptism. A goodly band of Savages who were present, not only did not interrupt him, but even listened to him with close attention. What a great advantage it is to have mastered their language, to be loved by these people, and to have influence among them! I do not think the Christian truths have ever been preached in this country on an occasion so favorable, for there were present some from nearly all the nations who speak the Huron tongue. The Father Superior found him so well-disposed that he did not consider it advisable to postpone any longer his baptism. This being accomplished, we withdrew from his presence to take a little rest. For my part it was almost impossible for me to close my eyes.

"The next morning, the prisoner again confirmed his wish to die a Christian, and he even promised the Father that he would remember to say in his torments, 'Jesus taïtenr,' 'Jesus, have pity on me.' About noon he made his Astataion, that is, his farewell feast, according to the custom of those who are about to die.

"The Sun, fast declining, admonished us to withdraw to the place where this

cruel Tragedy was to be enacted. It was in the cabin of one Atsan, who is the great war Captain; therefore it is called 'Otinontsiskiaj ondaon,' meaning 'the house of cut-off heads.' We took a place where we could be near the victim and say an encouraging word to him when the opportunity offered. Toward 8 o'clock in the evening eleven fires were lighted along the cabin, about one brass distant from each other. The people gathered immediately, the old men taking places above, upon a sort of platform, the young men below. Before the victim was brought in, Captain Aenons encouraged all to do their duty, representing to them the impor-

tance of this act, which was viewed, he said, by the Sun and by the God of war. He had hardly finished when the victim entered....

"For me to describe in detail all he endured during the rest of the night would be almost impossible; we suffered enough in forcing ourselves to see a part of it. Of the rest we judged from their talk. One thing, in my opinion, greatly increased his consciousness of suffering—that anger and rage did not appear upon the faces of those who were tormenting him, but rather gentleness and humanity, their words expressing only raillery, or tokens of friendship and goodwill...."[39]

**80.** Male dancer with snake. Polychrome ceramic vase from Altar de Sacrificios, Petén, Guatemala. Mayan Classic Period, A.D. 400-800. Museo de la Aurora, Guatemala.

Wearing trousers made of a jaguar skin with the animal's tail attached, the dancer is apparently in a mythic role. "Jaguar Sun," Balanke, was one of the Mayan names of the sun or sun-god.[17]

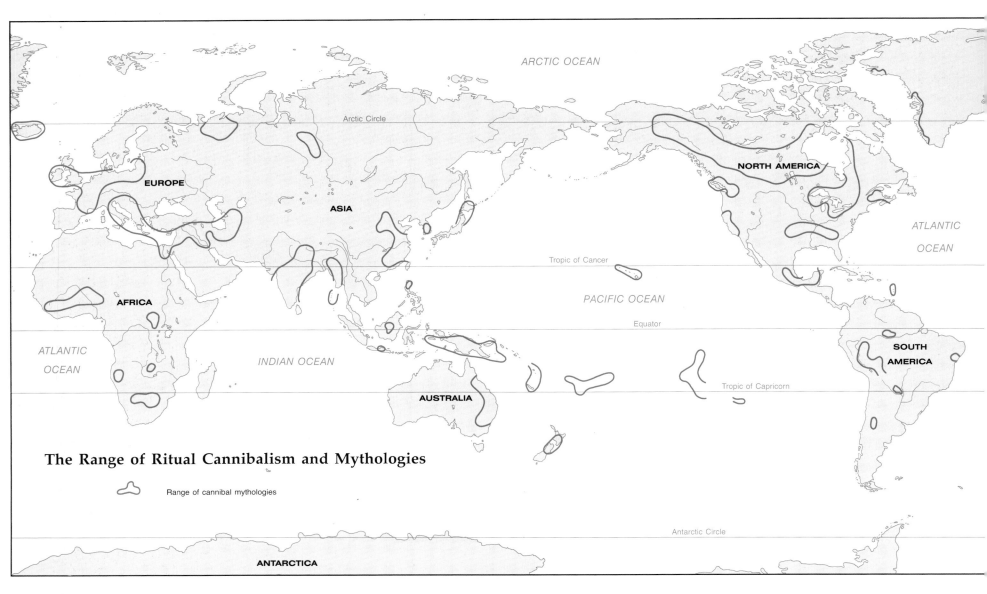

The Range of Ritual Cannibalism and Mythologies

⌒⌒  Range of cannibal mythologies

**Map 7** Although the ubiquity of cannibalism in myth suggests that the practice was once widespread, supporting evidence is notoriously unreliable. Even confirmed cannibals, aware of strong European taboos, were reluctant to admit the practice to early travelers, but they would happily attribute such activities to their neighbors. This map, based on the more reliable reports and on archaeological evidence, but not time specific, suggests a strong interrelationship between cannibalistic practices and the three agricultural matrices (see **Map 1**). Ritual cannibalism is today a rare occurrence, if not an extinct practice.

Cannibalism is a feature commonly associated with the ceremonies of agricultural tribes recognizing the mythological image of a primal being whose body became and is now the universe. There is a widely dispersed folklore theme related to this mythology, where a living person is slain, from whose buried remains the local food plants first appear (compare in I.1: 207–208, the Ojibwa and Seneca tales of the origin of maize). Psychologically (I suppose), cannibalism would be a natural — one might even say, inevitable — adjunct to any ceremonial wherein the motifs of such a myth would be translated into act. The infant at its mother's breast is (in fact) a little cannibal (innocent, as is nature) for whom the mother (whose substance it is there consuming) is the universe; and mythologies, accordingly, in which the universe is recognized as a living being from whose body all life and nourishment are drawn return the mind, by analogy, to an infantile (or, in Freudian terms, "pre-Oedipal") condition and situation.

Fundamentally different are the mythologies of primarily hunting tribes, where life is supported by deliberate acts of confrontation, killing, and ceremonious reconciliation. The psychology there

(in Freudian terms, "Oedipal") is of anxiety and tension (Spengler's *Spannung;* see above: page 33). The whole concern of Volume I, *The Way of the Animal Powers* (as, also, of Freud's *Totem and Tabu*) is in mythologies of this order; mythologies of *Spannung.* The concern, in contrast, of *The Way of the Seeded Earth* is in mythologies of *Abspannung (détente),* relaxation to a condition akin to sleep, or rather, nightmare. For the innocence of nature in its unmitigated manifestation of the voracity of life, which feeds on life, is something horrific to the waking mind committed to values of the light world, where things are experienced, not as of the one life, self-consuming, but as separate from each other. In the aboriginal festivals of those parts of the world where the silent cosmic feeding of the plant kingdom on the substances of its mother Earth is the one, ever-present, inescapable, immediate experience of the meaning of life in a living environment, there is always a moment of ultimate frightfulness, executed either in some hidden place, or in full view, as the pivotal climax of an enveloping, dreamlike revel of feasting and hilarity, masks, music and dance, in celebration of the sublime frenzy of this life which is rooted (if one is to see and speak truth) in a cannibal nightmare.

**81.** Yamāntaka, "Victorious over Yama," or the "Slayer of [the fear of] the Lord Death." Tibetan temple banner. A.D. nineteenth century.

Trampling underfoot figures symbolic of earthly fears and desires, holding as his drinking bowl a human cranium, filled with blood, this instructive manifestation of the Bodhisattva of Transcendent Wisdom, Mañjuśrī (pictured above), is surrounded by secondary manifestations. Below is Yama, Judge of the Dead, flanked by two of the kings of the world quarters. Above these (left) is the Great Black Protector of Religion, Mahākāla, and (right) Paldan Lhamo, his female counterpart. In the upper corners, right and left, are figures symbolic of lunar and solar consciousness: lunar being participation in the terrors of this temporal sphere; solar, of disengagment from the same, to rest in peace in what may be thought of as Eternity. The raised sword of Mañjuśrī is the keen blade of "discrimination" (*viveka*), which distinguishes the Knower from the Known, consciousness from its objects, true being from apparent becoming. Identification with the Knower is the way to transcendent peace.

Compassion, however, for the creatures of this world may move such a Knower, cleansed of the fear of death, to participation in their service (Philippians 2:6-8; see again above: **38**). This is the mode of the Savior, or in Buddhist terms, a Bodhisattva, as teacher of the Wisdom of the Yonder Shore, which is, that in the processes of eternity inheres, as in the light of the waning and waxing moon the unchanging light of the sun. In the upper corners of this banner the two orbs are of equal size, as when, on the fifteenth night of its cycle, a rising full moon confronts and reflects directly the light from the west of the setting sun.

Yama (below, center), here as Judge of the Dead among skulls, was in Hindu mythology the first mortal to die, and is in this sense a counterpart of Adam. As subordinate to Yamāntaka — the "Ender" (*antaka*) of [the fear of] Yama — he is revealed as but an infernal reflection of the grace of Mañjuśrī. (Compare the symbolic elements of **97**, below).

Nietzsche, in *The Birth of Tragedy* (1872), recognized in the art forms of classic Greece, and by extension, art forms generally, two antithetical modes of experience and expression: the "Apollonian," of delight in the light world and the beauty of individuated forms, and the "Dionysian," of rapture in the glory of the will in nature, into and out of which forms dissolve and reappear in the unending play of the one Being through all beings. Sculpture and music (specifically the dithyramb) are in Nietzsche's view the arts, respectively, of the Apollonian and Dionysian modes of experience; and in Greek tragedy the two, in his view, are balanced in the reciprocity of the agonies of the individuated characters on stage and the responses (in choral music and dance) of the homogenized satyr chorus. Whereas in diametric opposition to these two poetic orders of address to the world is the critical posture of what Nietzsche termed the "Socratic" mind, which is sealed off from all rapture except that of reasonable judgment and definition—which conduce in the end to a prosaic reign of mere proprieties emptied of life.

"In song and dance," states Nietzsche, "man expresses himself as a member of a higher community; he has forgotten how to walk and speak and is on the way toward flying, dancing into the air. His very gestures are of enchantment....He feels himself to be a god, going about in ecstasy, exalted, like the gods beheld in his dreams....He is no longer an artist, he has become a work of art. In a paroxysm of intoxication the creative power of all nature has come to light in him as the highest rapture of the One that is All. Nature, with its true voice undissembled cries out to us: 'Be as I am! I, the primordial ever-creating mother amidst the ceaseless flux of appearances, ever impelling into existence, eternally finding in these transformations satisfaction.' "[40]

**82.** Seal disk of a golden ring from Isopata, near Knossos. Crete, c. sixteenth century B.C.

A strange scene full of musical movement, representing apparently an epiphany among flowers beheld by the two worshipping figures, left. The movement starts from above, where a small female form is hovering in air as though descending, while the two large figures, center and right, appear to have just arrived. A single great eye is to be seen before the knee of the central apparition. Someone evidently is watching from another world, possibly below. Two serpents strangely hovering in air add to the mystery of the scene, as do the griffinlike heads of all four of the variously gesturing large females.[18]

In the religion of Crete, as in that of the Greek Dionysian mysteries, a distinctive feature was the prominence of women in giving form and substance to the worship. Music and the dance were essential to the rites, conducing to raptures culminating in visionary epiphanies. However, although an identification with the whole world of nature as itself an epiphany of divinity was fundamental to both orders, there are in the works of art of the pre-Homeric Cretan era no signs of anything like the violence, centuries later, of the Dionysian orgies. In Euripides' *The Bacchae* the god states that because the people of Thebes had rejected and denied him as a god, he now, returning, had "stung them with frenzy, hounded them from home to the mountains, where they wander, crazed of mind."[19] The centuries of dominance of the patriarchal Olympian gods that had intervened between the dates of the Cretan visionary dancers and Euripides' mad bacchae surely will have been the season, referred to by the god, when his divinity was impugned. For there is a basic psychological law that any living god unrecognized becomes a demon.

**83.** Apollo and the Nine Muses. Painting by Baldassarre Peruzzi (1481-1536). Now in the Pitti Palace, Florence.

Motivated by the light of the Apollonian mind, the Nine Muses dance, together with their lord, on the summit of Mt. Helikon. Hesiod (c. 800 B.C.), when pasturing his flock on a slope of that mystic peak where heaven and earth come together, opened his ears to their music. "We know how, both to lie, and to speak sooth," they told him, endowing him there with the power to sing of things both past and future. And in token of this initiation, they broke off (as he tells) and handed him a branch of olive.[20]

They are the nine daughters of Mnemosyne (the goddess "Memory"), by Zeus, and the arts of their endowment also are nine: bucolic poetry, from the Muse Thalia; history from Kleio; epic poetry from Kalliope; and from Terpsichore, the dance; tragedy from Melpomene; love song from Erato; Enterpe is the Muse of the flute; Polymnia, of choral sacred song; and Ourania, astronomy with knowledge thereby of the gods.[21]

**84.** Dionysos among satyrs, singing to a lyre.

**85.** Raging maenad wearing a serpent headband and fawnskin cape; in her right hand, the Bacchic thyrsus; in her left, a live animal to be torn apart. From a Greek kylix, fifth century B.C.

**86.** The arrival in Attica of Dionysos, after his years of travel and teaching in Asia. Red-figured vase, sixth century B.C. Museo Archaeologico, Orvieto.

In the god's own words, as imagined by Euripides: "Far behind me lie those golden-rivered lands, Lydia and Phrygia, where my journeying began. Overland I went, across the steppes of Persia where the sun strikes hotly down, through Bactrian fastness and the grim waste of Media. Thence to rich Arabia I came; and so, along all of Asia's swarming littoral of towered cities where Greeks and foreign nations, mingling, live, my progress made. There I taught my dances to the feet of living men, establishing my mysteries and rites, that I might be revealed on earth for what I am: a god."[22]

Euripides' play was composed 80 years before Alexander the Great's triumphant thrust (332–327 B.C.) through Persia into Bactria and the Punjab. Evidently it was already known that all the way from Greece, across the Near East into India, cults of a dionysiac kind were ubiquitous; so that when Alexander and his young officers, students all of Aristotle, then reached the Indus, they readily recognized in the Indian gods the counterparts of their own. And today, of course, it is apparent to every student of this subject that the Ras, for example, of the Lord Krishna and his gopis (above: **68**) corresponds in sense, as well as in form, to a bacchanalian rite.

The date of the Greek vase painting here reproduced is a full century and a half earlier than that of Euripides's *Bacchae*, yet its argument is already of the same mythology. Its season was of the founding of Persian Empire (the bounds of which extended from the Aegean to the Indus) by Cyrus the Great (d. 529 B.C.) and Darius I (r. 525-486 B.C.). That was the period in India of the life and teaching of the Buddha (c. 563-483 B.C.), and in Greece, of Pythagoras (c. 580-500 B.C.) and Herakleitos (c. 540-480 B.C.). The painting shows the god arriving attired as a noble Persian, but accompanied by a dancing ithyphallic silenus (a kind of modified centaur) lewdly capering behind his master's back before a woman who is standing with raised arms. What the intended relevance of the symbolic bird of prey bearing a serpent in its beak may have been to this incongruous scene is not immediately evident. However, almost certainly, it represents by analogy (which is the method proper to mythological thought) the mystic sense of the god's arrival with such an attendant.

For in Greece the eagle was the bird of heavenly Zeus and likewise of the sun, whereas Dionysos, begotten of Zeus, was an earthly incarnation of that god. Serpents, which in their going are fluent as the waters by which the earth is fertilized, with the constant flashing of their fiery forked tongues tell of the solar fire of which they are the earthbound vehicles. In Greece they were revered as epiphanies of Zeus,

who in the form of a serpent, according to a Cretan version of the legend, copulated with Persephone, his daughter; so that it then was she (not Semele) who bore Dionysos.[23] Serpents in bacchic orgies were essential, to be torn apart as sacrificial offerings, both of and to the god; while in art works celebrating these rites (as, for instance, **84**, opposite, of Dionysos singing), horse-tailed sileni, as well as satyrs and raging maenads, are the god's ecstatic companions.

Legends of the arrival in Greece of Dionysos bring him by sea to one or another of the wine-growing villages along the Attic coast between Marathon and Point Sounion. The vase painting (appropriately on a wine jar) suggests, besides the god's historic ar-

rival, the spiritual import of the gift of wine. For the bird and serpent symbol is an archetypal image known to many peoples over a great part of this earth, associated generally with a metaphorical sun-bird/moon-serpent theme, wherein the antitheses are connoted of heaven and earth, release and bondage, eternity and time. As applied to the present occasion, the relevant message would seem to have been, that with the arrival of this ageless god of ecstacies (fermentation being itself an ecstacy of the grape) there was given to Greece a means to break the hold on the mind of Apollonian form and purely rational discourse, releasing thereby, both the imagination to celestial flight, and the senses to participation in the rapturous spontaneities of the mystery that itself is life.

**87.** Orgiastic dance with serpents before Dionysos as Hades. Vase painting by Polygnotos. From Tomb 128 in the Valle Trebba, Spina, Italy.

The Hindu mother-goddess Kālī (Black Time), out of whom all things are born, is equally the cannibal ogress by whom all are consumed. The Indian saint and teacher Sri Ramakrishna (1836–1886), once beheld in vision a beautiful dark woman who came out of the waters of the Ganges, gave birth to a child, nursed it tenderly, opened her jaws, consumed the child, and returned into the river.[41] The oral aggression of the cannibal infant, we are told,[42] may give rise in its imagination to a talion, or retaliation in kind, by the mother, who becomes thereby the cannibal witch of the fairy tale. Thus, on many levels of symbolic association cannibalism is an expectable image, when the *Abspannung* of a Dionysian intoxication dissolves all disciplines of discrimination and releases in a possessed multitude the sense of an all-subsuming unity impelling them as one being.

Cannibalism, as far as I know, has not been reported of the North American tribes, though in the Caribbean it was rampant. Indeed, the word "cannibal" itself was in the fifteenth century derived from the name Carib, meaning "brave man, strong man," of the most feared canoe-warriors of that region.[43] Significantly, among the remains of the cultures (early snuffed out) of the southeastern United States, there is an engraved shell gorget from an excavated mound in Sumner County, Tennessee, showing a warrior, apparently dancing, holding a mace in his left hand and in his right a severed head (Figure 91, opposite). There is also a sculptured pipe bowl from Spiro Mound (Figure 90), in Oklahoma, showing a warrior ceremonially garbed beheading a naked victim. These are relics of the great agriculturally supported Mississippian Culture of c. A.D. 800 to 1600, remains of which have been found dispersed from Oklahoma to Georgia and north through Illinois, Indiana, and Ohio. As Frederick J. Dockstader, former director of the Museum of the American Indian, in which these two relics are preserved, has remarked of the beheading scene: "This pipe reinforces the many other indications that human sacrifice was common among prehistoric Southeastern peoples."[44]

The most immediate antecedents of the agricultural mythologies, festivals, and folkways of this widely dispersed Mississippean culture complex have been found, of course, in Mexico, whence the whole North American system of maize, beans, and squash agriculture derived. Among the known remains of that originating high-culture zone are a number of Precolumbian native books, known as codices, that have been preserved from the period of the Conquest in a scattering of European libraries. Treating largely of mythological, astronomical, and genealogical topics, they are inscribed in a painted pictorial script on strips of sized native parchment or paper, 8 or 9 inches wide and 10 to 15 yards long, which are then folded screenwise to form books of uncut pages roughly 8 or 9 inches square (Figure 89).

Among the recurrent images of the imperfectly understood pictorial script of these Mesoamerican codices there is one of a large cooking pot containing human heads and limbs (Figure 92), which has been interpreted by at least one authority as suggesting that dietary cannibalism may have been resorted to by the Aztecs to compensate for the lack of protein in their otherwise largely vegetable larder. What disposal, indeed, can have been made of the hundreds, even thousands, of bodies of those sacrifices whose hearts, still pulsing, ripped from their open chests, were offered daily to the ravenous Earth or Sun? We are told that the great temple plaza of the Aztec capital, Tenochtitlán, reeked of the rot of the trophy heads of the victims there displayed on racks. The glyph in the indicated codex does not

**88.** The Devouring Kālī. Carved wood. Nepal. A.D. eighteenth–nineteenth century. The body being consumed is of the god Śiva himself, Kālī's spouse.

**89.** Codex Vindobonesis Mexicanus I (Vienna Codex), a prehispanic Mesoamerican screenfolded "book," painted on thin deerhide sized with starch and gypsum. "Spread to its full length," states Jill Leslie Furst, "Codex Vienna is about 1350 centime-ters [about 14½ yards] long. The manuscript is folded into fifty-two pages, each measuring between 250 and 278 millimeters [10 to 11¹⁄₁₀ inches]; the height of the individual pages varies between 215 and 225 millimeters [8½ and 9 inches]. Wooden covers were glued to the backs of the first and last folds—whether in prehispanic or post-Conquest times is not known—presumably to protect the manuscript. After its arrival in Europe, metal clamps were added to the wooden covers to prevent splitting and separation."[24]

**90.** Stone effigy pipe from Spiro Mound, LeFlore County, Oklahoma. 5 by 10 inches. A.D. 1200–1600.

The scene is almost certainly not of the battlefield, for the victim is naked and the executioner fully attired. Spiro Mound is at the western term, Castalian Springs at the eastern, of the Mississippian culture range. (See I.2:211, Map 46.)

**91.** Engraved shell gorget, from a mound at Castalian Springs, Sumner County, Tennessee. Diameter, 4 inches. A.D. 1200–1600.

A warrior, possibly dancing, holds in one hand a mace and in the other a severed head. The forked eye is a characteristic Mississippian feature, prominent in engravings from the mounds of this culminating period of native American civilization in the North American Southeast. (See I.2:210–221.)

refer, however, to practical dietetics but to a deity, Xólotl, who was revered as god of the ball court, of twins, and of monstrosities.[45] So that if cannibalism is indeed indicated by this glyph associated with his name, it would have to have been of a *sacramental* meal: a partaking of the flesh and blood of the deity himself as incarnate in the sacrifice. Frazer, in *The Golden Bough*, brought together no end of examples from all over the world and every stage of civilization of the killing and eating of a god; and in summary of his interpretation of the sense of such ceremonials he invoked the idea of what he called *sympathetic magic*: "The savage commonly believes," he wrote, "that by eating the flesh of an animal or man he acquires not only the physical, but even the moral and intellectual qualities which were characteristic of that animal or man; so that when the creature is deemed divine, our simple savage naturally expects to absorb a portion of its divinity along with its material substance."[46]

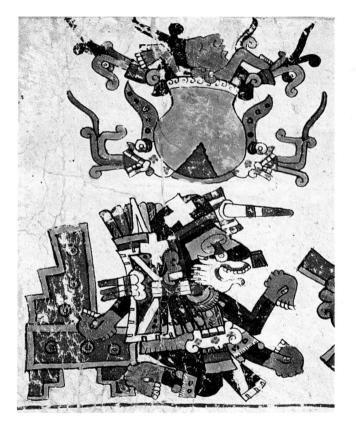

**92.** Xólotl, god of the ball court, of twins, and of monstrosities, and twin brother of Quetzalcoatl, here shown as regent of the seventeenth day of the Aztec twenty-day month: the day called *olin,* "movement." *Codex Borgia,* page 10; A.D. fifteenth century.[25]

A myth recorded by Sahagún[26] states that when the moon and sun were created they hung motionless in the sky until this frightened little god, who had tried to get away, was caught and sacrificed. "Weeping his eyes out of their sockets" (see the picture), he had changed himself, first, into a "double maize plant" (*xolotl*), then into a "double agave plant" (*mexolotl*), and finally, jumping into the water, into a kind of salamander (*axolotl*). (Such a flight and pursuit comparative folklorists know as a *transformation flight*.[27]) Seized in the water, the mercurial god was immolated, and time began. As Quetzalcoatl's sacrificed twin, he was especially associated with the downgoing, nightly aspect of the god as Evening Star, following the sun ball into the netherworld.

49

**93.** The "Lordly Dance" of Montezuma and his court, to maintain the cycle of the seasons.

As described by Bernadino de Sahagún (c. 1490–1590), this extraordinary dance of the dignitaries of the Aztec court took place in the grand plaza of Tenochtitlán (Mexico City) at the conclusion of an awesome festival of prayer and human sacrifice, called the *Izcalli*, which was celebrated every eight years, at that critical juncture when the 584-day cycles of the planet Venus and 365-day cycles of the sun came to termination on the same day (365 days × 8 = 2920 days = 5 × 584 days). The moment was of danger and dread; for the cycling might not be resumed, in which case the universe would fall apart. The "Lordly Dance," therefore, in simulation of the celestial round—performed by those dignitaries who in their social roles were counterparts on earth of the supportive lights of the sky—should by sympathetic magic contribute to the resumption of the rhythmic round. Richard Fraser Townsend, in his monograph *State and Cosmos in the Art of Tenochtitlán* quotes from Sahagún's account:

"And when they had completely ended the slaying [of sacrifices], all the chiefs and lords, who were men due great reverence, were ready, and stood waiting in complete array. Montezuma led them. He had put on the turquoise diadem, the royal diadem. . . . And in their hands were staves, which were small and shaped like weaving sticks and painted in two colors—red above and chalky white below. In either hand they grasped a paper incense bag. Thereupon they came down from the temple, dancing rapidly.

"And when they had descended, they circled [the courtyard] . . . four times. And when they had danced, they dispersed and went away, and thereupon all entered the palace in proper order. And this was known as the Lordly Dance; . . . it was the privilege exclusively of the chiefs that they should dance the Lordly Dance."[28]

**94.** New Year's Festival—Dance of the Monks—on a high plaza of the Potala, former palace of the Dalai Lama, Lhasa, Tibet. One feature of an annual month-long carnival known as Monlam,[29] formerly celebrated (before 1959) during the period from the end of January into February.

In the middle of the holy city of Lhasa, crowning a hill around which the city had, through centuries, become structured, the prodigious edifice of unnumbered chapels, chambers, and assembly halls, within which the living incarnation of the "Bodhisattva of Inexhaustible Compassion" known as Avalokiteśvara (Tibetan *sPyan-ras-gzigs*, pronounced "Chenresi") resided until 1959, represented in the local imagination the holy city of the gods on the summit of Mount Meru—which is the Indo-Aryan and Mahāyāna Buddhist counterpart of Homeric Mount Olympus. In this mighty palace at the summit of the pivot of the universe, where heaven and earth, eternity and time, come together and are one, the dedicated inhabitants of the great monasteries by which the city was for centuries surrounded (Dreprung, Sera, Gaden, Gyudto, Gyudme, Rato, Jang, Sangphu and many more: some housing only hundreds of monks, others eight to ten thousand) came together at the close of the cycle of each year to inaugurate an auspicious opening of the next round of eternity's play in the ephemeral yet ever-returning forms of cycling time.

In this valuable photograph the very powers symbolized in the temple banner of Figure **81** can be recognized in some of the costumes of the dancers. Their revolving circle (*mandala*) is an aesthetic composition grounded in a metaphysical realization (gained through meditation) of a way of seeing this whole world and its life as the eviternal epiphany of a rapture.

**95.** The Mystic Nativity. Painting by Sandro Botticelli, 1500.

"And in that region there were shepherds out in the field, keeping watch over their flock by night. And an angel of the Lord appeared to them, and they were filled with fear. And the angel said to them, 'Be not afraid; for behold, I bring you good news of a great joy which will come to all the people; for to you is born this day in the city of David a Savior, who is Christ the Lord. And this will be a sign for you: you will find a babe wrapped in swaddling cloths and lying in a manger.' And suddenly there was with the angel a multitude of the heavenly host praising God and saying,

" 'Glory to God in the highest,
and on earth peace
among men with whom he is pleased!' "
(Luke 2:8–14)

The ass and the ox at the manger have no place in the Gospel account, but appear first in Nativity scenes of the fourth century. In those years, these were the animals associated in Egypt with the dead-and-resurrected Osiris; for the bull was the symbol of Osiris himself, and the ass, of Set, his younger brother and slayer, the counterpart of Judas. Brought together at the manger and together breathing on the Child, they would seem to represent two themes: the first, the reconciliation of opposites in the spirit of the incarnate Christ ("But I say to you that hear, Love your enemies, do good to those who hate you, bless those who curse you, pray for those who abuse you" [Luke 6:27–29]), and the other, a voluntary passing on of their powers (their breaths) by the old gods, at the opening of a new age, to the one thus come in love to a new humanity.

Implicit in such a so-called magical act is the sense of an identification of the victim killed and eaten with the symbolized god and, thereby, of the sacrificing worshiper, not only with the consumed sacrifice, but equally with its implied divinity. The classic statement of this finally mystical, not simply "magical," way of thought is given in the following oft-quoted interpretation of Vedic sacrifice from the Hindu *Bhagavad Gītā:*

"Brahman [the Being of beings] is the act of the offering. Brahman is the oblation poured by Brahman into the fire, which is Brahman. By anyone thus recognizing in all action only Brahman, Brahman is attained."[47]

"Magical" beliefs and acts, one then must recognize, are but foreground manifestations (improperly interpreted) of that mystical experience of unity in multiplicity which has inspired, to one degree or another, all the mythologies and mystical philosophies of mankind. The sheerly rational (in Nietzsche's sense, "Socratic"), point of view of the nineteenth-century scientist as represented in Frazer's *Golden Bough*, holds at a critical distance not only the magical but also the mystical terms of the metaphysical experience and thus, for all its learning, consistently underinterprets the material of which it treats. Like-

wise, and for the same reason, congregations meditating for an hour a week, each family in its proper pew, on the mystery of the Crucified and his Sacrament of the Altar, may underexperience and consequently underinterpret the communion meal associated with their mythology.

Let us now contemplate the mystery scene of the Last Supper and Departure to the Cross as chronicled from the words, first, of one who had immediately heard of the event, and then, another who appears, indeed, to have been present. First: "And as they were eating, he took some bread, and when he had said the blessing he broke it and gave it to them. 'Take it,' he said, 'this is my body.'

"Then he took a cup, and when he had returned thanks he gave it to them, and all drank from it, and he said to them, 'This is my blood, the blood of the covenant, which is to be poured out for many....'

"And after psalms had been sung, they left for the Mount of Olives" (Mark 14:22–26).

And now, from the apocryphal Acts of John, an enlarged account of the psalm and singing of the Savior, "going to the Cross [to quote St. Augustine] like a bridegroom to the bride:"

He gathered us all together and said: *Before I am delivered up to them let us sing a hymn to the Father, and so go forth to that which lies before us.* He bade us therefore make as it were a ring, holding one another's hands, and himself standing in the midst he said: *Answer Amen unto me.* Then he began to sing a hymn and to say:

*Glory be to thee, Father.*
And we, going about in a ring, answered him:
     Amen.
*Glory be to thee, Word: Glory be to thee.* Amen.
*Glory be to thee, Spirit: Glory be to thee, Holy One:*
*Glory be to thy glory.*    Amen.
*We praise thee, O Father; we give thanks to thee, O*
*Light, wherein darkness dwelleth not.* Amen.
*Now wherefore we give thanks, I declare:*
*I would be saved, and I would save.* Amen.
*I would be loosed, and I would loose.* Amen.
*I would be wounded, and I would wound.* Amen.
*I would be born, and I would bear.* Amen.
*I would eat, and I would be eaten.* Amen.
*I would hear, and I would be heard.* Amen.
*I would be thought, being wholly thought.* Amen.
*I would be washed, and I would wash.* Amen.
*Grace dances. I would pipe. Dance you all.* Amen.
*I would mourn: lament you all.* Amen.
*The number Eight sings praise with us.* Amen.
*The number Twelve dances on high.* Amen.
*The Whole on high takes part in our dancing.*
     Amen.
*Who dances not, knows not what is coming to pass.*
     Amen.
*I would flee, and I would stay.* Amen.
*I would adorn, and I would be adorned.* Amen.
*I would be united and I would unite.* Amen.
*A house I have not, and I have houses.* Amen.
*A place I have not, and I have places.* Amen.
*A temple I have not, and I have temples.* Amen.
*A lamp am I to thee that beholdest me.* Amen.
*A mirror am I to thee that perceivest me.* Amen.
*A door am I to thee that knockest at me.* Amen.
*A way am I to thee, a wayfarer.* Amen.
*Now answer to my dancing. Behold thyself in me who speak, and seeing what I do, keep silence about my mysteries.*
*Thou that dancest, perceive what I do, for thine is this passion of the manhood, which I am about to suffer....*

Thus, my beloved, having danced with us the Lord went forth. And we as men gone astray or dazed with sleep fled this way and that."[48]

**96.** Xochipilli, Aztec god of the flower festival and of dances, games, love, and the arts. Codex Magliabecchiano, fol. 35′ (Cl. XIII. 3). Post-Columbian.

Adorned with flowers and butterflies and wearing his characteristic helmet mask of blue-plumaged, high-crested bird known as the quetzalcoxcoxtli, borne upon a litter of abundant maize and preceded by his herald, a musician, sounding the conch, Xochipilli holds in his hand the staff Yollotopilli, on which a human heart is impaled. Compare in I.2:219, and above: **45**, the procession in Florida of the young Timucua queen-elect being brought to the king. According to a native text translated by Sahagún, Macuil-Xóchitl and Xochipilli "were similarly worshiped and were the gods of those who dwelt in the houses of princes."[30]

**97.** Albrecht Dürer, The Great Crucifixion. Woodcut. 22½ × 15¼ inches, from The Great Passion Series. A.D. 1498 (book editions from 1511). Upper left, the sun of the spring equinox; upper right, the full moon of Easter (see above: **81**), at the foot of the Cross, a skull, the skull of Adam, the seed from which arose the Cross. *O felix culpa, quae talem ac tantum meruit habere Redemptorem!* "O happy fault, which deserved to possess such and so great a Redeemer!" (Words from the service for Holy Saturday: The Blessing of the Candle). Calvary (Latin *calvaria*, "skull"); Golgotha (Aramaic *gŭlgŭltha*, "skull"), the "Place of the Skull." (See above: **69**.) And from the right side of the Savior, pierced by the Lance of Longinus, flow the Waters of Life.

# THE FESTIVAL

The last great sanctuary of ritual cannibalism in the modern world was, until some five or six decades ago, New Guinea; and among the island's most vigorous exponents of this archaic religious practice were the Papuan Marind-anim. Until all but wiped out during the first decades of the present century by two European imports, syphilis and influenza, these relentless headhunters, dwelling in a scattering of villages along the torrid southernmost shore of what is now known as Irian Jaya (formerly, Dutch New Guinea), when not fulfilling the mythologically imposed function of harvesting their neighbors' heads, were either preparing for or actively celebrating a succession of Dionysian festivals that constituted the calendar of their lives.

During the years of World War I (while the master nations of Europe were locked in what now appears to have been the first seizure of an intermittent ecstasy of mutual immolation, as prefigured in Wagner's *Götterdämmerung* and, before that, in the mythology of the Icelandic *Poetic Edda*), the Swiss anthropologist Paul Wirz, residing among the Marind-anim as their guest, was chronicling every celebration and cataloguing every detail of their infinitely old, fast-disappearing culture—which in some of its details must have derived from before c. 20,000 B.C., when the waters of the sea rising toward the end of the last glacial

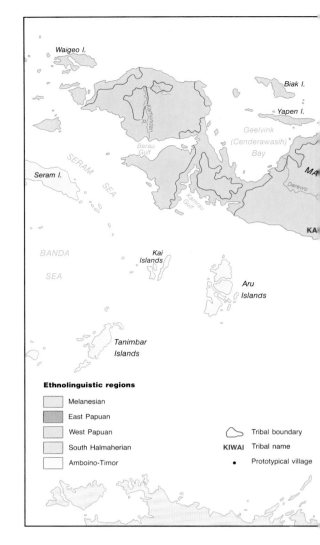

**Map 8** Until recently, New Guinea was the last great preserve of stone-age agricultural culture. Much of what is known about primal agricultural societies has been extrapolated from the study of present-day peoples who have preserved their ancient way of life into modern times. The ritual practices of the Marind-Anim of New Guinea, for example, have been essential to our understanding of the mythological function of cannibalism.

**99.** Ancestor skull with modeled features. Sepik River, New Guinea. Early twentieth century. Over the red clay modeling, traditional spirals are drawn in white earth.

**98.** Guardian figure from the lodge of a sacred enclosure. Iatnuil, Papua New Guinea.

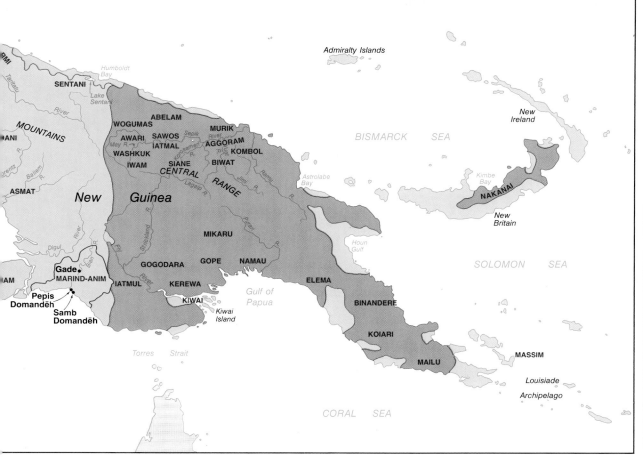

## New Guinea: Land Area and Local People

age began to separate New Guinea and Australia from the mainland, leaving stranded the Paleolithic hunting populations that during the centuries of low tides (from c. 50,000 B.C.) had entered those regions afoot (see I.1: 30–33). Around 7000 B.C. a knowledge of taro, sago, and yam horticulture had reached the island, by-passing Australia, and undoubtedly some of the most horrific of their cannibalistic celebrations of the energies and delights of the life that springs from death were thus vestiges from the period of mankind's first recognition of the mystery of vegetal regeneration.

The immediate source and base from which this unprecedented combination of an agricultural economy and associated system of rites had been carried to New Guinea and nearby Melanesia was the Southeast Asian mainland: specifically, the abundantly watered quarter comprising northeast India, Bangladesh and Assam, south and central China, Burma, Thailand and Malaya, Cambodia (now Kampuchea), Laos and Vietnam—a vast, unfathomed region that has only now (since the end of World War II) become an archeolo-

**100.** Skull sanctuary in Men's House. Urama, New Guinea.

**101.** Warrior's shield showing a threatening face with extended tongue: an apotropaic mask to avert evil. Compare the Classical Gorgoneion on the shield of Achilles (see below: **119**). Iatmul, Papua New Guinea.

gist's happy hunting ground. The discoveries have been sensational—of formerly unsuspected bronze and iron industries. However, the dating estimates and proposed schedules of the several schools of excavators are still in such confusion (1984) that no generally accepted chronology has yet been established.[49] Of the best attested datings for the mainland the following are especially interesting:

by 10,000 B.C., the cultivation of legumes and other crops[50]

by 6800 B.C., at a site in northwest Thailand known as Spirit Cave, a cord-marked, burnished pottery[51]

from c. 5000 B.C., somewhere in the Mekong drainage north and west of Ban Chiang, the invention of bronze[52]

by 4500 B.C., in the Ban Chiang area, bronze accompanied by a black pottery decorated in an already developed "Old Southeast Asian" style[53]

by 3500 B.C., the cultivation of rice[54] and the domestication of a bovine and (possibly) of the pig[55]

by 1340 B.C., the appearance of iron[56]

by c. 1300 B.C., at Non Nok Tha, in Thailand, use of the cire-perdue ("lost wax") method of casting.[57]

Carriage of the knowledge and techniques of tropical horticulture from the mainland to New Guinea occurred, evidently, *after* the separation of Sundaland and Sahulland into islands. According to Wilhelm G. Solheim II, of the University of Hawaii, director of the initial Thailand excavations (1963–1966), and founder of the journal *Asian Perspectives* (in 1957), there had been developing on the mainland from c. 8000 B.C. a local culture complex distinguished in the ornamentation of its artifacts by a combination of features that Solheim has termed the Old Southeast Asian Complex (OSEAC), while among the separating islands of that time, in what are now eastern Indonesia and the southern Philippines, there was coming into being a second formative center, which he has termed the Nusantao Culture Focus, where the outrigger and sail were coming into use, together with methods to increase freeboard and facilitate deep-water sailing. By 5000 B.C. significant population growth and pressures had begun to force people out of their ancestral homes into every available niche of Southeast Asia and out into the South Pacific. As Solheim represents the situation:

"New and more land was needed," states Solheim, "as agriculture became more important to the economy, and hunting and gathering less profitable and

**102.** From Ban Chiang, 3600 B.C. Black burnished and incised ring-foot vessel. Height, 15.5 cm (6³⁄₁₆ in.).

**103.** From Non Nok Tha. Cord-marked pottery Jar with ring foot. Height, 15 cm. (6 in.).

**104.** From Ban Chiang, 1600–1200 B.C. Red-on-buff incised and painted vessel. Height, 19 cm (7½ in.).

**105.** From Ban Chiang. Bronze socketed spearhead, c. 3600 B.C. Length, 15 cm. (6 in.).

**106/107.** From Ban Chiang, 1600–1200 B.C. Bimetallic spearheads: iron blades with cast-on bronze tang. Length, 28.5 cm (11¾ in.).

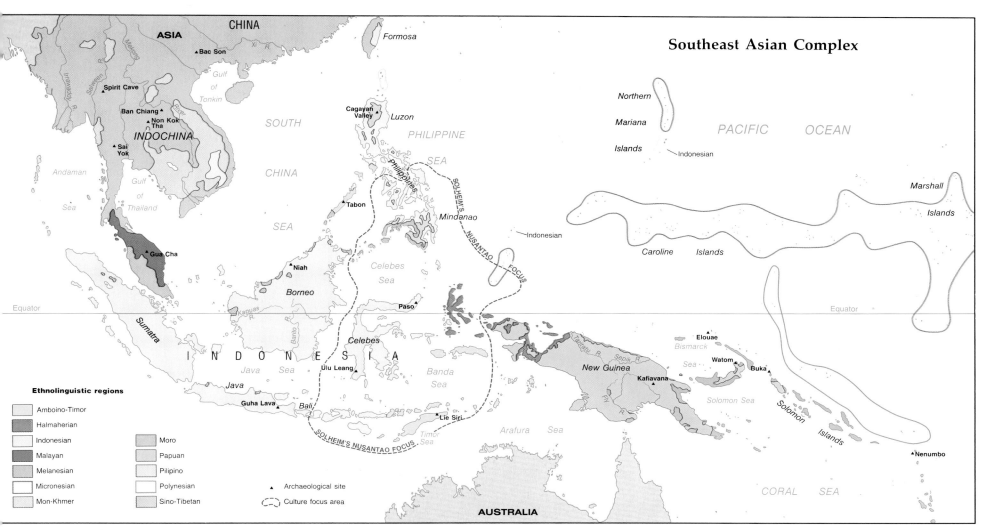

**Map 9**

easy. Trade in the metals needed for bronze, and possibly in the stone needed to make the molds, covered a considerable area. With no evidence so far of fortification of sites or warfare, there must have been developing some sort of political organization that would have maintained conditions needed for ease of movement required for their trade....In the east...the Early Nusantao people were becoming better long-distance and deep-water sailors and becoming more acquainted with seasonal winds and currents....Besides being good sailors and fishermen, I hypothesize, these people were acquainted with simple horticultural methods utilizing a stone, shell, and wood tool kit, but initially without pottery. Though they found no people on the islands of Island Melanesia beyond New Britain and New Ireland, they did find small populations along the coasts of the northern Philippines, possibly Taiwan, and the mainland. These they interacted with genetically and culturally."[58]

Also, of course, in New Britain, New Ireland, and emphatically, New Guinea, there were already present populations whose hunting-and-gathering ancestors had arrived before Sundaland and Sahulland had disintegrated into islands. These are the people known to anthropology as Papuans, in contrast to the seafaring Austronesians, who began settling along the island coasts c. 4000 B.C. New Guinea is the second largest island in the world (second only to Greenland). In 1980 its population of about 4,000,000 represented hardly 0.01 percent of the world's number; yet of the world's languages, no less than 15 percent are of this island: 700 in Papua New Guinea alone. Such a particularization of local dialects follows from long settlement over a large area by village-bound horticulturalists. (Something similar is reported from West Africa in the region of Upper Volta.)[59] And in contrast to their prehistoric contemporaries in Australia, whose ancestors also arrived before the drowning of Sundaland and Sahulland and who have retained to the present the customs, rites, and mythologies of a hunting-and-gathering culture (see I.2: 134–146), the Papuans of New Guinea are intensive horticulturalists, raising yams, taro, sago, the banana, and, in the Highlands, chiefly the sweet potato (see Figure 108)—which is a native American cultigen, whose appearance as a major crop in the almost inaccessible Highlands of one of the most culturally isolated areas of the South Pacific has confronted methodical antidiffusionists with a real stunner.

**108.** The women with their digging sticks plant sweet-potato cuttings in ground prepared by the men. Former Dutch New Guinea, now Irian Jaya.

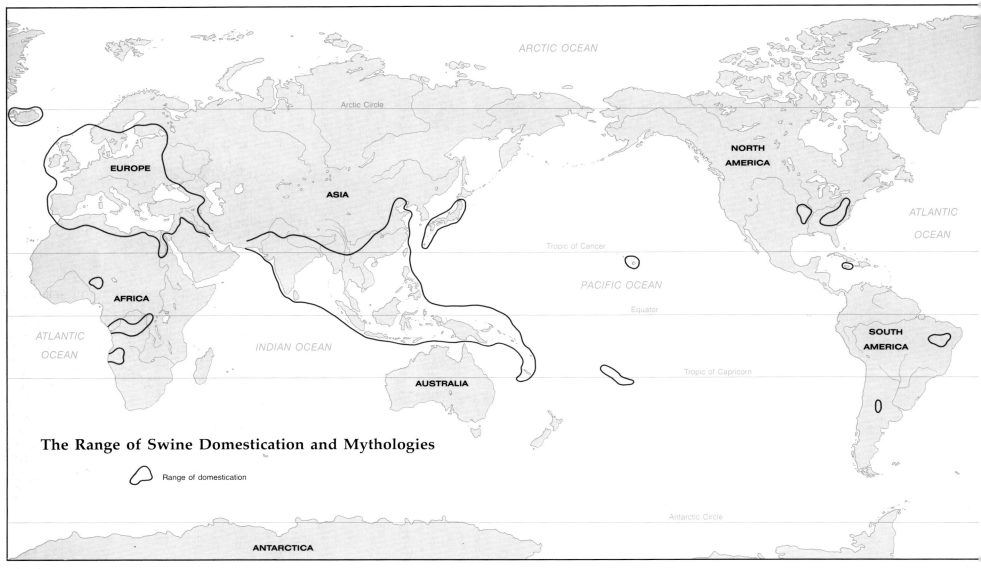

## The Range of Swine Domestication and Mythologies

 Range of domestication

**Map 10**

The prominence of domestic swine, not only in the practical economy, but also in the extravagant sacrificial festivals and associated mythologies, not only of New Guinea and the rest of Oceania, but also of an immense mainland zone of many distinct provinces, extending from the South China Sea to the Near East and ancient Greece, Celtic Europe, and the British Isles, attests to the early distribution

**109.** Celtic bas-relief from Beihingen, Württemburg, showing a pig being sacrificed to the horse goddess Epona, who is frequently associated with the Celtic *matres,* or earth goddesses, and was herself probably revered as a fertility goddess.

**110.** Vegetation goddess wearing a pig mask. Vinča civilization, Rastu, western Romania, mid-fifth millenium B.C. Figures of pigs impressed with grain have been found from the mid-fifth millennium B.C. in the upper valley of the Dniester. As remarked by Marija Gimbutas: "The fast-growing body of a pig will have impressed early agriculturalists; its fattening must have been compared to corn growing and ripening, so that its soft fats came to symbolize the earth itself, causing the pig to become a sacred

**111.** Head of a pig. Terra cotta, from the site of Leskavica, eastern Macedonia. Vinča civilization, c. mid fifth millennium B.C.

animal probably no later than 6000 B.C. An early Vinča Pregnant Vegetation Goddess wears a pig mask while the sacredness of the pig's body is indicated by Cucuteni pig sculptures which have traces of grain impressed upon them. Grain was impressed on the body of the pig just as it was impressed on the body of the Vegetation Goddess. These figurines and the pig masks imply that the pig was a double of the Pregnant Vegetation Goddess and was her sacrificial animal."[31]

**112.** Carved pig, ebony. Discovered in 1953. Trobriand Islands, northeast of New Guinea.

**113.** Woman sacrificing a pig. Red-figured vase-painting from a lekythos, fifth century B.C.

The woman holds in her left hand a basket, probably containing *sacra.* The torches indicate an underworld service, and the pig is held (apparently) over a ditch.

Jane Harrison has suggested that the occasion here represented was of an autumnal women's festival "of immemorial antiquity," the Thesmophoria, when pigs were thus sacrificed in memory of the abduction of Persephone to the underworld by Hades.[32] Frazer, in *The Golden Bough,* had already argued that both Persephone and her mother, Demeter, had in the past been pig-divinities and that the pigs thrown into caverns had been symbolic of the abducted goddess herself. "Further," Frazer adds, "it is to be noted that at the Thesmophoria the women appear to have eaten swine's flesh. The meal, if I am right," he concludes, "must have been a solemn sacrament or communion, the worshippers partaking of the body of the god."[33]

**114.** Ceramic pig from Nea Makri, Neolithic Proto-Sesklo settlement in Attica, Greece, c. 6000 B.C.

**115.** A sow, sacred to the sky goddess Nut, suckling her piglets. Green blazed pottery. Egypt, c. 600 B.C.

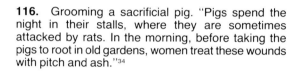

**116.** Grooming a sacrificial pig. "Pigs spend the night in their stalls, where they are sometimes attacked by rats. In the morning, before taking the pigs to root in old gardens, women treat these wounds with pitch and ash."[34]

**117.** Youth feeding the pig that he will sacrifice in his initiation rite, c. 1914, Atchin Island, Malekula, New Hebrides.

**118.** Ritual slaughter of pigs by the men of the Dani tribe of Irian Jaya. After the slaughter, the men walk among the carcasses and raise a great shout to placate the ghosts of the pigs. The pigs' ears are then roasted and eaten, while the tails are made into neck ornaments and worn as talismans.

**119.** The shield of Achilles, bearing the apotropaic mask, with the extended tongue, of the Gorgon (the Gorgoneion). Beneath the victorious warrior's couch lies the body of the Trojan champion, Hector, whose old father, Priam, has arrived with gifts to buy back for burial his son's remains (Iliad XXIV, ll. 477 ff.).

over an immense portion of the globe, not of the material benefits alone of pig husbandry with agriculture, but also (more enigmatically) of an associated mythological insight of some kind. The most striking feature of the rites is their fundamental cruelty, obliterating individuals, whether animal or human, with apparent indifference to their value. Ritualized torture, mutilation, rape, murder, and cannibalism are common features. The head trophy is ubiquitous, whether of an ancestor deceased or of some alien tribesman slain. The ghostly hum of the bull-roarer is frequently an ominous accompaniment, and a release of orgiastic abandon the usual culmination. In contrast to all of which is the second striking feature of this general tradition, which is, namely, a ritualized depersonalization of the whole population of the local tribe or village through an application of such strictly graded rules of attire and conduct that everyone is converted, so to say, into an archetype.

Friedrich Nietzsche, in *The Birth of Tragedy* (1871), wrote of the paralyzing spiritual catastrophe known to mystics as *illumination:* that glimpse into the ground of being that transforms the spectacle of this world into a display of unsubstantial appearances. India's ''veil of Māyā,'' the Buddha's ''all life is sorrowful,'' and Shakespeare's ''to be or not to be'' are expressions of the insight of this moment; so also, the existentialist ''nausea.'' But

how should anyone struck with such a sense of the senselessness of any form of action in this field of deluding forms be ever recalled to an affirmation of life in this world?

Nietzsche's reply is, by art! And of art there are two aspects: that of the god Dionysos, of rapture in the violence of that will in nature that pours through time like a torrent, annihilating even while generating the ephemera of what we take to be reality; and that (in contrast) of the god of the light world, Apollo, of delight in the beauty of the forms even as they pass—as though to plead, ''If this be a dream, then let me dream!''

Dionysian art is of the impulse; Apollonian, of measure. But impulse without measure is chaos, while measure without the impulse of an illuminated rapture ends in rigidity. Accordingly, the more catastrophic the initiating realization and consequent violence of the Dionysian rapture, the more compelling will the requirement be of a proportionate Apollonian hold to measure. In Nietzsche's view, in the classic arts of the Greeks, the contributions of these two gods were equivalent, whereas in the ''barbaric'' arts of their immediate neighbors the Dionysian frenzy, unrestrained, generated that ''horrible witches' brew of sensuality and cruelty,'' to use Nietzsche's phrase, by which the cults were inspired of such blood-reeking Asian divinities (not to mention India's Kālī) as the Phrygian god-

dess Cybele and that Taurian virgin who was the attending priestess (according to Euripides's *Iphigenia in Tauris*, the already sacrificed daughter of Agamemnon) at her temple's altar soaked with human blood crowning a precipice on the northern shore of the Black Sea.

''The Tauri,'' states Herodotus, ''have the following customs. They offer in sacrifice to the virgin goddess all shipwrecked persons, and all Greeks compelled to put into their ports by stress of weather. The mode of sacrifice is this. After the preliminary ceremonies, they strike the victim on the head with a club. Then, according to some accounts, they hurl the trunk from the precipice whereon the temple stands and nail the head to a cross. Others grant that the head is treated in this way, but deny that the body is thrown down the cliff—on the contrary, they say, it is buried. The goddess to whom these sacrifices are offered the Tauri themselves declare to be Iphigenia the daughter of Agamemnon. When they take prisoners in war they treat them in the following way. The man who has taken a captive cuts off his head, and carrying it to his home, fixes it upon a tall pole, which he elevates above his house, most commonly over the chimney. The reason that the heads are set up so high, is (it is said) in order that the whole house may be under their protection. These people live entirely by war and plundering.''[60]

In one stride we're back in New Guinea.

**120.** Relief made from beaten bronze, originally used as a chariot covering. Length about 11½ inches. Greek Archaic Period, sixth century B.C. Now in the museum Antiker Kleinkunst, Munich.

The relief shows the Mistress of the Lions, a Gorgon, squatting with her legs widespread, her arms extended at shoulder height. In her hands she holds two lions, as if throttling them; the lions stand upright with their right hind paws on her knees. A bird and a seahorse are on her left, suggesting her dominion over air and sea.

**121.** Labyrinthine lintel, carved wood, Maori, New Zealand, showing a Gorgon-like female threshold-guardian with extended tongue, in squat position, four secondary masks at knees and shoulders, another at the vulva, a sixth, inverted, lower right (below the base line), matched symmetrically by a seventh, lower left (which has been removed), four birdlike figures attacking (apparently) convolutions of the serpentine, and everywhere a balanced organization of spirals, left side matching right, as though the perfectly matched wing-panels had swung open of the portal to a forbidden precinct, thus manifesting its guardian.

And our first realization on turning from Nietzsche's Greece to the anthropologist Paul Wirz's account of the plundering, headhunting Marind-anim is of the extraordinary force and pervasiveness through the context of their culture of that delight in the beauty of measure and form which Nietzsche in his celebration of the Greeks associated with Apollo. Their notion of beauty was not that of Phidias or Praxiteles. Indeed, to the European eye it was outlandish. Yet the dedication of energy and concern to the transformation of nature and production of symbolic effects engaged every bit of their waking life not devoted to horticulture, hunting, fishing, and the massacre of neighbors.

"The whole social order of the Marind," states Wirz, "is built of two institutions: the ranking in *age groups* of members of the same generation, and the mythological-totemic *clan formation*. Over and against the age groups the family is left all but isolated. One could even say that the age group makes for so much stronger boundings than the family that it inhibits its development."[61]

Of these age groups there are nine, progressed according to sex along separated lines and defined by changes of costume bestowed in family ceremonials, namely:

(1) newborn infant (*honakon*)

(2) infant in its carrying cradle (*kantara*)

(3) little boy or girl (*papis-patur* and *papus-kiwasum*)

(4) bigger boy or girl (*musnakin-patur* and *musnakun-kiwasum*)

(5) young adolescent (*mokraved* and *wahuku*)

(6) developed adolescent (*ewati* and *kiwasum-iwag*)

(7) youth or maid of marriageable age (*miakim* and *iwag*)

(8) married man or woman (*amnan-gib* and *sav*)

(9) old man or woman (*samb-anim* and *mes-iwag*)[62]

**122**

**122–124.** *Kantara*: Age grade of the infant that can sit up but not yet walk, who, in a little family ceremony, has been given its own carrying cradle (*vaseb*). As here is evident, the manner of carriage is of the mother's choice. All the following photographs were taken c. 1916, at Domandeh, former Dutch New Guinea (now Irian Jaya).

**123**

**124**

Each advance in age rank is marked by an instructive family ceremonial through which, not only a new appearance, but also a new way of life, is laid upon the person; so that upon entering any native village, what the visitor would behold would not be a miscellany of unpredictable individuals, but a local typologization of the stages of human growth as signalized in the local rules and forms of behavior and of attire.

But it is, in fact, through such formal typologization that myth and ritual operate everywhere. Historical and local differences follow from the differing orders of insight by which the mythologies are inspired; and these, in turn, are influenced largely, among aboriginal peoples close to nature, by the *paideumatic* powers—to use again Frobenius's term—of their environments (see above: page 9).

Among nomadic hunters, for example, where individual courage and prowess, insight and decision, greatly count, these faculties are not only fostered by way of mythologies of the vision quest, shamanic power, animal familiars, and so forth, but also honored in celebratory festivals and signalized in ornamental tokens of attire (feathers, medals, emblematic staffs, and the like). Whereas, in contrast, within the bounds of a settled agricultural community, where the conditions of life are relatively stable and the social unit is a prosperous village, the accent shifts from the gifted individual to the group, from creativity to maintenance, from merit, so to say, to conformity; so that, instead of heroic values, those recognized in the myths and cultivated in the relevant rites are of participation in the common ground, which is defined in terms appropriate

**125/126.** *Patur* and *kiwasum,* age grades of the "boy" and the "girl," each of which is of two stages: first, *papis-patur* ("little boy") and *papus-kiwasum* ("little girl"), when the child just able to walk is given, again in a family ceremony, its first ornament, an upper-arm band (*barar*) of rattan, the girl receiving in addition a simple string (*kakim*) to wear about her waist; and then, *musnakim-patur* ("big boy") and *musnakun-kiwasum* ("big girl"), when the youngster's ears are pierced by a maternal uncle.

The four *kiwasum* here pictured have been given besides, again in family ceremonies, necklaces (*baba*) of nautilus shell (*samond*).

125

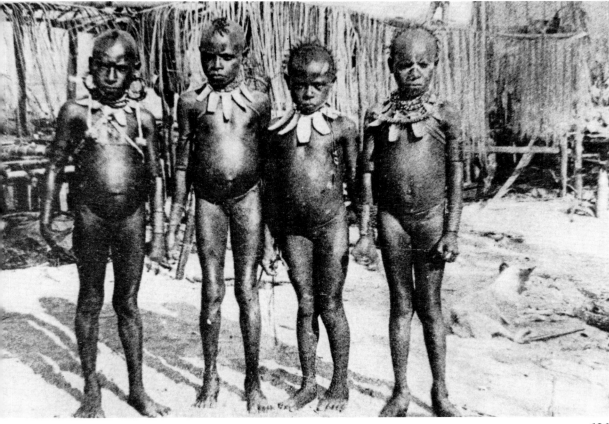

126

127

rather to the planet than to the animal world.

The first order of values recognized by the Marind-anim was thus of the stages of human growth, which of course are about the same for human beings all over the world. One may think of them as universal archetypes (Jung) or elementary ideas (Bastian). Applied by the Marind-anim to the structuring of their society, they were accommodated to local village practice by way of family ceremonials.

**127.** *Mokraved,* age grade of the young male adolescent resident in the Men's House under supervision of his foster parent. His hair now grown long enough to be braided with pandannus fibers and thus lengthened to the shoulder in the fashion known as *angar wahukak* ("pandannus braided"), he has received from his maternal uncle a bone hairpin to wear; large upper-arm bands and ear plugs further mark his rank. His life is now to be of participation exclusively in the enterprises, deliberations, and entertainments of the Men's House. Relationships with females of the village are forbidden.

**128–130.** *Wahuku,* age grade of the young adolescent female. She has been presented in the requisite family ceremonial with a pubic shield (*noah*), stained black, of the inner bark of a certain shrub (also called *noah*); her hair has been braided with strips of the inner bark of a sort of hibiscus (*mumbre*) and may, on occasion, be flounced variously and extended down the whole back, to which effects strips of cocofrond (*beisam*) and of coconut bark (*eva*) contribute. Bracelets, shell necklaces and any number of earrings now appear, and the painful ordeal of scartattooing commences.

129

128

130

132

131

13[1]

**131–135.** *Ewati,* age grade of the mature male adolescent, still resident in the Men's House. The time for his promotion from *mokraved* to this degree depended on a joint decision by the youth's foster and natural families, which in turn depended on their readiness to support the considerable expense of the large banquet of pork, bananas, sago loaves, taro, coconuts, yams, and miscellaneous adjuncts that a festival in celebration of their's son's coming of age required.

The principal sign of the young man's new estate was then to be the penis shield by which his elevated member was thenceforth to be shielded. Other effects required a blackening of the teeth, piercing of the septum of the nose to recieve either a piece of bone (of bird or kangaroo) or the tusk of a boar, distinctive upper-arm bands, and special arrange-

ments of the treated hair with spectacular feather effects.

Though resident still in the Men's House and forbidden to visit the village by day, the *ewati* was free to participate in nightly dances, where he would appear in full regalia to the admiration of all. On the headhunt forays, in which youths of this grade participated, they were the most courageous and dangerous of the killers. Also, it was at this stage that they were initiated into secret cults. So that, in sum, as Paul Wirz soon realized "the life state of the *ewati* was the fairest [*der schönste*] of Marind-anim life."[35]

At the end of his required term, the fulfilled *ewati* left the Men's House by way of a graduation festival, to become what in the West could have been termed an "eligible bachelor" (*miakim*), ready for marriage.

**136–138.** *Iwag,* age grade of the young female ready for marriage. A number of secondary stages between the *wahuku* and *iwag* grades were marked chiefly by elaborate changes in the dressing of the hair, for to beauty-culture a vast amount of time was devoted by these imaginative young people, full of play and of delight (as Wirz knew and described them) in their everlasting celebration of the wonder of their own lives. In the way of work nothing was expected of young women of the *iwag* grade, only the preservation and celebration of their beauty until marriage. "Officially," states Wirz, "premarital sex was unacknowledged; but one would not go wrong in supposing that it was actually the rule. In any case," he adds, "it was not seriously regarded unless it led to pregnancy. Its enjoyment, however, was in secret." "Principally," Wirz concludes, "it was with personal adornment and sweet nothing-to-do that the young woman ready for marriage passed her time of day."[36]

136

137

134

138

135

139

140

141

**139–143.** *Sav,* age grade of the married woman. She has moved to the village of her husband, usually at first into her mother-in-law's hut, and gradually, piece by piece, her ornaments have been laid aside, until little more than her scar-tattooings remain.

For now has begun her time for work: in the gardens, planting and harvesting; at home, raising her family (see above: **122–125**); and whenever (which is frequently) a festival is in prospect, participating seriously in the endless preparations, which involve gathering produce from the gardens, baking innumerable sago loaves, and so on. Unless an effect can be achieved of inexhaustible abundance, there will have been no Marind-anim feast.

The woman's hair, however, as a personal concern continues to be of interest. The *sav* may retain for a time the mode of her premarital years or move on to one of the so-called *dahamata* styles proper to her age (**140, 141**). The extraordinary, artificially greatly lengthened arrangement known as *bongbonga-ahamata,* which is shown (**139**), would usually be assumed only by a mother, following her confinement, as a way of returning to the society adorned.[37]

142

143

144

145

146

**144–146.** *Amnangib,* age grade of the married male adult, here in full ceremonial attire.

It was from such thirty-second degree masters (so to say) as these that the anthropologist Paul Wirz learned of the headhunt as a religiously inspired and required ritual of sacrifice prerequisite to the generation of children. Out of death comes life, whence, specifically, according to Marind-anim belief, before a child could be named, a head had to be taken and the name of the victim bestowed, then, on the infant.

"A head without its name," Wirz learned, "is worthless."[38]

Not for glory, therefore, nor out of economic need, neither for conquest nor for defence, were the devastating head harvests of these night raiders accomplished. Like the Aztec wars for the acquisition of captives to be sacrificed, those of the Hebrews for the acquisition of Canaan, of the Christian crusades to release the "holy land" from the infidel, or of the Muslim "holy war" (*jihad*), the headhunt—and not

only that of New Guinea—was a religious exercise.

So the disciplines of the Marind-amin Men's House were at once military and religious (which is a combination of terrible destiny to neighbors), and all the cheer of the great festivals of abundance, charm of the adorned age groups, and rules of decorum of Marind-anim life, rode (so to say) on a spiritual tide sustained by the unceasing rites of sacrifice by those priests of death.

67

147

148

147–151. Like the ancestral "dream time" of the Australians (see I.2: 135–146), the mythological "time of the Dema" of the Marind-anim and their neighbors, not only was of the past, but also is still present both behind and within the world's appearances; and in the great totemic masks of the village festivals the everlasting generative potencies which in that mythological age were everywhere manifest, but have since withdrawn from direct view, are again made known. These are the Dema, by which the forms both of tribal life and of the natural world are structured and maintained. To the sound of drums they appear, and to singing.

Figure 147, Ndik, appears in the shape of a bird in flight, *Xenorrhynicus asiaticus*, distinguished by its long yellow beak. The bent elbows, flapping, are its wings. The two long lines behind are to be carried, as a train, by its female attendants, the *nakari* (see 148). As the first of the Dema to arrive on the festival scene, Ndik heralds the approach of others.

Figure 150 is the Bamboo-Dema; Figure 151 an example of a type known as the Gari, which appears, beating its drum, in the midst of a cloud, the *humum*; Figure 149 is the Dema of the cocopalm; and Figure 148 is an apparition known as Mongumer Man, here shown followed by his *nakari*, moving about the festival scene beating his drum.

Watercolors were painted by Paul Wirz, c. 1916, at Domandeh, former Dutch New Guinea, now Irian Jaya.

The second order of vital energies to be recognized by these people was then of the local powers of nature: specifically, of a torrid coastal landscape, with its rank tropical flora, monsoon seasons, mangrove swamps, slowly zigzagging rivers, slimy and frequently flooded flats, ragged beaches, and offshore reefs and isles. And as the energies of the human archetypes were held in harmonious social play by the nuclear family and its rites, so it was by way of totemic clan formations and their numerous, elaborate, and excitatory village festivals that the socially relevant powers of nature and their gifts were brought to mind and held in regard.

These powers were theatrically impersonated in magnificent masked-costumes representing what were known as Dema: the ancestral givers of live, which inform all things and in the Mythological Age were all that existed. They were at that time simultaneously of animal or plant and of human likeness, endowed with supernatural powers and characteristics, and able to transform themselves and to accomplish all sorts of astonishing things, such as people today can no longer attempt. The landscape itself and all that then existed had the character of Dema. But in time those faculties were lost, so that people, animals, and things today, all of which are derived from the Dema, are greatly reduced in power. The myths tell

of the transformations of the Dema into the forms of the world as now perceived, and in the festival masks they are again revealed, to be recognized as the indwelling powers, not only of all things round about, but also of the Marind-anim clan system. "Everything is Dema," say the Marind-anim; "by which is meant," states Wirz, "that all things have come from the Dema and that in their psychic qualities and powers there is still something of the Dema as the source....Such powers find their application in magic, since related spiritual substances influence each other.

"The mythological Dema," Wirz goes on to explain, "are thought of chiefly as beings in human form that can nevertheless change shape. Some are seen as incarnate in actual human beings, who are nevertheless immortal and possessed of extraordinary powers....In representations of the Dema the essential part is the head, often simply the eyes (which is why the eye ornament is so widespread), but frequently, also, the heart or entrails, which are regarded as seats of the soul.

"As ancestors, the Dema participate in the objects derived from them, and accordingly are sometimes looked upon as beings of a kind intermediate between their totemic and their human aspects. Or they may be perceived as of a human form underlying a natural object or an artifact. In a bow, for instance, there is such an

**149**

**150**

underlying human form; for it too is derived from a Dema….In the coconut, signs can still be seen of the head of the Dema out of which the first palm tree grew, in that its three nodular indentations correspond to the eye sockets and mouth. The legs of the Coco-Dema are now the stems; the hair has become fronds and pinnules; and in the rustle of the fronds the Dema's voice can still be heard. 'That,' the Marind-anim say, 'is how the Coco-Dema once talked.' And so in all things there is a more or less evident relationship discoverable to the Dema who stand to them as authors.

"The first creatures and natural objects that came forth from the Dema, however, were in no way like those of today. There was still about them something weird and extraordinary. They were still to a certain degree Dema, although looking like creatures today. Only in the course of time and through generations did they lose, gradually, their extraordinary attributes and become the mortals, animals, and perishable objects of the present."[63]

Thus it was in the visionary mythic appearances of the Dema in their elaborate village festivals, together with the age-grade costumes by which the archetypal stages of human maturation were made visible on their own persons through all seasons, that the Marind-anim were held constantly to the recognition of those "forms"—to quote again Robinson Jeffers's memorable lines:

*The phantom rulers of humanity*
*That without being are yet more real than*
*    what they are*
*born of, and without shape, shape that which*
*    makes them:*
*The nerves and the flesh go by shadowlike, the*
*    limbs and the lives shadowlike,*
*    these shadows remain, these shadows*
*To whom temples, to whom churches, to*
*    whom labors and wars,*
*    visions and dreams are dedicate.*[64]

Such are the figments of that Appollonian dream of which Nietzsche tells, by which the mind exploded by an appalling realization is recalled to participation in this effluvium of unsubstantial appearances. "It was to be able to live," wrote Nietzsche, "that the Greeks, out of a profound need, brought forth their gods."[65]

And he suggests thereto an apt analogy:

"When we turn away blinded after a forced attempt to gaze at the sun, black spots appear before the eyes, as it were as a cure. Conversely, the projected luminous images of the masking Apollonian display….are the effects of a glimpse into the inmost horrors of nature: brilliant spots to heal, as it were, eyes damaged by terrible night."[66]

**151**

* * * *

69

What, then, was the catastrophic metaphysical insight into the inmost horrors of nature which had inspired among the Marind-amin such an elaborate, masking, ceremonial display in celebration of the gifts and joys of existence in their tropical world? Little family and great totemic festivals took care of the masking Apollonian forms. The unmasking, Dionysian side of the revelation was solemnized, in contrast, only apart, in extreme ceremonials, in sanctuaries of the men's secret societies—of which there were, in the period of Wirz's residence in the region, five, concerning which he was able to gain information, and one, of which he had the direct experience.

"In most cases," he concluded, "one remains unable to decide where the primary motivation of the secret cults is to be sought, whether it be in the sex drive, in the desire of the young men to give themselves over unhindered to occasional, bloodthirsty, horrible debauches that could lead even to endocannibalism; or whether it be out of religious grounds that these secret cults have arisen. One finds almost always the two motives together: sexual debauches are never missing, but neither, apparently, are religious grounds requiring the regular celebration of such ceremonials. One can interpret them as fertility rites or explain them as supposedly required by the Dema. In any case, it can be assumed that there is a common root from which they all have sprung, namely the one myth. Even the obscene orgies are said to be institutions of the demonic ancestors and founders. They rest upon primordial traditions, not to be questioned, and have thus the religious savor."[67]

The single event that Wirz was privileged to witness took place in a village on the upper Bian River, where it was celebrated to the humming of bullroarers, which is a dangerous sound to women, here interpreted as the voice of a Dema bearing the curious name Ezam (Husband). A second sound—equally dangerous—was of a Dema named Uzum (Wife) and was produced by a secret kind of bamboo drum called *nakok*, made of two lengths, about 2 feet long, of a particularly hard bamboo, 4 inches in diameter, plugged with wood at one end, left open at the other, and struck together at the blocked ends, to give forth a dull, drumlike tone. The origin of this society was given in a legend (withheld from Wirz) about the Dema, who was a dwarf dwelling with his wife, Uzum, underground; whenever he came to the surface, this ceremony had to be performed.

"The little that I was able to learn of the Ezam Secret Society," Wirz wrote in the report of his adventure, "I shall recount from my journal of an excursion to the upper Bian.

"It was a rainy morning when we came

**152.** Drum from Finschafen, Cape Cretin, Papua New Guinea.

to within reach of the village of Gadé, rested a little, and, after a half-hour tramp through a swampy savanna, arrived at the settlement.

"Here, according to what we had heard from the natives of another village, an Ezam ceremony was about to be enacted. We were greeted by a company of young and older men, who conducted us to an area that had been completely divided in two by a high hedge of bamboo and palm fronds, in such a way that the hedge cut directly through a large hut of the double-roof type [see Figure 153], which was also divided thus in two parts. This was known as the *Ezam-aha*, "Ezam house." Beyond the hedge the women and children were encamped. On this side there were only initiated men and the youths about to be initiated. The hedge was high and so thick that there was nowhere the slightest opening through which any woman might peer, and had anyone tried to do so, the youths and men would have been immediately alarmed by a crackling of leaves. There were but two very small openings through which one would have to crawl on all fours if one wished to pass from one side of the village to the other without going around the hedge, which reached at both ends well into the forest. The whole

thing was covered with painted ribs of sago-palm fronds as a clear sign of warning to the women that everything this side of the division and all that was about to happen here was to them tabu.

"I was conducted directly to the men's side and into the *Ezam-aha*, where there were sitting and lying about a large number of youths and older men, including some, apparently, from neighboring villages. All conversing was in whispers. And I was struck particularly by the sight of two long, thick peeled tree trunks, so thick that one's arms could hardly reach around them. They were set parallel to each other at a slope, in such a way that the lower ends reached into the women's half, resting there on the ground, while the elevated ends reached out from under the hut's high roof, supported by a horizontal beam that was upheld, in turn, by three upright supporting staves, the one in the center hollowed out in a special way and carefully painted. Unfortunately I neglected to sketch the handsome designs. The two long, thick tree trunks were named *uk*, the name of the trees from which they were cut. They had been set to each side of the central upright, but so close to each other that one could hardly have squeezed between. Within the hut a little platform had been fixed upon the slope of each of the two large *uk* beams, and on these there had been placed some thirty or forty Ezam-drums. Also, hanging from them were the bullroarers, outfitted with the cords and sticks by which they were to be swung. One stood out, larger than the rest and especially ornamented.

"With the talk in whispers and every sound of any kind suppressed, I could not even crack open a coconut. The others, too, were being careful to be quiet, conversing in low tones. The large assemblage of men, the ominous silence, the whole hut with its curious equipment, produced an uncanny impression. I had known something of the kind before in relation to other secret cult situations and could imagine approximately to what sort of end it was all pointing. Before the hut there were sitting apathetically some old men, around whom there were lying ready a scattering of cudgels, bows, and arrows. My attention was called to these with grimaces of warning and drastic gestures of beheading, keeping my mouth shut, and not touching the bullroarers or drums.

"From time to time, on command of the old men, everybody stood up. The bamboo *nakok* were taken cautiously from their place, and here, too, the making of unnecessary noises was avoided. The instruments were handled with such care as is addressed only to sacred things. The old men then began a monotonous, solemn chant in which the young men joined, beating time by striking the bamboos together, repeating over and over again:

"The whole thing made upon me a deep, somber impression. What did this chant and drumming signify? What, the deadly silence that was otherwise to prevail? What connection did these have with what was to follow: the grisly, bloodthirsty ceremony soon to begin? These questions were not answered for me, but I gained the conviction that behind all the brutality and bloody ferocity that unquestionably constituted the main point and essential feature of this whole affair, there was something else; also, that the intimidation of the women on the other side of the hedge was not the main reason for these preliminaries. More probably, they had actually to do somehow with initiating the young men, or preparing them for the coming orgy by exciting them. When I returned to the coast and there questioned the natives, I learned that those to be initiated were required during this period to abstain from certain foods, as indeed is usual in the practices of secret cults.

"There followed a pause, during which each was free to do as he liked. They went and came as they pleased. Only a few of the old men remained to keep watch in the village, so that nothing unpermitted should take place; the bullroarers and bamboo *nakok*, for example, were not to be mischievously handled. It would have occurred to no one, however, to do such a thing. Every now and then one of the old men would pick up a bullroarer and in a squatting position swing it around. This was not done to be funny. One had the impression, rather, that this was a well-established ceremony and deliberate performance. Presently the young men came together again and took up the bamboo *nakok,* and again the monotonous, melancholy chant resumed, to the accompaniment of the dull drumbeats of the bamboo tubes. This went on with regulated pauses until evening and darkness had gathered, when the whole company assembled in front of the hut and sang until about midnight: this time, also, to the accompaniment of the *nakok,* but a different song.

"Meanwhile, erotic events were occurring in the forest, and each initiate, on returning, to signify that coitus had been accomplished, carried a broken branch, which he placed upon the elevated end of the *uk,* so that in a very short while a great heap of leaves and branches had accumulated. The custom was a familiar one, common to all the major Marind festivals, when every woman was free to every man. Usually in the villages one would see in front of the Men's House a forked branch on which lay heaps of twigs and bunches of grass from the last celebration.

"Around midnight the singing stopped, and everybody rested. Then, later in the night the young men were roused by the elders, the bullroarers began humming, and to the accompaniment of the bamboo drums, the monotonous chant resumed.

"And so it went on through several days and nights without anything special happening. The end of the ceremonies I must report from accounts that I received from the natives. They are undoubtedly correct, for although from completely separate places and unrelated parties, all are in full agreement. European bird-of-paradise hunters who had witnessed the event gave the same account, unanimously. An unforseen event had forced me, unfortunately, to return in haste to the coast.

"Men arrive from near and far, for all are admitted to the *Ezam-aha.* The din is terrific. For days and nights the chant and the boom of the bamboo drums continues, almost without interruption. Between is the humming of bullroarers. People appear to have become worked up to a fantastic state of excitement, so that everything has gone wild. Already during the time of my stay there had reigned among the initiates, and even more obviously among the novices (those in the *Ezam-aha* who were about to be initiated), an erotic tone that was expressed, for example, in obscene manners of speech. Also, during the entire period, absolutely unlimited freedom in sexual intercourse was allowed—except to the novices, who were forbidden participation, so that their craving should be increased.

"The drumming had become ever more violent, the singing, wilder and more excited. More heftily were the bullroarers being swung. One had lost all ordered sense of sight and sound, when at last the appointed moment arrived, known only to the old men and to those already initiated. It was at night. A young woman (or perhaps more than one) of the seventh age class (an *iwag,* or "nymph," of marriageable age), in full ceremonial attire, dripping with oil and fresh paint, came conducted by a group of old men to the *Ezam-aha.* Eucalyptus bark was spread on the ground beneath the two great beams of the *uk,* and the conducted *iwag,* without knowing what was before her, was required to lie down there. Immediately, the orgy commenced of the released novices, in sequence, throwing themselves upon her. But there was one (unknown to himself) who had been appointed to become the offering of the festival. And when he and the *iwag* were at one, the prodigious beating of drums arose, and at a given signal, two men, standing ready, ripped away the uprights supporting the great beams, which dropped with a dull thud on the couple beneath.

"A general hideous howl went up. The two were quickly pulled from beneath the dropped beams, dragged to a shed, chopped to pieces and roasted. And the bloodthirsty horde then had its feast.

"I was unable to learn," Wirz comments in conclusion, "whether the offerings in this ceremony were members of the tribe or headhunt captives raised from childhood to this end."[68]

**153.** Ezam-Aha (House of the Dema Ezam). Scene of the mythological event. Village of Gadé, Bian Valley.

# THE OFFERING

The contrast between such a sacrifice as that of the Marind Ezam-Uzum festival and any of the types of sacrifice described in Volume I corresponds to that represented in the terms "sacred" and "profane," or as Nietzsche has characterized the contrast, in the Dionysian and Socratic states of mind. The reindeer and dog sacrifices of the northeast Siberian Koryak and Chukchi, for example (see I.2: 158), are reasonable, pragmatical, commutative transactions in the sense of *do ut des* ("I give in order that thou mayest give") or *do ut facias* ("I give in order that thou shouldst do"). When a personal god, "out there," is supposed to receive and respond to such an offering, the transaction is said to be religious. Where there is no such god, but an impersonal source of power that is supposed to be touched and tapped (as in Raven Man's white-reindeer sacrifices to bring his brother-in-law back to life; see I.2: 180), the transaction may be said to be magical.[69] In either case, a rational decision has been made to procure a specific good and a practical procedure undertaken (in terms of the current reading of the laws of nature) to procure that good. When in the recent Occident the laws of nature became interpreted in terms of the mechanistic sciences, so that technological methods could be developed for obtaining what had formerly been the usual aims of magic and transactional religion (health, wealth, and progeny), the results were so gratifying that magicians and clergymen have lost in recent centuries much of their former influence in the direction of human affairs. I would suggest, therefore, that where rites, whether of sacrifice or of prayer, are performed as being directly causal of such specifically intended secular results as today are rendered by the practical sciences (fertility, prosperity, success in war, and so on), they should be recognized as "profane," which is to say, not only ordered to temporal ends, but also understood in terms of the usual temporal laws of cause and effect.

Moreover, the sacrifices noticed in Volume I are, without exception, addressed to entities, whether visible or invisible, close by or remote, that are "out there." In the Ainu bear sacrifice, where the offering made is not *to* a god but *of* a god, and the sacrificed animal is itself the very divinity which is being honored and consumed (see I.2: 152–154), the bear is understood to be a voluntary visitor from the spirit world who in order to appear on earth had to put on the appearance of a beast, from which it is now being relieved in a friendly family party of bon voyage and return home. The whole affair is conducted and interpreted in terms of light-world consciousness, where (to use a post-Kantian philosophical term) the "principle of individuation" (*principium individuationis*; time, space, and causality constitute the formative modes of perception and cognition by virtue of which "things," so called, are experienced as separate and distinct from each other) is in full effect. There is no frenzy, no loss of the sense of when, where, and how. The mode is consistently of the light world, Apollo's realm of distinguishable forms, whether of waking or of dream. All rites properly of the animal powers are of this order, except where they pass into shamanic trance, which, however, is not of any group, but of the gifted individual, who then becomes the inspired and inspiring Dionysian personality of his tribe.

In contrast, the whole intent of the week-long season of preliminaries to the catastrophe of the Ezam-Uzum feast was the generation of a group frenzy, such a transformation of consciousness as should constitute some kind of initiatory experience. We are not told of the content or import of this experience. The old men of the Marind-anim could not be brought to talk of it. Indeed, Wirz had all he could do to learn anything at all of their secret lore. But if the aim of the males of that urgently sexed tribe of cannibals had been simply to gang rape and eat another young female, they would not have had to make it all so difficult for themselves, so mysterious, so theatrical.

In short, those were not rites voluntarily undertaken by reasoning individuals to gain intended ends. Nor were they primarily transactional (*do ut des*), but transformative (*tat tvam asi*), imposed furthermore by a tradition from of old and founded in myths of the ancestral Dema of the Mythological Age out of whom all things of this temporal world are derived. In fact, it was the Dema who first performed the rite of which this orgy was but a replication. The anonymous young woman (*iwag*), ceremonially costumed and theatrically introduced as the epiphany of all that could be desired, was the Dema whose life is the life of this world. And the novices who ravished and consumed her were not rationally motivated, freely willing individuals, but her own creatures, beside themselves, overtaken totally by the life that she represented to them: the life that lives on lives.

It is significant for the argument of the present volume that this Papuan festival of untrammeled participation in the zeal of the vegetal powers of the seeded earth may date back as far as to c. 7000 B.C. and thus represent one of the first formative, bonding insights of the earliest plant-supported village communities. The contrast with the state of mind represented in hunting rites, where there is always an I and a Thou, is evident and striking. Even the trance state of the shaman is of an I, an ego, not dissolved but confirmed; indeed, become belligerent. The Lapps, for example, interpret the northern lights as a reflection of the energies of two shamans who in trance have somewhere met and are fighting.[70]

Spengler's recognition (see above: 8–9) of the contrast between the conditions of the animal and the plant—the animal as a microcosm in relation to a macrocosm and the plant as something cosmic; the animal free to determine its position with respect to the All, the plant in bondage to the All—is verified and enforced by this contrast between the mythologies of nomadic hunters and of settled planters: the one being of a tension (*Spannung*) of subject and object within the hold of the *principium individuationis*; the other, of a détente (*Abspannung*), following a shattering of the hold upon the mind of that same principle of individuation, whereupon the willing subject may lose all sense of himself as a separate being and dissolve into the cosmic All. The experience of things separate from each other in space and time then yields, in a moment of conversion, to an insight of them all as of one life: "I am the vine, you are the branches" (John 15:5). "Zeus is all things and whatsoever is higher than all things" (Aeschylus, *Heliades*, fragments 70). "By anyone recognizing in all action only Brahman, Brahman itself is attained" (*Bhagavad Gītā* 4:24). "There is really nothing strange in that reduction [of all selves] to One; though it may be asked, How can there be only One, the same in many, entering into all, but never itself divided up" (Plotinus iv.9.4,5, condensed). "Harkening, not to me, but to the *Logos*, it is wisdom to confess that all things are one" (Heraclitus, fragments 50,1). The vocabulary of bondage and freedom then goes into reverse, bondage becoming interpreted as entrapment in the hold of the *principium individuationis*, with freedom (or salvation) understood, accordingly, as release from individualism into identification with the All or its symbol (the deity or the tribe)—in the sense of those well-known sayings of Paul: "Who will deliver me from this body of death" (Romans 7:24) and "It is no longer I who live, but Christ who lives in me" (Galatians 2:20).

All very well! But is it proper to bring in, at this point, such exalted thoughts and authorities in explication of such a barbaric debauch as that of the union of Ezam and Uzum?

The question is appropriate and was, of course, to be expected. It brings up the delicate problem as to whether in a mythic image there may be an implicit meaning, for the mythological image that is rendered in this shocking rite is the same as that of the sacrifice of the mass. The archetype or elementary idea (*Elementargedanke*) is in both ceremonials the same: the sacrifice of an incarnate divinity and a communion meal of its flesh (*Hoc est enim corpus meum*). The secondary, local settings and interpretations (*Völkergedanken*) differ, but the psychological impact and therefore the transformative power of a myth derive from the image, not its explanation.

This is a fact universally recognized among peoples familiar with the service of myth to meditation. The verbal discourse, the explanatory legend, is functionally a lure to conduct the mind to, and to prepare it for, an experience of the image as an archetype of some aspect of one's own mystery. The image comes to one as though from afar, yet from within, as an opener of the way to release from the tension of separateness in space and time, the anguish of temporality, and one goes to it as a bridegroom to his bride or as an infant to the breast. Space, time and reasoning fall away: the *uk* beams drop, and there is peace.

The *uk* beams correspond in function, thus, to the Cross, as threshold agents between time and eternity, enabling the passage. In the Ezam-house, the bullroarers and bamboo drums are laid upon the *uk* beams. For they, too, are threshold agents, conveying to mortal ears ancestral voices. Hence the care with which they are to be handled. Though fashioned of materials of this temporal world, they are vehicles of a timeless call. Moreover, the Ezam-house itself is equally of that intermediate zone where time and eternity come together, as are all sanctuaries. Hence the requirement for silence: that the noises of this world should be hushed and the presence of that other experienced, as though from within and from all about. For all beings are threshold beings, and the function of a ceremonial is to provoke in the participant the recollection of his own immortal part.

The name of the Marind-anim festival, Ezam-Uzum (Husband-Wife), suggests the *yab-yum* symbolism of Tibet, where the image of the male (*yab*) and the female (*yum*) in embrace denotes (according to a relevant Tibetan text) the yogic realization of the essential unity of all apparent dualities whatsoever—eternity and time, freedom and bondage, birth and death, sorrow and joy—in the one great passion of the universe-embracing love divine.[71]

Could the old men of the Marind-anim have intended anything of this kind?

What else is registered in their symbols?

That the acts of sexual intercourse performed in the forest by those already initiate were not of lust simply, but symbolic of the sense of the festival as well, is indicated by the ceremonious placing of the broken twigs as tokens upon the *uk*. What sign more explicit of the solemnity of the act and of its relationship to the mystery of the ceremony could have been contrived? The very special form of the bam-

**154.** Two bamboo runners. In pairs they arrive on the festival ground from the Men's House, solemnly to the beat of their drums. Then breaking into a run, they encircle a chanting, drumming chorus of the old men. As apparitions of the Dema, they hold their drums, which are their tongues (their voices), by handles joining the two halves; as likewise, in their coming they are revealing, as one, the two worlds, invisible and visible, of the Dema and common day. Their hands beating the drums are tied to the tall plant sprays above their heads by long lines, so that with each stroke there is a corresponding swaying dance of the totemic sign.

boo drums that were sounded full force at the sexual climax, furthermore, was of two separate lengths of bamboo brought together. The sound that they made was called *uzum* ("wife"): it was the sound of her voice in response to that of the bullroarers. Their humming was named *ezam* ("husband"), the name of the ceremony itself. And just as in the *yab-yum*, the Tibetan "great symbol," the unity in duality is not only of male and female, but also of energy and form, heaven and earth, eternity and temporality, and more, so also in this "great symbol" of the Papuan Marind-anim: the *iwag* is the ancestral Dema, emptied of herself, having "assumed the condition of a slave," obedient unto death; and the novice, immolated in her eternalizing embrace, is the godward-yearning mortal who has reached his goal. In the Christian "great symbol" of the savior crucified, the mystery of the two that are one is typified both in the doctrine of the incarnation of the word as at once "true god" and "true man" and in the metaphor of the "son" returning to the "father" with whom he is "consubstantial." (Consider the form of the Papuan drum represented in Figure 152, above.)

But again we ask: Is it proper to compare such different and widely separated symbolic traditions in this way? The answer was given half a century ago by Ananda K. Coomaraswamy in a paper entitled "Primitive Mentality," which opened with a quotation from Euripides: "The myth is not my own, I had it from my mother" (fragment 488).

"By 'folklore' we mean," he wrote, "that whole and consistent body of culture which has been handed down, not in books but by word of mouth and in practice, from time beyond the reach of historical research, in the form of legends, fairy tales, ballads, games, toys, crafts, medicine, agriculture, and other rites, and forms of social organization, especially those that we call 'tribal.' This is a cultural complex independent of national and even of racial boundaries, and of remarkable similarity throughout the world; in other words, a culture of extraordinary vitality. The material of folklore differs from that of exoteric 'religion,' to which it may be in a kind of apposition—as it is in a quite different way to 'science'—by its more intellectual and less moralistic content, and more obviously and essentially by its adaptation to vernacular transmission: on the one hand, as just cited, 'the myth is not my own, *I had it from my mother*,' and on the other, 'the passage from a traditional mythology to "religion" is a humanistic decadence.'"[72]

As Coomaraswamy notes further: "The content of folklore is metaphysical. Our failure to recognize this is primarily due to our own abysmal ignorance of metaphysics and of its technical terms."[73]

# THE HISTORICAL FORMS

**155.** *Venus of Laussel, "The Woman with the Horn."* Carved limestone block, 17 inches high. From a rock shelter (Laussel) in the Dordogne, France, c. 20,000 to 18,000 B.C. (See I.1:66–68.)

**156.** Symbolic scene from the Shaft or Crypt of the Temple cave at Lascaux, Dordogne, France, c. 20,000 to 18,000 B.C. (See I.1:64–66.)

Of the many ways in which mythologies may be classified and thereby interpreted, that chosen for the present historical atlas —as appears in the titles of the four volumes—has been according to what have been called their *paideumatic*, or pedagogical, models: *The Way of the Animal Powers, The Way of the Seeded Earth, The Way of the Celestial Lights,* and *The Way of Man.*

The earliest model was of the animal world and the hunt, where the animals slain were the sacrifice, and the associated rites were of the order of a practical, commutative transaction: *do ut des,* "I give in order that thou shouldst give," which is to say, "shouldst be appeased and return, according to the order of nature, as a willing victim for another kill."

The earliest evidences of rites of this kind, from the period of Neanderthal Man (see I.1: 54–56), were contemporary with the earliest evidences of burials—both of which signs attest to a notion of life beyond death for both man and beast. The animals killed were venerated, furthermore, as teachers of the way of life according to nature, and were thus the life sustainers of mankind, as well spiritually as physically. Accordingly, as messengers of

**157.** Visionary mask from Spiro Mound, Leflore County, Oklahoma. Wood, 11½ by 7 inches, c. A.D. 1200 to 1600. (See I.1:3)

the supporting powers of the known world, they constituted the whole content of the religious art of the Late Paleolithic temple caves for a period of some 30,000 years.

The psychology of hunters inhabiting such a world was necessarily of that "tension" (*Spannung*) of which Spengler tells; namely, of an *I* confronting a *Thou*. Individuals (whether animal or human) were experienced as separate from each other within a field of space-time. However, informing and supporting that field was a mystery, experienced as a power, which might (or might not) be imagined as a personal being with the name of some assumed god. In immediate experience it was recognized with especial force in the two confounding mysteries of (1) the menstrual cycle of the female in its relevance to birth and (2) the visionary trance states of the shaman, who became thereby supernaturally empowered. Known variously as *ntum, megbe, orenda, wakan, manitou,* and so on, this ground of being was equivalent, finally, to that which in India is known as *brahman* (a Sanskrit neuter noun that can be defined as "the essence from which all created things are produced and into which they are absorbed").[74]

The recognition of such a force as the supporting consciousness of all things is the fundamental theme of *The Way of the Animal Powers*. It is nobly expressed in the native American ceremonial of the calumet, as well as in the statements quoted in Volume I of Chief Seattle, Letakots-Lesa, and Black Elk. *Mutatis mutandis*, it is equivalent to the Homeric (Apollonian) insight by which the Greek worldview was inspired and which Walter F. Otto, in his appreciative celebration of the spirit of Greek religion, has characterized as "the ability to see the world in the light of divinity—not a world wished for, expected, or as known mystically in unusual ecstatic experiences, but the one into which we are born, of which we are a part, woven into it through our senses and engaged to it in mind for its abundance and its life."[75]

The second *paideumatic* model to exercise the human imagination was of the plant world as experienced and interpreted by those primary planting cultures, to the exposition of whose mythologies the present volume is dedicated. The dating of their first appearances, very roughly, is c. 10,000 B.C., in three parts of the world. Accordingly, their exposition in this volume is to be of three parts: (1) the Americas, (2) Southeast Asia and the Pacific, (3) Africa and Southwest Asia. In all three of these the dominating idea of the sacrifice is that already noted, of a reciprocal dual offering: an eternal being is given to life in this world, and temporal lives are returned to an eternal being. Through various modulations it is thereby suggested that an original downcoming or self-emptying of this kind produced the universe and that through properly conducted ceremonials reproducing that original act, life in this world is renewed. The sanctuary in which such a ceremonial takes place is removed symbolically from the conditions of secular time, since enacted there is an identification of the cult

**158.** A Prayer to the Mystery. (See I.2: 192–193.)

**159.** George Catlin's sketch of a Blackfoot shaman illustrates the principle of man's acquisition of medicine power through identification with the energies that certain animals command. In addition to the pelt of a yellow bear (a great rarity), there are the skins of snakes, frogs, and bats; the beaks, toes, and tails of birds; the hoofs of deer, goats, and antelopes; "and in fact," quoting Catlin, "the odds and ends and fag ends and tails and tips of almost everything that swims, flies, or runs, in this part of the wide world."[39]

**160.** Rain Sacrifice. Rock painting, Rusape District, Zimbabwe (formerly Rhodesia). Period of Great Zimbabwe, fourteenth and fifteenth centuries. Copy by Leo Frobenius.

With upraised arms, a priest wearing an ornamented penis-sheath stands before a tree beneath which a female body lies, while above, a larger female form, as though responding with uplifted arms, leans over a standing field of 9 parallel lines, below which rain descends.

offering with the primeval offering of which it is the replication. As in the Roman Catholic sacrifice of the mass, where the offering of bread and wine is believed to have been transubstantiated (that is to say, to have become, through the magic of the words of consecration, transformed *literally* into the body and blood of Christ

Jesus),[76] so, too, in every sacrifice of this kind, *the victim is understood to be an incarnation of the god,* transubstantiation having taken place when the ceremonial costume was assumed. Furthermore, as in every celebration of the mass the sacrifice on Calvary is not simply symbolized, or referred to, but repeated, so likewise in all sacrifices of this order, both space and time are annihilate in an eviternal act.

The idea is not easy to grasp or to hold to by the faculty of reason. Indeed, in order to yield to it, reason must be wiped out. That is what all the so-called mystifications of myth and ritual are designed to achieve. But on the other hand, once the requirements of reason and the normal conditions of experience in the light world of separate things have been by one means or another removed, the experience of participation is not only easy to come by,

but inevitable; as though an earlier condition of mind, antecedent to that of birth into the field of the knowledge of space and time had become re-cognized, with a leap of joy in the recovery of a realization which had been lost. In contrast to the Apollonian mode of participation in the mystery of being, this now is the Dionysian. Apollo is of the light world, the sun, the wonder and beauty of separate things in the field of space and time. Dionysos, in contrast, is the lord of the vine ("I am the vine, you are the branches," [John 15:5]), and his blood is the vital, dizzying liquid of the vine, which opens the heart.

Under the life conditions of a hunting race, where the fundamental fact of life is the confrontation of the hunter and his prey, the mystical experience out of which religious forms arose was necessarily of this light world and of waking consciousness in tension, in relation to things separate from one another. With the development, on the other hand, of agriculture and the transfer of interest from the hunt to planting and harvesting, the darker *mysterium* of the seeded earth and the observed metamorphoses of living forms became the pedagogical model of human life, with rituals compelling a relaxation to the primary impulsions of the vegetable nature of the body, as to the will that moves through all things, where nothing holds its form but all is in flux.

The third *paideumatic* model to take possession of the human mind and will, reshaping all to its order, was of the planets and the moon and sun in the measured regularities of their courses through the constellations of fixed stars. This radical transfer of attention from the messages of a stable earth to those of the revolving sky occurred first in Mesopotamia, c. 3500 B.C., with the appearance there of the first city-states in the history of civilization. The arts of writing and of higher mathematics were invented there at that time; also the institutions of kingship and priestly orders; monumental architecture with especial attention to symbolic temple forms; elaborately symbolic, hieratic court procedures; and the whole complex of military and bureaucratic authorities, tax collection, chronic warfare, and controlled labor. The historic transfer of the spiritual focus from animal powers and the seeded earth to the celestial lights occurred when it was realized that those enigmatic travelers of the star-strewn heavenly vault were moving through constellations at various mathematically determined discoverable speeds and that these constituted in concert *the revelation of a cosmic order mathematically determined.*

This was a completely new idea in the world. There had been plenty of interest, before, in the sun, the moon, and certain stars. Personified, they had figured in many myths, and there had been rituals

**161.** Rain gods carved on a door. Dogon tribe, Mali. Now in the Musée de l'Homme, Paris. The connection between falling rain (or sacrificial blood, its mythic corollary) and rising crops was observed by agricultural societies worldwide and transfigured by them into ceremony and art. Compare the outstretched arms of the Dogon rain gods with those of the supplicant in Figure **160** and the two stalks of growing grain in Figure **162**.

**162.** Our Mother the Fertile Earth, bearing Our Mother Maize (represented as a dove). Huichol Yarn Painting (yarn on plywood, affixed with beeswax), by Cresencio Pérez Robles, Nayarit, Mexico, mid-twentieth century.

Above, center, is the sun; above, right and left, are two of the four Rain Mothers of the four directions. (Compare **160,** opposite.)

**163.** The beautiful Step Pyramid of the Pharaoh Djoser (or Zoser), the first tomb complex built entirely of stone, c. 2686–2613 B.C., at Saqqāra, southwest of modern Cairo. Designed with its elegant compound of white limestone chapels, colonades and galleries by Imhotep, the Pharaoh's chancellor, physician and architect (the earliest artist's name known to history), the radiant white apparition is symbolic of the two kingdoms of Upper and Lower Egypt united under one incarnate god, the everliving Pharaoh.

celebrated, as well as observatories instituted, to mark the summer and winter solstices, spring and fall equinoxes. Never before, however, had anything like this *mathematical* concept of cycles within cycles of time, marking harmoniously a supernatural program for the organization of all things, been known. It immediately became in those Mesopotamian city-states the key to a supernaturally authorized organization, not only of the calendar of festivals by which the common life was regulated, but also much more especially, of the now highly symbolic decorum of the court. The king and his queen or queens, as well as the members of his high council, were identified with the sun, the moon, and one or another of the planets: Mercury, Venus, Mars, Jupiter, and Saturn—the names of which suggest to this day some of the roles that they may already have represented: as Treasurer, Queen Consort, Troop Commander, Civil Magistrate, and Executioner. The comings and goings of the king and his queens, in particular, were regulated by the movements, appearances and disappearances, of the celestial spheres to which they were assigned, so that at certain critical junctures, interpreted as representing the termination of an eon, *the king and his entire court were killed.*

This was the form of sacrifice, known as "Sacred Regicide," to which Sir James G. Frazer dedicated many years of his scholarship and the twelve large volumes of a cardinal work, *The Golden Bough.*[77] It is a form of total sacrifice that can be identified in modified forms in evidences from every one of the archaic high civilizations, all of which had received seminal influences from Sumerian Mesopotamia; namely, Egypt, Crete and early Greece, India, and China—with an extension to Mesoamerica which is evident already in Late Olmec sites, c. 400–300 B.C., where writing, a system of mathematics on base 20, and an astronomically controlled calendar have been identified. In the present volume, therefore, I am not including the high cultures (Mayan, Toltec, Mixtec, Aztec, etc.) of Mexico. In terms of the *paideumatic* influences represented in their monuments, they qualify for a place in Volume III, *The Way of the Celestial Lights.*

**164.** Mayan Pyramid. "The House of the Magician," Uxmal, Yucatan. Late Classical Period, A.D. 600–900. Built, according to legend, in one night.

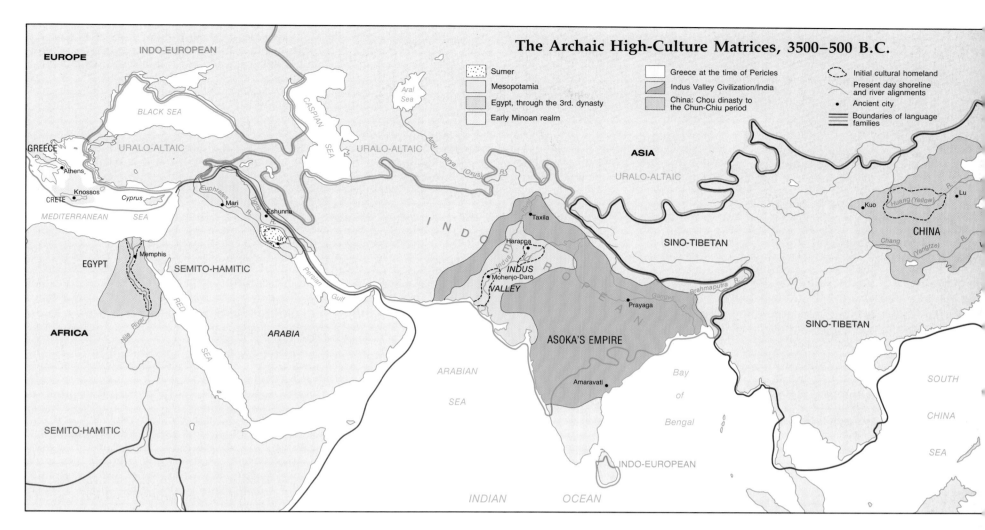

Sumer

Mesopotamia

Egypt, through the 3rd. dynasty

Early Minoan realm

Greece at the time of Pericles

Indus Valley Civilization/India

China: Chou dinasty to the Chun-Chiu period

Initial cultural homeland

Present day shoreline and river alignments

• Ancient city

Boundaries of language families

**Map 11.** About 3500 B.C., when agriculture had firmly taken root in areas roughly coinciding with the hearths of the earliest cultivators, along the fertile river valleys of north Africa and Asia, evidence appears of what we would now call civilization. In Egypt along the Nile, in Sumer between the Tigris and the Euphrates, in the Indus Valley along the river of the same name, and along the Yellow River in China, the first great cities were born. As the focal points of the agricultural societies around them, the cities inevitably became seats of political power. Across the globe, like the sun and the moon with their attending stars, the early kings and queens organized their realms on the model of the heavens, ushering in the first knowledge of mathematics, and with it a new mythological perspective: our third *paideumatic* model, the Way of the Celestial Lights.

The primal myth of the Sacrifice, however, retained its power. The actions of the king, the queen, and the court were dictated by a priestly caste that arose to interpret the movements of their celestial counterparts, so that when the stars came into certain alignments that represented the end of an era, the king and his entire court were sacrificed in order that a new one could be born to take its place.

**165.** Remains today of the Ziggurat of Ur, which was built of broch and clay as the earthly residence of the Moon-god Nanna, c. 2112–2004 B.C., by the Sumerian kings of Dynasty III of this city of the Moon-god's special favor.

And it was from exactly here, according to Genesis 11:31, that the patriarch Abram (later, Abraham), together with the rest of his family or clan, was led fourth by Terah, their father, (whose name means, "Who takes them out"), to settle in Harran. Whence again, according to Genesis 12:1–3, Abram at the age of 75 was summoned by his personal or family god (known to the biblical scribes of a thousand years later as yahweh) to father a people that should become to all the families of the earth a blessing.

Modern scholarship tends to favor the earthly second millennium B.C. as the likely period of the patriarchal age of Abraham, Isaac, Jacob, and Joseph, a season that culminated c. 1674 B.C., when the Asian Hyksos (an invading horde of largely Semitic and Hurrian tribesman) entered to govern Egypt until expelled a century later by the native rulers of Thebes.

**166.** Reconstructed group burial from the "death pit" of one of 16 "Royal Tombs" uncovered in the precinct of the Ziggurat of Ur. At the back is the vaulted burial chamber of the king, whose name, given on a cylinder seal, was A-bar-gi. Against the wall of this vaulted chamber stood a company of the women of his court with two harpists, a female and a male. The pillar of each of the instruments (each about 4 feet tall) bore a magnificent bull's head of gold with lapis lazuli beard, projecting forward from the sounding box, which thus became the bull's body. Soldiers guarded the welled-up door of the tomb; others stood all about against the matting-draped sides of the excavation; while among the crushed remains of two heavy chariots drawn by yoked oxen lay the bones of their drivers and of soldier attendants. Reins decorated with huge lapis lazuli beads had been attached to silver rings in the animals' nostrils. Silver collars had graced their necks. And above their backs, attached to the chariot shafts, were two little bulls of silver surmounting rings through which the reins had passed.

In the foreground, left, we see the end of a downward-sloping broad ramp, guarded by helmeted soldiers, along which this elite company of 65 individuals had come in full ceremonial attire to the sound of harp tones and of women chanting, to be interred alive with their deceased Lord and become reborn, like the moon, immortal. Earth was shoveled in upon them, packed down, level upon level, and when all was silence beneath, there descended into the same deep pit along a second, higher ramp, a second festive company—of the queen.

Her name, Shub-ad, is given a lapis lazuli cylinder seal. Her body, shrouded in beads of gold and silver, lapis lazuli, agate, chalcedony and carnelian, was found lying on a bier in a second vaulted chamber, with a gold cup by her hand, and with two ladies-in-waiting crouched, one at her head, the other at her feet. Her crushed skull was covered by a large ceremonial wig encircled by a massive hair-ribbon of gold, gold chaplets, and with the five-flowered hairpin of a queen. At her side, on a shelf, lay a second ceremonial wig, bound by a broad fillet of lapis lazuli beads, against the blue background of which, marvelously wrought little gold figures were sewn of animals, fruit, and ears of wheat. The imagery is that which later became identified with the Great Goddess known as "Lady of the Wild Things," who in the classical tradition was Artemis. Among the numerous precious articles strewn about the chamber floor was the head of a cow in silver (obvious answer to

the golden bull), while outside the blocked chamber door were the remains of animals sacrificed. Beside a large flat chest which had held the royal garments lay the bones of the Keeper of the Wardrobe. Forming a little cluster apart was the queen's choir of female voices, together with her young female harpist, the bones of whose hands lay still in place (after 4500 years) at the pillar and strings of her instrument. And there were grooms still in attendance on the gaily adorned and inlaid sledge-chariot, drawn by two asses, upon which the queen had been brought alive to the burial place of her lord. And the number of her company was 25.[40]

The interpretation of this amazing discovery is unsettled. That Queen Shub-ad was alive when she proceeded with her court into her dead king's burial pit is suggested by the gold cup at her hand. Other cups of the kind have been found in these tombs, and as Sir Leonard Wooley, director of the excavation has conjectured: "Presumably some kind of service was held…and at its end each took a little cup….and drank a draught of a narcotic and lay down in his place and slept."[41] That the king was buried before his queen is evident from the fact that his tomb is on the lower level: how long before, however, is unknown. Nor do we know whether, he, too, had been ceremonially slain; for his tomb chamber had been broken into and plundered (apparently by those building the chamber of his queen), so that no such undisturbed display of the circumstances of his death has appeared as of his queen—who, in any case, will have gone to him, together with her court, and joined him in Eternal Life, in the way of saté ("suttee," see above: 38–39).

The dating of the 16 "Royal Tombs" of Ur was assigned by Wooley to the period of Dynasty I of the city, c. 2500–c. 2350 B.C., which was antecedent to the building of the Ziggurat as now known. And Leonard then proposed the interesting question, which remains to this day unresolved, as to why, during that century and a half, no more nor less than 16 of such burials were celebrated. What could possibly have been their occasion?[42]

To which my own modest suggestion would be, that, since the planet Venus has long been associated in both Classical and Near Eastern mythologies with a great goddess by that name (known, also, as Aphrodite, Isthar, and Inanna), and since 5 synodical revolutions of that planet, of 584 days each = 2920 days, while 99 lunar months of 29½ days each also = 2920; whereas, moreover, 8 solar years of 365¼

days each = 2922 days, while 8 × 16 = 128, which is about the number of years of the period of Dynasty I or Ur (c. 2500–2350 B.C.): the scheduling of those 16 royal festivals must have been determined by observations of the heavenly cycles and conjunctions of the three brightest of all celestial lights: the sun, the moon, and the star of the goddess of love.

Frazer, in *The Golden Bough*, has noticed that the tenure of the royal office was formerly limited in Sparta to eight years; likewise in Crete and in a number of other Greek city states.[43] And the reason, he suggests, "is probably to be found in those astronomical considerations which determined the early Greek calendar…Thus, for example," he explains, "it is only once in every eight years that the full moon coincides with the longest or shortest day; and as this coincidence can be observed with the aid of a simple dial, the observation is naturally one of the first to furnish a base for a calendar which shall bring lunar and solar times into tolerable, though not exact, harmony. But in early days the proper adjustment of the calendar is a matter of religious concern, since on it depends a knowledge of the right seasons for propitiating the deities whose favor is indispensable to the welfare of the community. No wonder, therefore, that the king, as the chief priest of the state, or as himself a god, should be liable to deposition or death at the end of an astronomical period."[44] Add the cycle of the planet of the goddess Venus to the scenario, and the great mystery play of the Queen of Heaven following in death her Lord of the Night, the Moon-bull, for an eternal rebirth, is explained.

By chance a fragment has survived from the period of the Zigguarat of Ur III of such a hymn as may have been sung by her women to the tones of Queen Shub-ad's young harpist:

> Mayest thou go, thou shalt cause him to rejoice,
> O valorous one, star of heaven, go to greet him,
> To cause Damu to repose, Mayest thou go,
> Thou shalt cause him to rejoice.
> To the shepherd Ur-Nammu mayest thou go,
> Thou shalt cause him to rejoice.[45]

Damu (Damuzi-absu) being the Sumerian name of the ever-dying and resurrected god; Ur-Nammu, the name of a Third Dynasty king who will have died in the godly role.

And we have, also, an epic document of the Queen of Heaven's response:

> From the "great above" she set her mind toward
>   the "great below,"
> The goddess, from the "great above" she set her
>   mind toward the "great below,"
> Inanna, from the "great above" she set her
>   mind toward the "great below."
>
> My lady abandoned heaven, abandoned earth,
>   to the nether world she descended,
> Inanna abandoned heaven, abandoned earth,
>   to the nether world she descended,
> Abandoned lordship, abandoned ladyship,
>   to the nether world she descended
>
> The seven divine decrees she fastened at her
>   side, to the shugurra, the crown of the plain,
>   she put upon her head.
> Radiance she placed upon her countenance,
>   the rod of lapis lazuli she gripped in her hand.
>
> Small lapis lazuli stones she tied about her neck,
>   sparkling stones she fastened to her breast,
> A gold ring she gripped in her hand,
>   a breastplate she bound about her breast.
>
> All the garments of ladyship she arranged
>   about her body,
> Ointment she put upon her face.
>   Inanna walked toward the nether world.[46]

**168.** Gold vessels from Queen Shub-ad's tomb.

**169.** Stone vase from Queen Shub-ad's tomb.

**167.** Rein-ring and mascot from Queen Shub-ad's chariot.

**170.** Girl musician of the sacrificed court. From the "great death pit" of King A-bar-gi and his Queen Shub-ad, in the Royal Cemetery of Ur, c. 2500 B.C. The wax head reproduces the features of Sumerian women of the period, *as estimated from their skulls.*

**171.** Symbolic headdress of the sacrificed Queen Shub-ad. From the Royal Cemetery of Ur, c. 2500 B.C.

81

**172.** Gold wreaths from Queen Shub-ad's headdress.

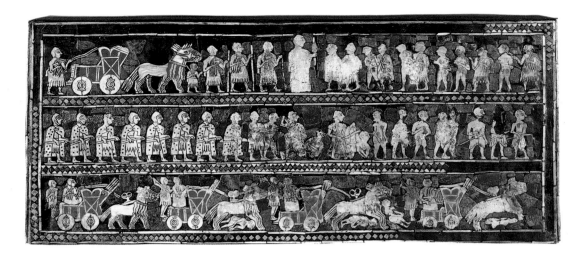

**173.** "The Standard of Ur," the War Campaign. From a tomb in the Royal Cemetery, c. 2500 B.C.

**174.** Gold dagger and a toilet case from the Royal Cemetery of Ur, c. 2500 B.C.

**175.** The "Bull of Heaven," gold with lapis lazuli beard. Symbolic ornament on a harp from the Royal Cemetery of Ur, c. 2500 B.C.

**176.** Gold helmet of Meskalam-dug. From a tomb in the Royal Cemetery of Ur, c. 2500 B.C.

**174.** "The Standard of Ur," the Victory Banquet. From a tomb in the Royal Cemetery, c. 2500 B.C.

**178/179.** Inlaid gaming boards with the "men" and dice.

**180.** Panel from the pillar of a harp showing animal-fable scenes (see opposite page: **175**).

**181.** A ram standing erect, its forefeet secured to the branches of a flowering thicket by silver chains (now decayed). 19½ inches high, made of gold, lapis lazuli, and white shell.

**182.** The Sacrifice of Isaac (Genesis 22), detail from the floor mosaic of the Beth Alpha Synagogue, near Galilea, A.D. sixth century.

The Akedah, Abraham's "binding" of his son, is the archetype, the legendary prototype, of Israel's submission to God's will. Historically it represents a radical introversion of the idea of The Sacrifice. For Abraham had already in his mind and will given his son to god when the heavenly voice stayed his hand. The sacrifice, that is to say, had been spiritually accomplished. The submission, moreover, had been of an individual in response to an unprecedented divine summons, and in that sense it has stood for centuries as the prototypical sign of Israel's disengagement from the whole ritualized mythic context of The Way of the Celestial Lights, not only as this was represented in the Royal Tombs of that city of Ur from which Abraham is described as having departed, but also as it has been modified and continued through the subsequent historical development of religions and ideals among the nations of the Gentile world. Abraham's two servants stand at the left. "Stay here with the ass," he had said to them. "I and the lad will go yonder and worship" (Genesis 22:5). The one-hundred-and-ten- or -twelve-year-old patriarch, his son, and the ram that is to serve, finally, as a substitute burnt offering, are labeled in Hebrew, and beside the hand of God are the first words of the prohibition: "Do not stretch forth…" The hand reaches from a dark cloud that is sending four rays of light to the world below and three into heaven above, the orderly nature of God's heaven being signified by the regular spacing of its trees, while on earth there is an irregular scattering of vegetation. As interpreted in a well-studied elucidation of the symbolism of the scene: "The cloud is the source, and the hand, along with or without the rays, is the symbol of the procession of divinity from the source to mankind and the world in general. So while the hand is entirely below the line of heaven in the Beth Alpha scene, the round dark source, which we may by a compromise call the 'cloud of unknowing,' is properly only in part below that line, and it casts its purest rays above it."[47] The altar, already blazing, is at the right.

A fourth *paideumatic* model becomes first evident in India, in the Vedic Upanishads (c. ninth century B.C.), where all phenomenal forms whatsoever, whether of earth, of sky, or of the imagination, are recognized as created, pervaded, and upheld by the same will or power that can be experienced within as the very life, finally, of oneself; whereupon attention is turned—again radically—from the whole spectacle of the universe "out there," whether of beasts, of plants, or of the circling spheres, to a fathoming of the light within—to its source. The challenge is already sounded in the two earliest of these scriptures, the *Brihadāranyaka* and *Chāndogya*.

"This that people say: 'Sacrifice to this god! Sacrifice to that god!'—one god after another. . . . These are but It's names according to [differing] functions. The worshiper of one or the other knows not; for in each It is incomplete. One's meditation should be on the Self [*ātman*] alone, wherein all such are united. For this Self is the imprint of the All and through it one knows the All, just as by [following] footprints one finds [the animal]."[78]

"OM! Now, there was Svetaketu, the son of Aruna. . . . whose father said to him: 'Bring me a fig from yonder fig tree.' 'Here it is, Sir.' 'Divide it.' 'Sir, it is divided.' 'What do you see?' 'These tiny seeds, Sir.' 'Divide one.' 'Sir, it is divided.' 'What do you see?' 'Sir, nothing at all.'

"Then Aruna said to his son: 'My dear, that finest essence which you do not see: from that, this immense fig tree has grown. My dear, believe me,' said Aruna, 'that finest essence which you do not see: of that is this whole world. That is the reality. That is the Self [*ātman*]. That is what *you* are [*tat tvam asi*], O Svetaketu.'"[79]

It is remarkable, but by about 500 B.C. such a turn of the mind deliberately from the heavens to the search, not only for an inward truth, but also and at the same time for specifically human values in the social-political sphere, had become general across the whole field of the great Eurasian high civilizations. In India the dates of the Buddha were c. 563–483 B.C.; in China, of Confucius, c. 551–478 B.C. (Lao-tzu's dates, though apparently of about that time, are unknown); in Greece, corresponding dates are of Pythagoras, c. 580–500 B.C., Heraclitus, c. 540–480 B.C., and Aeschylus, c. 525–456 B.C. In the main,

the philosophies of these very great sages agree in the recognition of a transcendent metaphysical ground, or "void," of which all things are apparitions, and to which the mind and will are to be brought, one way or another, to accord. Here are words from the *Tao Te Ching*, attributed to Lao-tzu:

> He who knows the male,
>   yet cleaves to what is female
> Becomes like a ravine,
>   receiving all things under heaven,
> And being such a ravine
> He knows all the time a power that
>   he never calls upon in vain.
> This is returning
>   to the state of infancy.
> He who knows the white,
>   yet cleaves to the black
> Becomes the standard by which all
>   things are tested;
> And being such a standard
> He has all the time
>   a power that never errs,
> He returns to the Limitless.
> He who knows glory,
>   yet cleaves to ignominy
> Becomes like a valley that receives
>   into it all things under heaven,
> And being such a valley
> he has all the time
>   the power that suffices;
> He returns to the state of the
>   Uncarved Block.
> Now when a block is sawed up
>   it is made into implements;
> But when the Sage uses it,
>   it becomes Chief of all Ministers.
> Truly, 'The greatest carver does the
>   least cutting.'[80]

And from the other end of the ecumene, here are a few fragments from the little that is known of Heraclitus:

"This world, the same for all, was not made by any god or man, but was always, and is, and shall be an everliving Fire, with measures of it kindling and measures being extinguished" (fragment 30). "We must know that War is common to all, and Strife is Justice, and that all things come into being by Strife" (fragment 80). "What is at variance comes to terms with itself—a harmony of opposite tensions, as of the bow or the lyre" (fragment 51). "To God all things are fair and good and right; but men hold some things wrong and some right" (fragment 102). "Good and evil are one" (fragment 58). "God is day and night, summer and winter, war and peace, surfeit and hunger; but he takes various shapes, just as fire, when it is mixed with spices, is named according to the savor of each" (fragment 67). " It is the same thing in us that is alive and dead, awake and asleep, young and old. For the former shift and become the latter, and the latter shift back again and become the former. For as

**183.** Aeschylus, c. 525–456 B.C. Roman copy of a Greek original from c. 325 B.C. Now in the Ny Carlsberg Glyptotek, Copenhagen.

**184.** The Buddha, c. 563–483 B.C. Fine white sandstone, Sārnāth, A.D. fifth century, Sārnāth Museum.

The hand posture (mudrā) is of the Teaching Buddha, "Turning the Wheel of the Law" *(dharmacalcra-mudrā)*. Below are his first disciples, listening in the Deer Park of Benares ( = Sārnāth) to his first sermon. The "Wheel of the Law" *(dharmacakra)* is shown among them, turning. Above are two heavenly beings *(gandharvas)*, listening as well. The rampant winged lions *(śārdulas)* at the Buddha's elbows represent both the resonance of the "lion roar" *(simha-nāda)* of his teaching and the response to it of the powers of nature; while the beautiful aureole about his head is of the sunlike radiance of his revelation, by which the night of our dream-time is terminated.

**185.** Confucius, c. 551–478 B.C. Stone rubbing, nineteenth century. Museum of Fine Arts, Boston.

out of the same clay one can mold shapes of animals and obliterate them and mold them again and so on unceasingly, so nature from the same matter formerly produced our ancestors, and then obliterated them and generated our parents, and then ourselves, and then others and yet others, round and round. The river of birth flows continually and will never stop, and so does that opposite stream of destruction which the poets call Acheron and Cocytus. So the same first cause that showed us the light of the sun, brings also the twilight of Hades" (fragment 88). "Hearkening not to me but to the Word, it is wisdom to confess that all things are one" (fragment 50).[81]

On the whole, across the whole field, such pronouncements of what has been termed the *Philosophia perennis* ("or Perennial Philosophy") of mankind accord in general sense with the messages of myth, being as it were translations of the import of the archetypes of myth into verbal discourse: *mythos* into *gnosis*, image into word.

\* \* \* \* \* \*

THE FOUR DOMAINS.

**183–187.** Europe, the Near East, India, and the Far East: along the date line of c. 500 B.C. there appeared in each of these high provinces a historical personality in whom its spiritual character was epitomized and defined.

Aeschylus (c. 525–456 B.C.) disclosed in *Prometheus Bound* the European tragical archetype of the heroic protagonist of humane values challenging the tyranny of brute laws, whether of nature, of the tribe or state, or of God. Having tricked and outwitted Zeus to bring to mankind the gift of fire (compare in Volume I: the Fire-theft theme), and along with that, knowledge of letters and the art of civilization, the Titan had been nailed, in revenge, to a remote high crag in the Caucasus range.

"I shiver when I see you," the sympathetic Chorus sings, "wasted with the thousand pains, all because you did not tremble at the name of Zeus: your mind was yours, not his."[48]

Advised to give up intransigence, to bow and to show regard to Zeus, lest the sufferings, already great, be increased, the unbroken champion of values specifically human answered with unconcealed disgust:

"Worship him, pray; flatter whatever king is king today; but I care less than nothing for Zeus. Let him do what he likes."[49]

In India, where a prime concern for centuries had been to gain through yoga release from engagement in exactly that unending agony which is life and which Prometheus voluntarily was enduring, Gautama Sakyamuni (c. 563–483 B.C.), the Buddha, proclaimed his eightfold way to release through *psychological* disengagement; while in the Far East, Confucius (c. 551–478 B.C.), profoundly distressed by the general chaos in China of 500 or more warrior states in continuous combat, proposed as the only hope for mankind the cultivation of a governing class refined and shaped to the ideal of the "Superior Man": one possessed, that is to say, of the character of "benevolence" *(jen)* and "sincerity" *(ch'eng),*[50] practiced in the forms of social decorum through which mutually respectful relationships are cultivated—of which there are five types that are fundamental: between prince and minister, father and son, husband and wife, elder and younger brother, and between friends.

"What Heaven confers *(ming)* is called the inborn

85

nature (*hsing*)," we read in the Confucian classic known as The Doctrine of the Mean (*Chung Yung*). "The following of this nature is called The Way (*Tao*). The cultivation of this way is called education."[51]

"Only he who is possessed of the most complete sincerity," we read further, "can give to his nature its full development. Able to give its full development to his own nature, he can do the same to the nature of other men. Able to give its full development to the nature of other men, he can give their full development to the natures of animals and things. Able to give its full development to the nature of creatures and things, he can assist in the transforming and nourishing powers of Heaven and Earth. Able to assist the transforming and nourishing powers of Heaven and Earth, he may with Heaven and Earth form a group of three."[52]

The Way of Man, then, as a new possibility and discovery announced, c. 500 B.C., from three distinct points of view in three of the four great Eurasian provinces of civilization, came to light with the realization by certain seers and prophets teaching in those parts that the adult human being is properly an autonomous organism, rightly capable of self-government, the proper aim of instruction being, therefore, not the imposition of laws from without, but the opening of each to the knowledge from within of his own genius, whether as an independent mind (Prometheus), the expression of an inborn nature (Confucius), or an ephemeral reflex of enlightening delusion (the Buddha).

In contrast, in the Near Eastern quarter of the world, where at that time the newly founded Persian Empire was in fresh career, Darius I, its King of Kings (521–486 B.C.), under protection of his universal God of light and the Righteous Order, Ahura Mazda, saw to it with all force that the idea of a system of law to be imposed from without upon submissive subjects should not be relaxed. As from of old, therefore, in that part of the world where the first city states had arisen and, on one hand, the Royal Cemetery of Ur had swallowed every eight years an entire court, while on the other hand, the patriarch Abraham, submitting to the order of a god of his own, had sacrificed (effectively, in his mind) his lawfully begotten son, the tyrannical principle of law, and of laws and laws and laws to be obeyed without question or reason, remained—and to this day remains—in force.

**186.** Darius I, the Great, c. 522-486 B.C. Detail of a panel from the Persepolis Treasury.

By the will of Ahura Mazda, King of Kings, King of Persia, King of the Lands, Master in fact of the entire Near East, from Thrace to the Ionian isles, and river Nile to the Indus, he was nevertheless stopped at Marathon, September 490, and when the battle ended there lay dead on the field (according to Herodotus, Bk. VI. 117) 6400 Persians and 192 Greeks. The poet Aeschylus, aged 35, was carried from the battle, wounded.

**187.** The great carved monument on a lofty rock wall at Behistun (or Bisutun), Iran, commemorating the victory of Darius in September 522 B.C. over Gaumata the Magian, last rival claimant to the Persian throne. Darius's foot is on his rival's belly; hovering above is Ahura Mazda, by whose will Darius became king; and in three languages—Old Persian, Elamite, and Babylonian—the whole history is recorded of the victor's rightful claim, the wickedness of his rivals, and the good works of his own reign.

**188.** The Seal of Darius the Great, 522–486 B.C. British Museum.

The king in his hunting chariot, wearing his crown, aims at a lion beneath a palm tree. Another lion lies under the horses. The inscription reads, in Babylonian and Persian cuneiform: "I am Darius, the Great King." Above, in the winged sun disk, is Ahura Mazda.

In the Near East, on the other hand, at that time part of the recently founded Persian Empire, a totally contrary point of view, philosophy, and supporting myth came into force. Darius I, who reigned as King of Kings, 521–486 B.C. (compare the dates just now reviewed), controlled a piece of the world that extended from the Greek Ionian isles (Satrapy I) to the Punjab and the Indus (Satrapy XX). All the ancient worlds of Egypt, Mesopotamia, Phoenicia, the Asiatic Greeks, and the Indus Valley had been absorbed into one progressively and aggressively inspired, international nation; the first of its kind in the history of the world. The Persian answer to the question of the way of life proper to mankind was in the building and enlargement of a humanely governed world empire under God. The prophet of this mandate, Zarathustra (in Greek, Zoroaster), who has been characterized by the historian Eduard Meyer as "the first personality to have worked creatively and formatively upon the course of religious history,"[82] is nevertheless a personage of such indefinite outline that his proposed dates range from 1500 to 550 B.C.

The outline of his mythological innovation, however, is distinct and impressive. It is of two contrary creators, a good and an evil, Ahura Mazda and Angra Mainyu. Good and evil are therefore at the ground of being. They are not merely relative, referential, but are opposed absolutes. They are final terms. Zoroastrianism is thus the earliest *ethically* based religion in the whole history of this subject. The term "beyond good and evil," in this system, makes no sense and is thus deceptive, itself evil, and of Angra Mainyu.

Ahura Mazda created in the beginning a world of Truth, of Light, and of the Righteous Order, into which, however, Angra Mainyu maliciously poured his own darkness, ignorance, and deception. There was a fall from Righteousness, so that all of nature (and the nature of man as well) is now corrupt, a mixture of light and dark, good and evil, truth and deception. *One is not to put oneself in accord with such a world, but to correct it.*

For three thousand years, according to this mythology, the conflict of good and evil within every particle of nature continued unabated, until in the mythic central land of the seven lands of the earth, Eran Vej, there was born of a pure virgin the prophet Zarathustra, to teach the Righteous Order. "Hear ye then with your ears!" he called. "See ye the bright flames with the eyes of the Better Mind! It is for a decision as to religions, man and man, each individually for himself. Before the great effort of the cause, awake ye to our teaching."[83] Especially and directly against the caste system, the yogic inward turning, and the ever-revolving cycles of time of the religions of neighboring India Zarathustra's challenges were hurled.

"Verily I say unto thee, the man who has a wife is far above him who begets no sons; he who keeps a house is far above him who has none; he who has children is far above the childless man; he who has riches is far above him who has none; and of two men, he who fills himself with meat is filled with the good spirit much more than he who does not do so; the latter is all but dead; the former is above him by the worth of a dirhem, by the worth of a sheep, by the worth of an ox, by the worth of a man. It is this man that can strive against the onsets of Death the Bone Divider, Death the Self-Moving Arrow; that even with thinnest garments on, can strive against the winter fiend; that can strive against the wicked tyrant and smite him on the head; it is this man that can strive against the ungodly deceiver and deceived, who does not eat."[84]

The age-old ways of yielding to the laws of nature, whether as represented in the ancestral social order, in messages of earth and sky, or in the inward path to identification with *brahman*, are all here deliberately brushed aside, and a summons is sent forth to each, as a freely choosing, self-directing, ethically responsible individual, to forget his imagined bondage to what is in fact deception, corruption, and the work of Angra Mainyu, recognize Righteousness, and engage on the side of the Good in this cosmic conflict with Evil.

I would say that we are here at the historic threshold of the modern separation of West from East.

For by virtue of the gospel of this prophet of Truth, those who had ears to hear engaged themselves in the battle, the tide in fact turned, and there was instituted a progressive course toward the restitution of that world of Truth, of Light, and of the Righteous Order which was originally of Ahura Mazda. "May we be such," runs a Persian prayer, "as those who bring on the renovation and make this world progressive, till its perfection shall have been achieved."[85] At Behistun (or Bisotun), Iran, there is a celebrated rock inscription in three languages, Old Persian, Elamite, and Babylonian, recounting the history of the accession of Darius I to the Persian throne, "by the will of Ahura Mazda." Thus the Persian Empire, under the hand of this King of Kings, became the historical agent of the progressive renovation, that was to be consummated three thousand years following the death of Zarathustra in a culminating universal war, whereby all the agents and works of Evil, including Angra Mainyu himself, would be annihilated. A virgin bathing in Lake Kansava would have conceived of the seed of Zarathustra the incarnation of his Second Coming, Saoshyant by name, who would appear at that time to accomplish the end of the world. The dead would be resurrected, and when all had resumed their bodies, each would know his father, mother, brother, wife, and others of his kind. And all would be light, truth, and righteousness forever after.

**189.** King Hammurabi of Babylonia (r. 1792–1750 B.C.) receiving from the sun-god Shamash the lawgiving authority of a universal tyrant. Bas relief at the top of a black diorite stela 6 feet in height, found in 1901 by Jacques de Morgan at Susa (Shush, in Iran), and now in the Louvre.

Below this heavenly scene, 51 columns of text in Akkadian cuneiform register in nearly 300 paragraphs the schedule of laws and punishments of what is now known as the Code of Hammurabi. Here the enthroned sun-god, wearing a turban ringed with horns and with rays of light rising from his shoulders,

presents to the king the emblems of his reign, a staff and a ring: the ring, full circle of the world horizon, which the king as its pivotal staff is herewith ordained to establish and maintain in justice: "that the strong might not oppress the weak and that justice might be dealt the orphan and the widow."

**190.** Ezra showing the Law to the People. Detail of an engraving by Gustave Doré (1823–83).

When the Persian, Cyrus the Great, in the year 539 B.C. entered and took possession of the city of Babylon, the people of Judah, who had been resident there since the fall of Jerusalem, in 586 B.C., to the Babylonian King Nebuchadnezzer II were permitted to return to rebuild their city and temple, and the captured treasures of the house of Yahweh were returned (Ezra 1:7-11).

About a century later (whether 458, 428, or 397 B.C., under Artaxerxes I or Artaxerxes II, is debated), the priest Ezra, "a scribe skilled in the Law," was dispatched from Babylon with a large company of the faithful and authority from the Persian emperor to take charge of the city's affairs, and on arriving, he was scandalized by what he found. As stated in his own report (Ezra 9:1-3): "The officials approached me and said: 'The people of Israel and the priests and the Levites have not separated themselves from the peoples of the lands with their abominations, from the Canaaites, the Hittites, the Perizzites, the Jebusites, the Ammonites, the Moabites, the Egyptians, and the Amorites. For they have taken some of their daughters to be wives for themselves and for their sons; so that the holy race has mixed itself with the peoples of the lands. And in this faithlessness the land of the officials and chief men has been foremost.' And when I heard this, I rent my garments and my mantle, and pulled hair from my head and beard, and sat appalled." An assembly was called, meetings were conducted, Ezra threw the Book at them, and in the end: "all the men who had married foreign women…put them away with their children" (Ezra 10:44).

For the reforms instituted on this occasion, which amounted to a reconstruction of the community of Israel on the basis of Pentateuchal law (which was represented as divinely revealed) Ezra has been called *a second Moses*. There were to be no more mixed marriages and no work on the Sabbath, there would be taxes paid for support of the Temple and strict observance, henceforth, of *all* provisions of the law.

Clearly, we are here in the progressive West, and the form of the sacrifice now is of a moral order: the dedication of one's life to the undoing of every agent of evil, and to good works. The explanation of the obvious resemblance of this program for the reform of the universe to both the Jewish program and the Christian rests on the recognition of all three as variant productions of a single, tightly bounded portion of the globe, where there have been through the millennia crossings and recrossings among races and related civilizations. The Old Testament story of the Fall (Genesis 2:4b through 3:24) dates from not later than the ninth century B.C., the period of the Two Kingdoms, Israel and Judah. The Assyrians conquered Israel in 721 B.C., and its people were deported. Nebuchadnezzar of Babylon took Jerusalem in 598 or 587 B.C., and the next year he destroyed the city, deporting its people to Babylon, where, as we read in the psalm, "By the waters of Babylon, there we sat down and wept when we remembered Zion" (Psalms 137:1). That was not to be for long, however; for in the year 539

B.C., Cyrus the Persian conquered Babylon and two years later gave orders that the Jews should return to Jerusalem and its temple be rebuilt.

Jewish monotheism, which came to maturity in this period, has been derived by some (Sigmund Freud, for example, in *Moses and Monotheism*[86]) from the monotheistic Aton cult of the pharaoh Akhnaton, who reigned from c. 1377 to 1358 B.C. There was, however, no such formidable ethical code associated with Aton as with Yahweh; no chosen people or program for world history. Jewish monotheism, no matter what there may have been of earlier influences, was in its final form unique and unprecedented, deliberately held apart from every system of belief in the surrounding nations by the simple device of identifying the local tribal patron god or ancestor with the creator of the universe ("Hear, O Israel, the Lord is our God, the Lord is One"), who, after the usual mythological separation of creator-god from the earth of his creation (of which we have had in Volume I numerous examples), here represented as the Fall, did not

abandon his people but retained in them an interest and concern comparable to that of a demanding husband in a difficult wife (Hosea 2).

The corollary of all this (which became through the histories of the two daughter faiths, Christianity and Islam, a terrible destiny for the peoples of the world) was that the gods of the gentiles were not gods, but devils and abominations to be destroyed together with their idolators. The *locus classicus* of this fate-bearing notion of righteousness is to be found already in II Kings 5:15 *"Behold, I know that there is no god in all the earth but in Israel."* The earliest historical effects of this manner of thought are chronicled in such accounts of the massacres by the Hebrews of the populations of whole cities as those, for instance, of the cities of the Midianites (Numbers 31), of Jericho (Joshua 6) and of Ai (Joshua 8), as well as the cities, kings, and armies of the Amorites (Joshua 10), that day when the sun and moon stood still and the Lord himself "threw down great stones from heaven upon them. . . . and they died."

\* \* \* \* \* \*

**191.** The Alexander Mosaic, from the floor of a house in Pompeii (A.D. 79). Roman copy of a Greek original from the fourth century B.C. Museo Nazionale, Naples.

Alexander the Great, 23 years old, at the Battle of Issus, 333 B.C., overwhelms the army of the Persian Darius III, who in his chariot takes flight. The Macedonian cavalry and startling spears, 13 or more feet long, dominate the field. Three years later, Alexander is "Lord of Asia." Again, three years later, 327 B.C., he enters India and with a fleet (built on the spot) of 800 to 1,000 ships sails down the Indus to its mouth. The Persian Empire has fallen; Europe, India, and the Far East have been joined.

In the year 332 B.C., Alexander the Great overwhelmed the army of Darius III, and the Empire of Ahura Mazda fell. The young conqueror passed through with his army into India, and there followed a period of mutually profitable exchanges of Buddhist, Classical, and Upanishadic ideas. The Buddhist king Asoka of northern India, for instance, who reigned c. 268 to 232 B.C., sent teachers of the Buddhist faith to the kings Antiochus II of Syria, Ptolemy II of Egypt, Maqas of Cyrene, Antigonas Gonatas of Macedonia, and Alexander II of Epirus.[87] By 100 B.C. the Old Silk Road between Rome and the Jade Gate of the Great Wall of China was already in service, and by A.D. 100 it reached from Cadiz, on the Atlantic coast of Spain, to Shanghai on the Pacific. Not only silk, but also ideas, were transported along that route. Nestorian Christian as well as Buddhist shrines and monasteries have been uncovered, punctuating the length of it. There was commerce by sea, also. South of Madras, for example, where at a site called Arikamedu, the remains have been excavated and reported of a large Roman trading station from the period of the birth of Christ, and we have also from that time the log of an Egyptian-Greek mariner of Roman citizenship who sailed the coasts of southern Arabia, Per-

sia, western India, and East Africa, describing in detail the active ports and harbors, wherein there were to be seen, variously at anchor, the merchant ships of China, India, Rome, and the Arabs.[88]

In the city of Madras itself the Roman Catholic Cathedral built by the Portuguese in 1504 rests, it is said, on the remains of Christ's apostle to the Indies, St. Thomas, who it is believed was martyred while kneeling in prayer upon a flat stone at the top of a hill (eight miles southwest of the city) now known as St. Thomas's Mount (but to Indians as *Faranghi Mahal*, "Hill of the Franks"). There is a little church at the top of this hill, built by the Portuguese in 1547, with the reputed stone in its treasury, together with a portrait of the Virgin and Child which is believed to have been painted by St. Luke—though when I saw it the style looked very much to me like High Renaissance.

Now it was during the first and second centuries A.D. that Mahāyāna Buddhism arose in India, as representing an advanced order of insights, beyond those represented in the strictly monastic Buddhist schools of the preceding five centuries since the *parinirvāna* (release from *samsāra*, the round of rebirths) of Gautama Sakyamuni, the historical Buddha. But the first and second centuries

**192 a–f.** Coins issued by the Greek tyrants of Bactria, c. 225–135 B.C.[53]

**a.** Euthydemus I

*Obv.* Euthydemus I, first independent tyrant of Bactria, diademed, border of dots.

*Rev.* ΒΑΣΙΛΕΩΣ ΕΥΘΥΔΗΜΟΥ, "King Euthydemus" Heracles seated on a rock, grasping with right hand his club, lower end of which rests on a pillar of stones.

Attic Tetradrachm, c. 220 B.C.

**b.** Demetrius I, son of Euthydemus

*Obv.* Demetrius I, draped, wearing headdress of elephant skin, border of dots.

*Rev.* ΒΑΣΙΛΕΩΣ ΔΗΜΗΤΡΙΟΥ, "King Demetrius." Heracles standing to front, placing wreath upon his head with right hand holding club and lion's skin.

Attic Tetradrachm c. 190 B.C..

**c.** Antimachus, continuator of Euthydemian line.

*Obv.* Antimachus drafted bust, wearing *kausia*, border of dots.

*Rev.* ΒΑΣΙΛΕΩΣ ΑΝΤΙΜΑΧΟΥ, "King Antimachus." Poseidon, naked to waist, standing to front, leaning with right hand on trident and holding palm in left. (possibly in commemoration of a great naval victory).

Attic Tetradrachm c. 150 B.C.

**d.** Eucratides, usurper of Demetrius' Bactrian throne.

*Obv.* Drafted bust of Eucratides, diademed, wearing helmet adorned with horn and ear of bull; bead-and-reel border.

*Rev.* ΒΑΣΙΛΕΩΣ ΜΕΤΑΛΟΥ ΕΥΚΡΑΤΙΔΟΥ, "King Eucratides, the Great." The Dioskouroi (Twin Heroes, Castor and Pollux) wearing pilei (pileus, a sort of close-fitting, pointed cap) and carrying palms, prancing on horseback with spears at rest.

Attic Tetradrachm, c. 165 B.C.

**e.** Heliocles, possibly Eucratides' son, by whom he was murdered.

*Obv.* ΒΑΣΙΛΕΩΣ ΗΛΙΟΚΛΕΟΥΣ ΔΙΚΑΙΟΥ, "King Heliocles, the Just."

*Rev.* Zeus, draped, standing three-quarter face toward left, holding thunderbolt and leaning on scepter.

Attic Tetradrachm c. 140 B.C.

**f.** Menander, culminating continuator of the Euthydemian line, r. c. 160–135 B.C. (other authorities have placed him, however, c. 125–95 B.C.)

*Obv.* ΒΑΣΙΛΕΩΣ ΣΩΤΗΡΟΣ ΜΕΝΑΝΔΡΟΥ "King Menander, Savior." Bust of king.

*Rev.* Maharajosa tratarosa Menandrasa, "King Menander, Savior" (Pali, in early Indian Kharosti script). Athene Promachos (Athene, Protectress).

A.D. were also those of the development of Christianity at the western end of what had formerly been the Persian Empire. Highways that in the Persian period had been opened between the Mediterranean coast (Satrapy I) and the Indus Valley (Satrapy XX) were still in operation, and their viability may be judged from the fact

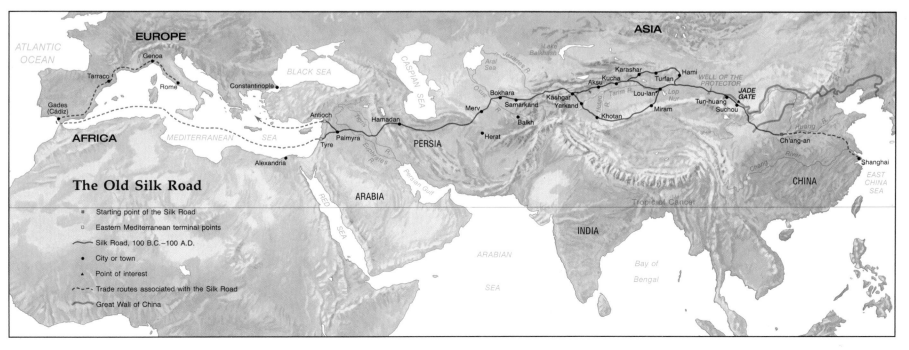

The Old Silk Road

- ■ Starting point of the Silk Road
- □ Eastern Mediterranean terminal points
- — Silk Road, 100 B.C.–100 A.D.
- • City or town
- ▲ Point of interest
- ⌁⌁⌁ Trade routes associated with the Silk Road
- — Great Wall of China

**Map 12**

91

**193.** A portion of the vast underground tomb built for the Chinese emperor Qin Shi Huang. Discovered in March 1974 in the city of Xi'an in Shaanxi Province, it houses over 100 war chariots, 600 clay horses, and 7,000 terra cotta warriors, as well as an immense quantity of real weaponry. This massive sacrifice to the dead emperor testifies not only to Qin Shi Huang's personal fear of death, but also to his search for immortality.

In 221 B.C. Qin Shi Huang founded the Qin (or Chin, as it was formerly spelled) Dynasty, from which the name China is derived. With the aid of his chief minister Li Su, the emperor established the country's first centralized administration. He standardized weights, measures, and coinage, and formalized the Chinese alphabet and rules of literary composition that have remained essentially unchanged up to the present day. He also tried to enforce uniformity of thought by banning philosophical debate and by burning all books except those in the Imperial Library. In a continuing effort to secure his northern border, he sent multitudes of laborers to interconnect scattered sections of wall fortifications left from previous kingdoms into what we now call the Great Wall.

that in the year 301 B.C. the emperior Seleucus himself, who had been busy in India mending fences at the eastern bound of his empire, was able to hasten back to Syria, 2,500 miles, with a squadron of 500 war elephants in time to crush a rebellion that was brewing there under Antigonus I, his rival.[89]

From the year of Alexander's entry into the Punjab, 327 B.C., the Greeks had maintained in the rich country between the Oxus (Amu Dar'ya) and the Indus a colonial territory of prospering communities known as Bactria, at the juncture of the caravan ways into India and to China. For nearly three hundred years (a period almost half again as long as the life, to date, of the United States) their kings and emperors issued coinages of their own,

bearing elegant portrait profiles of themselves. One handsome youth, Demetrius I, who in his coin portrait is represented wearing as headdress the head of an elephant (as though to identify himself with Indra), conquered the whole Indus Valley, c. 197 B.C., and settled there; whereupon his earlier Bactrian capital was seized by Eucratides, another Greek, so that for the next hundred years there were two contending Hellenic empires at the gate to India from the West, where a dazzling compound of Hindu, Greek, and Buddhist beliefs had come together. With their ready understanding of symbolic forms, the Greeks identified Indra with their own Zeus, Shiva with Dionysos, Krishna with Herakles, and the goddess Lakshmī with Artemis. (Contrast the likelihood of Josh-

ua's identification either of Zeus or of Indra with Yahweh!) Moreover, one of the greatest of these Hellenistic kings, Menander (c. 125–95 B.C.), if not himself a Buddhist, was at least a lavish patron of the Faith. The Buddhist Wheel of the Law appears on his coins; Plutarch states that the cities of his realm contended for the honor of his ashes,[90] and there is a major Buddhist text (in part, perhaps from c. 50 B.C.), *Milindapañha* "The Questions of King Milinda", in which this king (Milinda = Menander) is described arguing with a Buddhist monk, Nagasena, by whom he is defeated and converted.

"The king was learned," we read, "eloquent, wise and able, a faithful observer—and that at the right time—of all the various acts of devotion and ceremony enjoined by his own sacred hymns concerning things past, present, and to come. . . . And as a disputant he was hard to equal, harder still to overcome; the acknowledged superior of all the founders of the various schools of thought. Moreover, as in wisdom, so in strength of body, swiftness, and valor, there was found none equal to Milinda in all India. He was rich, too, mighty in wealth and prosperity, and the number of his armed hosts knew no end."[91]

Greek rule in both Bactria and the Indus Valley ended with the arrival of a horde of central Asian nomads from the vicinity of the Chinese Great Wall, called by the Chinese Yueh-Chi, by the Indians Kushanas, classified by some scholars as Mongols, by others as Turkomen of a sort, and by still others as some kind of Scythian-like Aryan folk. They had been dislodged and set in motion by a group of Huns ranging the country between the southern reaches of the Great Wall and the Nan Shan. Their migration across the wastes of Kuku Nor and Sinkiang lasted about forty years (c. 165–125 B.C.), causing major displacements of population in the areas traversed, and therewith hard pressures on the Bactrian border. The Greek defenses broke. First Scythians, then the Kushanas themselves poured through and, crossing the mountains from Bactria into India, possessed themselves of the greater part of the Gangetic plain, southward as far as to the Vindhya hills.

**194.** Clay horses and terra-cotta soldiers in Qin Shi Huang's tomb. In the time leading up to the founding of the Qin Dynasty, clay figures had become increasingly popular in sacrifices as substitutes for real persons and things. A heavy emphasis was placed on realism, and practically all objects buried with the dead were carefully modelled beforehand.

**195.** Terra-cotta soldiers under excavation at the great tomb in Xi'an. Thanks to the accuracy and realism of the rendering of both their features and their dress, Chinese archaeologists have been able to identify these soldiers as being from different parts of China.

**196.** A fragment from *The War of the Sons of Light and the Sons of Darkness,* a Dead Sea Scroll (first century B.C.–A.D. first century) found in the Qumran caves in Jordan in 1947. The document is a campaign plan for the battle of the last judgment. Based quite closely on Roman patterns of military organization, Theodore Gaster calls it "a kind of G.H.Q. manual for the guidance of the Brotherhood of 'Armageddon.' "[54]

**197.** Panel from the Arch of Titus, Rome, A.D. 81, commemorating the "pacification" of Judea, destruction of the Temple of Jerusalem, and confiscation of its treasures (A.D. 70).

It would have been during the first century of their empire that St. Thomas would have arrived in India and traveled to Madras, to be martyred there where the little chapel stands on the top of St. Thomas's Mount. The emperor Kanishka, whose dates are variously reckoned as c. A.D. 78–123 and as c. A.D. 120–162, was the greatest of their monarchs and, like Menander, not only a convert to the Buddhist faith, but also a lavish patron both of monks and of the arts of the partly Greek lay community. There is a tradition—questioned, though generally accepted—that it was under his patronage that a great Buddhist council launched the Mahāyāna on its career. The cultivation of Sanskrit as an elite literary language and of the classic Kavya (''poetic'') literary style, commenced apparently in the Kushana courts[92]. And in the sphere of religious art, a number of developments took place that were among the most notable in the history of the Orient.

Of these, the most important was the sudden appearance in Buddhist art of images of the Buddha. Before Kanishka's time, the human form of the Buddha had never appeared on the elegantly ornamented Buddhist monuments, his presence being symbolized simply by a Bodhi tree, the Wheel of the Law, an empty throne, footprints, or a shrine. For he was the one who had realized in himself the Void (that essence that Aruna's son, Svetaketu, came to know on dividing first the fig and then one of its seeds). What the Buddha had realized and what he therefore represented was that he was ''empty—without being.'' Therefore, as we read in a text from that earlier period: ''There is nothing anymore with which he can be compared.''[93]

Then, suddenly, in the second century A.D., we have his images in two distinct yet contemporary styles: one from the Indian city of Mathura (pronounced ''Muttra''), on the holy river Jumna, and the other from Greek Bactria. And in both the head of the Savior is shown framed by the earliest known halos in the history of art.

In Hellenistic images of the sun-god Helios and in Roman portraits of emperors the heads may be crowned with sun rays. Those, however, are not halos. The circular, simple disc of the authentic halo, or nimbus, such as one sees *behind* the heads of the second-century Buddha portraits, first appear in the West in Christian art of the late third and early fourth centuries, at first framing the heads of Christian emperors and then, about the middle of the fourth century, the head of Christ.

In India the phenomenon was directly associated with the appearance in the period of Kanishka's reign of that second body of Buddhist doctrine known as Mahāyāna—the ''Great'' (mahā)'' Vehicle ''(yāna)''—which in the later arts of medi-

**198.** Statue of Kanishka, Mathura, A.D. second century.

**199.** Statue of a Kushana king. Mathura, A.D. second century.

**200.** The radiant sun-god Helios. Detail of a metope from the Temple of Athene at Ilion, Asia Minor (Turkey). Third century B.C. Staatliche Museum zu Berlin.

eval Tibet became typified in the image of the "great symbol," the *Yab-Yum*, of the male (*yab*) and female (*yum*) in embrace. For the yogic realization of duality in unity which this symbol signifies implies that not only male and female, heaven and earth, energy and form, are one, but also *saṁsāra* (life in this world of rebirths) and *nirvāṇa* (extinction in the Void). All things, that is to say, are void. There is nothing special, therefore, about the Buddha, except that he has realized this fact, and accordingly, there is no longer any point in not representing especially him, since everything else also is void. What the halo represents, therefore (and it appears appropriately around the head) is his realization of *the ultimate sacrifice, which is the idea of selfhood,* there being no self to be released from the world and no world from which to be released. All is of the mind, *tathāgata,* "thus come":

> Stars, darkness, a lamp,
>   a phantom, dew, a bubble.
> A dream, a flash of lightning
>   and a cloud—
> Thus should we look
>   upon the world. [94]

\* \* \* \* \* \*

**201.** The Invisible Buddha in early Buddhist art. The Buddha crossing the Nairañjanā. Panel from the ruined great stupa at Amaravati, c. A.D. second century. British Museum.

Since what is revered in the Buddha is not his body but his buddhahood, which is invincible, he was not pictured in early Buddhist art, but indirectly implied by the reverential attitudes of worshipers addressing his footprints, an empty throne or shrine, or the Bo tree. In the bas-relief here reproduced we see only his footprints on the water, a flight of wild geese circling above him as he passes, heavenly damsels *(apsarases)* attending his departure, and a serpent king *(nāgarāja)* with 2 wives welcoming his arrival on the Yonder Shore. Note the halo of seven cobra hoods around the naga's head and the cobra hoods, like an ornamental comb, above the heads of his wives. In the background is another nāga.

**202.** Buddha beneath the Bo Tree, seated on the Lion Throne, attended, above, by *gandharvas* (heavenly musicians) and below, by *yaksas* (earth divinities), each of the latter bearing a chauri, or fly-whisk, in his service, as attending royalty. Front Mathurā (pronounced Muttra), sculptured in the red sandstone characteristic of images from this center, A.D. mid-second century. Museum of Archaeology, Mathurā.

The vigorous style of this Buddha-form is of a native Indian art tradition owing nothing to the art of the contemporary Graeco-Roman shapes producing images for the shrines and temples of neighboring Bactria. The scalloped border of the halo may be reminiscent of cobra hoods (compare the nāga-king, **201**, opposite). Serpents shed their skins to become, as it were, reborn: the Buddha, shedding attachment to the world, is at one with the immortal light of consciousness within all. The raised right hand is in the "fear not" posture (*abhaya mudrā*). The lotus-wheel on its palm and those on the soles of the Buddha's feet are among his birth-signs prophetic of buddhahood. Others are the hair-tuft (*ūrnā*) between the eyebrows and the strange bump (*usnisa*) on the crown of his head. The long ear lobes suggest royalty, as having once held the jeweled ear-plugs of a young prince.

Symbolic beneath the teaching Buddha's throne is the roaring lion, at the sound of whose voice all the grazing animals of the plain take flight. So too, at the sound of the Buddha's voice, life's delusions are dispelled.

**203.** Standing Buddha, Graeco-Roman style, Gandbara. Black, slate-like mica-schist, from Jamalgarhi Monastery, A.D. first century. Earliest appearance of the halo in the history of art. Natural History Museum, Chicago.

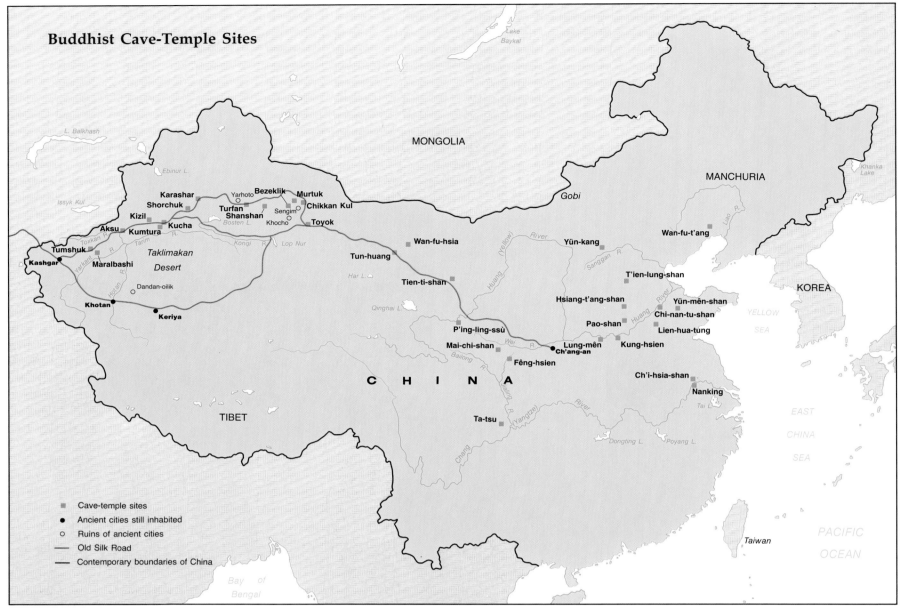

## Buddhist Cave-Temple Sites

Map 13

Legend:
- ■ Cave-temple sites
- ● Ancient cities still inhabited
- ○ Ruins of ancient cities
- Old Silk Road
- Contemporary boundaries of China

**204/205.** Two (of seven) Gandharvas. Fresco fragments from Miran, A.D. third century. Now in the British Museum.

Since Oriental gandharvas do not have wings, Sir M. Aurel Stein reflected long on these amazing figures found on the crumbling wall of a little chapel buried under wind-blown sand in the middle of an empty desert. "And what," he asked himself, "had these graceful hands, recalling cherished scenes of Chris-

tian imagery, to do here on the walls of what beyond all doubt was a Buddhist sanctuary?"

Their historical importance was to him immediately evident. As he recorded in his journal: "These frescoes marked an *étape* of exceptional interest in the history of classical pictorial art as transmitted to innermost Asia under Buddhist auspices…Nowhere in the Hellenized East, not even in Egypt, have graphic representations of angels survived from a sufficiently

early period to throw light on the question as to where and when the Acpids of classical mythology underwent transformation into that type of winged figures which the painter of the Miran fresco dado made use of for decoration of a Buddhist shrine. Yet there is so distinct a suggestion of Semitic traits in most of these faces that one's thoughts are instinctively carried to regions like Syria, Mesopotamia, and Western Iran as likely ground for that original adaptation."[55]

Amoghasiddhi, whose name means "Unerring Achievement (of Nirvāna)," is a Buddha purely of the mind, a "Meditation (Sanskrit, *Dhyāni*; Chinese, *Ch'an*; Japanese, *Zen*) Buddha," of no "reality" except as typifying, inspiring, and supporting a specific state and discipline of the mind in meditation, which mental state is then his reality.

This purely spiritual Buddha is represented in Mahāyānā thought as attended by two equally spiritual Bodhisattvas: *Dipanī,* "Remover of Obstructions," and *Vajrapāni,* "Thunderbolt Bearer." The eyes of the latter, as here shown, are fixed on Amoghasiddhi. The chauri or fly-whisk of his service is in his elevated right hand, while in his left is the *vajra* ("thunderbolt") symbolic of that blast of Enlightenment by which attachment to the world-illusion is terminated. (Its unusual form in this early Central Asian painting has not, as far as I know, been explained.) Note the halo, the *ūrnā,* and the long earlobes, which, however, in contrast to those of the historical Buddha, still contain the jewels of a prince.

For in contrast to the ascetic ideal represented by the Buddha Sakyamuni, who renounced his throne to seek enlightenment, the Mahāyānā ideal of the Bodhisattva—whose "being or essence (*sattva*) is enlightenment (*bodhi*)"—is of one who, while remaining in life in his earthly role, is yet fixed in mind in the knowledge of transcendence, holding the *vajra* firmly in grasp, while yet humbly serving as a chauri bearer. The implied non-duality of this simultaneous experience of the "sorrows of the world" (*samsāra*) and "release from sorrow" (*nirvāna*) is allegorically suggested by the two falconlike birds at the Bodhisattva's side, one on the ground, the other in flight, but descending.

**206.** The Bodhisattva Vajrapani contemplating the Meditation-Buddha Amoghasiddhi, part of whose leg is visible (above, right) resting on the cushioned throne upon which he is seated. Fresco fragment from a cave sanctuary at Kizil in the Kucha area (see **Map 12, 13,** above), c. A.D. 500.

**208.** Head of the Buddha Sakyamuni. Wood, gilded. Height 4⁵⁄₁₆ inches (11 cm.). From Tumshuk, midway between Kashgar and the Kucha area (see **Map 12, 13,** above), A.D. fifth to sixth century.

When Prince Siddhartha, having in his mind renounced his inherited throne, rode forth at night from his palace and, dismounting, had sent his horse, Kanthaka, riderless back to the palace, with his right hand he grasped his scimitar and with his left the princely top-knot of his hair, which he cut off, together with the diadem. Whereupon, as told in the Pali account of The Great Renunciation, "his hair became two finger-breadths in length and, curling to the right, lay close to his head. As long as he lived it remained of that length, and the beard was proportionate. And never again did he have to cut either hair or beard."[57]

Hence the classic convention represented in this beautiful little head, of showing the Buddha's hair in tight little curls.

"Then," the narrative continues, "the Future Buddha seized hold of his top-knot and diadem, and threw them into the air, saying, 'If I am to become a Buddha, let them stay in the sky, but if not, let them fall to the ground.'

"The top-knot and jeweled turban mounted for a distance of a league into the air and there came to a stop. And Sakka (Indra), the king of the gods, perceiving them with his divine eye, received them in an appropriate jeweled casket, and established this in the Heaven of the Thirty-three Gods as the 'Shrine of the Diadem.'"[58]

**207.** The Buddha, six monks, and the arm of a worshiper tossing flowers. Fresco fragment from Miran, a long-abandoned way station in the Taklimakan desert, some 75 miles southwestward of Lop Nor. A.D. third century.

Note the halo, already two-thirds of the way across Asia, the Buddha's raised hand in *abhaya-mudrā,* his *usnisa,* and the long ear lobes; also, the chauri, or fly-whisk, in the hand of one of the monks (probably Ananda). The foliage suggests that the occasion illustrated may be of a sermon delivered in a garden. This precious fragment was discovered and with extreme care removed from its crumbling wall by Sir M. Aurel Stein during his 1906–1908 expedition into the Taklimakan Desert.[56]

**209.** The Future Buddha Maitreya in the Heaven of the Thirty-three Gods. Wall painting from a rock-cut cave at Kizil, in the Kucha area (see **Maps 12, 13,** above), c. A.D. 600–650.

The essential Hindu-Buddhist idea of "creation" as a continuous event, producing universes without number which appear and vanish throughout space and time (both of which are without bounds), is complemented by a belief in Buddhas also without number that have appeared and shall continue to appear as teachers of the way to release from attachment to ephemeral forms through the recognition of oneself as of the nature, not of the forms, but of their ground (which is of no form). The sacrifice required, that is to say, is of one's commitment to phenomenality.

Gautama Sakyamuni was the teacher of the present cycle of time of our local universe. The teacher of the next cycle will be Maitreya, the "Loving Kindly One" (Chinese, Mi-lo-fo; Japanese, Miroku; Tibetan, Byams-pa; Mongolian, Maidari), who is already waiting in the highest of the storied heavens there teaching, meanwhile, the resident gods, whom we here see moving their hands in reflective response to his thrilling voice. (The joys of such a heaven are so great, however, that detachment is for gods a far more difficult achievement than for the creatures of this earth.) Note the haloes. The crossed ankles of Maitreya, seated on a throne, is characteristic of his appearances in Buddhist art. His right hand is here in *abhaya-mudrā* ("Do not fear the step to renunciation!"), while his left is in the "bestowing posture," *varada-mudrā*, bestowing both the grace "not to fear" and the boon of fulfilled enlightenment.

**210.** Dignitary seized by soldiers. Fragment of a wall painting found among the debris of a temple. The context, whether legendary or historical, is unknown. Kunitura, in the Kucha area (see **Maps 12, 13,** above), A.D. eighth to ninth century.

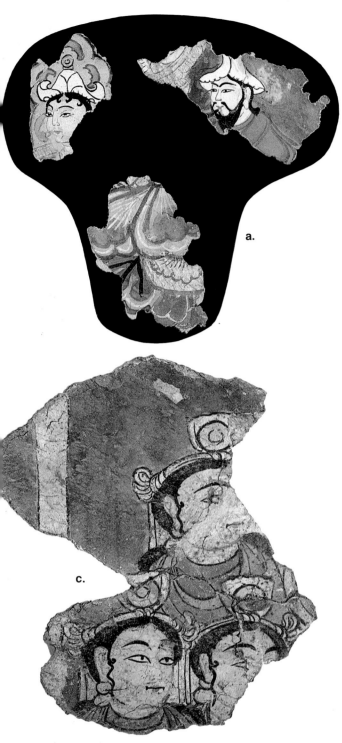

a.

b.

c.

**211 a-f.** Fragments of Manichaean books from Khocho in the Turfan area (see **Map 12, 13,** above), A.D. eighth to ninth century.

The spectacular success and spread throughout northern Asia, the Near East, North Africa and Europe of the Gnostic religion of purity and hope conceived and taught by the Persian visionary Mani, or Manes (A.D. 216–276), was marked especially by the North-African St. Augustin's youthful acceptance and then rejection of the faith, 373-382; its appearance in Central Asia and China in the eighth and ninth centuries; and its appearance with such effect in southern France in the twelfth century that Pope Innocent III proclaimed against it the Albigensian Crusade of 1209–1244.

Briefly, its theme was of the release of the world's potential for truth, harmony, and justice from entrapment in the actual context of universal violence and suffering; the means to this end to be a disciplined non-participation in the violence and the living of lives totally dedicated to the re-cognition, and thus release to light, of the spirit. Its end everywhere (as in thirteenth century Europe) was in violent suppression by local authorities, Mani himself having died enchained in a Persian prison. The Europeans burned at the stake went, together with their leaders, chanting hymns even as the flames enclosed them.

Pictured in the book fragments here assembled from their eighth to ninth century center in Kocho, Central Asia, we see what appear to be members of the lay community (**a, b** and **c**); a college of their leaders (**d**), the Perfected Ones, of exemplary lives, all writing; two heavenly musicians on a truly beautiful page (**e**), and two demons (**f**), identified by their fangs.

d.

e.

f.

**212.** The First Palm Sunday. Nestorian wall painting at Khocho, in the Turfan area (see **Map 12, 13,** above), A.D. ninth century.

From Cairo to Ch'ang-an, from the fifth to the sixteenth century, the Christianity of Asia was predominantly Nestorian, the initiating crisis having occurred at the Council of Ephesus in the year 431, when Nestorius, the Patriarch of Constantinople, refused to accept the designation of Mary by the Council as *Theotokos*, "God-bearer," "Mother of God." He was deposed from his see and banished to an Egyptian desert, there to die in obscurity.

But those Christians of Syria and Asia Minor who adhered to his position (namely, that Mary had not conceived of God, but gave birth naturally to a man who became "the chosen vessel of the Godhead," as appeared at the time of his baptism by John in the river Jordan, when "he saw the heavens opened and the Spirit descending upon him like a dove" [Mark 1:10]) migrated to Persia; and it was from there that their missions went out, through Persia, and to Egypt, Arabia, Ethiopia, India, Central Asia and the farthest East.

**213.** Bodhisattva. Kocho, A.D. ninth to tenth century. Painting on silk, 13½ by 10⅕ inches.

**214.** A Uighurian Prince. Painting on a cloth banner, 4 feet 6 inches by 1 foot 7 inches. Kocho, A.D. ninth century.

The Uighur are a Turkic people who between the eighth and ninth centuries A.D. maintained in eastern Turkistan and Mongolia a kingdom of considerable power and (as appears in the person of this nobleman) civilized elegance. The banner is to the memory of an ancestor deceased, the spray of flowers indicating that the bearer has died.

**215.** Colossal Buddha, height 44 feet, carved into a red-sandstone cliff at Yün-kang, Shensi, late fifth century A.D.

The niche is No. 20 of a series of 42 rock-cut shrines along the face of a great rock wall. The Buddha intended is probably Sākyamuni. In the radiance of his halo appear the Buddhas of earlier world cycles, together with saints and worshipping heavenly beings. The standing figure at the meditating Buddha's side is possibly Maitreya, his right hand lifted in the "fear-not" gesture, *abhaya-mudrā*.

The legend of the entry of Buddhism into China begins with a prophetic dream of the emperor Han Ming Ti, of a golden man arriving from the West. A welcoming embassy was sent out; and coming eastward along the Old Silk way were two Buddhist monks conducting a white horse bearing on its back an image of the Buddha and a packet of Mahāyāna texts. The date was about A.D. 65. In Lo Yang, the imperial capital, a monastery was built, named for the animal on whose back the honored image had arrived; and it was there, in that White Horse Monastery, that the long project began of rendering Sanskrit sūtras into Chinese.

The image, undoubtedly (considering the date), was of the Graeco-Roman, Gandhāran type. Unmistakable signs of influences from that Late Classical center remain evident (as in the image here reproduced) throughout the history of Far Eastern Buddhist art.

216. Daibutsu, the "Great Buddha." Tōdaijii, Nara. Bronze, height 53 feet 6 inches; pedestal of 56 bronze lotus petals, each 10 feet high; stone platform, 7 feet high; each ear, 8 feet 6 inches long; each eye, nearly 4 feet long; weight, 452 tons. Casting commenced, A.D. 743, finished, 749; image dedicated 752 by Emperor Shōmu. Gilt wooden halo bearing 16 Buddhas added, date unknown, probably Genroku Era, 1588–1703.

The great figure is in a teaching posture; right hand in *abhaya mudrā* (Japanese, *semui-in*), left in *varada mudrā* (Japanese, *yogan-in*). Engraved in hairlines on the pedestal is the text of a sermon—"The Lotus Realm" (*Padmaloke-dhatu;* Japanese, *Rengezō-kai*—which is supposed to have been delivered by the Buddha Sakyamuni while still seated beneath the Bo-tree. Too profound to be understood at the time, it was followed, later, at Sārnāth, the "Deer Park of Benares," by that generally known as the "First Turning of the Wheel of the Law" (see above: **184**).

Represented in this awesome image is the "Meditation (*ohyāni*) Buddha" Vairochana, whose name means, "Belonging to, or Coming from the Sun," and to whose doctrine, known as the "Flower Wreath" (Japanese, *Kegon*), the Buddha Sakyamuni gave voice in his Bo-tree sermon. No single being—so runs the argument—can be said to exist in and of itself. Instead, there is a "mutual arising," a derivation, not only from antecedents through time, but also from interdependencies throughout space, and even backward, as it were, from intentions for a future. So that through both space and time everything is linked to everything else, like flowers to each other in a garland encircling, as it were, this great Solar Presence, "thus come" (*tathāgata*), who is at once revealed and concealed in all.

The Mahāyāna text in which this "Doctrine of the World of Totalistic Harmony Mutually Relating and Penetrating" is disclosed in the *Avatamsaka Sūtrā*, a work that was translated between 317 and 420 from Sanskrit into Chinese.

the sorcery of art, by which the paralyzing experiences either of absurdity or of horror become converted into thoughts with which one can live: in the comic, a discharge through art of the nausea of absurdity; in the sublime, an overcoming through art of the spell of horror. Ataraxy (ἀτᾰραξία "calmness, intellectual detachment") while yet regarding things with aesthetic enchantment, is the life-restorative resolution. The miracle of the Greeks is that in their classic arts the raptures both of energy and of form, Dionysos and Apollo, are in balance, whereas in the wild rites of many of their barbaric neighbors Dionysian force prevailed, and in the neoclassic arts of certain later European periods form for itself became the high concern without the informing life.

Returning to the Near East we find that the healing there proposed for the recognized evil and evils of life has been by way of the invention of a god "out there" who is not himself in any way a part of or contaminated by these terrestrial evils, which, although he is the creator of the world, are not of his creation; and who through prophets or incarnations has projected onto this troubled earth a unique community which, like himself, is of a

In *The Birth of Tragedy,* Nietzsche asks how any mind so exploded by a catastrophic illumination might be summoned back to participation in the sorrows of an illusory life thus rendered meaningless. He compares the baffled state of the mind to that of Shakespeare's Hamlet, stunned by a realization of the iniquity of his mother, which he has been called upon

by his father's spirit to avenge. Experienced as an intuition of iniquity at the root, not only of all life, but also of all action to correct it, the insight fills the youth with an existential nausea by which his own life (and that of everyone he should be loving) is undone.[95]

The cure proposed by the Greeks for such confusion was, in Nietzsche's view, supernatural order that is incorruptible. Membership in this community is the cure. For there is no evil within it; all evil is outside. And the work to be undertaken, once one has been either cured of evil by conversion or born and raised in righteousness as an uncorrupted representative of God's purpose for the world, is, first, to obey his ritual laws, and second, to extend his domain, so that, as foreseen by the prophets Zechariah and Zephaniah: "The Lord will become king over all the earth: on that day the Lord will be one and his name one" (Zechariah 11:9). " 'Therefore wait for me,' says the Lord, 'for the day when I arise as a witness. For my decision is to gather nations, to assemble kingdoms, to pour out upon them my indignation, all the heat of my anger; for in the fire of my jealous wrath all the earth shall be consumed. Yea, at that time I will change the speech of the peoples to a pure speech, that all of them may call on the name of the Lord and serve him with one accord' " (Zephaniah 3:8–9).[96]

The most explicit formulation of the prospect of this pious aspiration is to be seen in the Muslim vision of the earth as of two realms: "the territory of Islam" (*dār al īslam*) and "the territory of war" (*dār al-harb*), with believers required to take part in the holy war (*jihād*) "on the way of Allah" (*fī sabil Allāh*), in order violently to convert the heathen to the true faith, or at least to subject them to the yoke of Islam.[97] The manner of the Christian execution of the ideal is amply illustrated in the present volume. And with one more community of zealots now added to the list—in the name, not anymore of that one and only God, but of the one and only authorized order of social justice, according to the revelation of Karl Marx—an imminent fulfillment of the desiderated day of eternal rest in one community with one language is by many believed to be at hand.

Psychological, if not social, release from the increasing stress of this imbroglio of historic tensions arising from the deluding concepts of "Good" and "Evil" (mostly, "We are good," "You are evil") may be found in the genial "Forest of Pencils" of the early Chinese philosophical schools, where the first revelation to greet

**217.** Horyuji, Nara, Japan. seventh to nineteenth century.

The oldest existing temple in Japan, consisting of 4 buildings from the Asuka Period (552–645), 5 from the Nara Period (645–710), and 24 more, from every period to the fall of the Shogunate in 1867.

A.D. 552 had been the year of the introduction of Paikche/Buddhism, when the King of the Paikche Kingdom of Korea sent to the Imperial Court of Japan a gift of Buddhist images and sutras, along with a company of monks and nuns, architects and sculptors, to assist in the foundation in the islands of a Buddhist civilization. A brief period of resistance on the part of the native Shinto families terminated with the recognition of Buddhism as an enrichment, no displacement, of the native religious order; and in the region, then, of the Empress-Regent Suiko (r. 592–628), her nephew, the Crown Prince Shotoku (572–621)—through whose faith and influence Buddhism had become the religion of the Court—in the year 607, by order of the Empress-Regent, founded what is now the temple complex of Horyuji. The Five-storied Pagoda and the large Koudo, or Main Hall, are two of the oldest wooden buildings in the world.

**218.** Interior of the Church of "Divine Wisdom," Hagia Sophia, as converted in the year 1453 into a mosque. The Byzantine mosaics were then over-painted with arabesques and the walls hung with calligraphic emblems. Since 1931, however, the Byzantine Institute of America has been uncovering the mosaics, and in the year 1935 the mosque was converted into a museum.

The great dome, 105 feet in diameter, is 189 feet high; the floor, 252 feet long by 234 feet wide. Founded by Constantine the Great on the site (it is said) of a pagan temple, the original building burned in the year 415. Rebuilt by Theodosius II, it was again burned along with much of the city, during an insurrection in the year 532. The present glorious structure dates from the reign of Justinian I (527–565) and

celebrates, both the rebuilding of the city as a political as well as a spiritual center of Christendom, and the achieved unification of the Christian world under Byzantine control—disregarding the Nestorian East, Coptic Ethiopia, and the unresolved claim to authority of the Pope, the Bishop of Rome.

**219.** The Infant King of Kings enthroned on the knees of his Virgin Mother receives from the Emperor Constantine (r. 334–337) the city of Constantinople (right) and from the Emperor Justinian (r. 527–565) the gift of the city's cathedral, Hagia Sophia. Mosaic from Hagia Sophia, south vestibule, A.D. ninth century.

Thus here, at the Western end of the ancient trans-Asian Silk Road, we see again the halo framing the head of a World Teacher and Savior. The enigma of the nature of this infant born in Bethlehem in the reign of Herod I the Great (r. 37–4 B.C.)—whether he had been human or divine, or both, or neither, an apparition, or a fact—had by the year A.D. 500 split the Christian world apart. For in the Near East there was at that time (as there is, in fact, to this day) no separation of Church and State. For example, the Emperor Theodosius II (r. 408–450) was addressed by St. Cyril of Alexandria as the "image of God on earth," and reciprocally, the idea of God in that part of the world was a Universal King, *Pantokrator*, seated either on a throne in heaven or, as here, on his Virgin Mother's knee. (Compare Darius I, above, **186.**) Unity of the Empire required unity in religious belief, and the votes of bishops in council determined what the belief was to be. Heresy was a civil offense, and anything like a private opinion was heresy, not to be taught. (Consider the history of Nestorius, (see above: **212**) or centuries later, in Roman Catholic Europea, Galileo.)

**Map 14** The rapid spread of Islam out of Arabia cannot be explained in terms simply of military violence and prowess. There must have been a readiness throughout the neighboring Near East to bear and to live by the relatively simply message of the Prophet who in his fortieth year, while meditating (as was his custom at that time) in a cave in the side of Mount Hira (three miles north of Mecca, his city), had heard a voice. "Proclaim! In the name of the Lord and Cherisher, who created man from a clot of blood: Proclaim!" the compelling voice had said. "For thy Lord is most bountiful who has taught man the use of the pen—taught man what he had not known before!" (Koran, Sura 96).[59]

The received message was again essentially that of the original monotheist Abraham, whose elder son, Ishmael, the legendary ancestor of the Arabs, had been dismissed as a child into the desert, along with Hagar, his Egyptian mother, after Abraham's second

son, Isaac, had been born to his aged wife Sarah (Genesis 21:8–14). The delivered message, that is to say, was again of the one and only God and his laws—*lā ilahā illa-liāhu:* "There is no God but God!"—now to be addressed, however, not alone to the children of Isaac, but to all those in the world who in their hearts submit (*islām*, "I submit") to the will and laws of the one God as here proclaimed.

Mohammed died in 632, and immediately, inspired armies went out to instruct the world. By 634 all of Arabia had been conquered; Palestine and Syria, by the year 636; 637, Mesopotamia; Egypt by 642. Eastward, Persia was overrun, 642 to 643; western Turkestan and the Punjab by the year 664. Through Egypt, westward, a thrust along the North African shore brought the message to the Berbers, who in the year 711 entered Spain and by 732 were

approaching Paris when confronted and turned back by Charles Martel at Poitiers. So that the history of the Occident for the next 700 years was of the wars on every front, from the Pyrenees to the Jordan, of the champions of the Crescent and the Cross.

The conquest of India began in 1001, and continued through six and a half centuries of merciless slaughter, plunder, vandalism, and religious satisfaction in the execution of God's will, until in 1565 the last remaining Hindu capital, Vijayanagar, in the south, was taken and destroyed. Muslim merchants, meanwhile, had colonized Indonesia, so that when the sixteenth century Spaniards arrived in the Philippines with their own edition of the necessary message, once again the familiar confrontation of the banner of the Crescent and the Cross was put on stage.

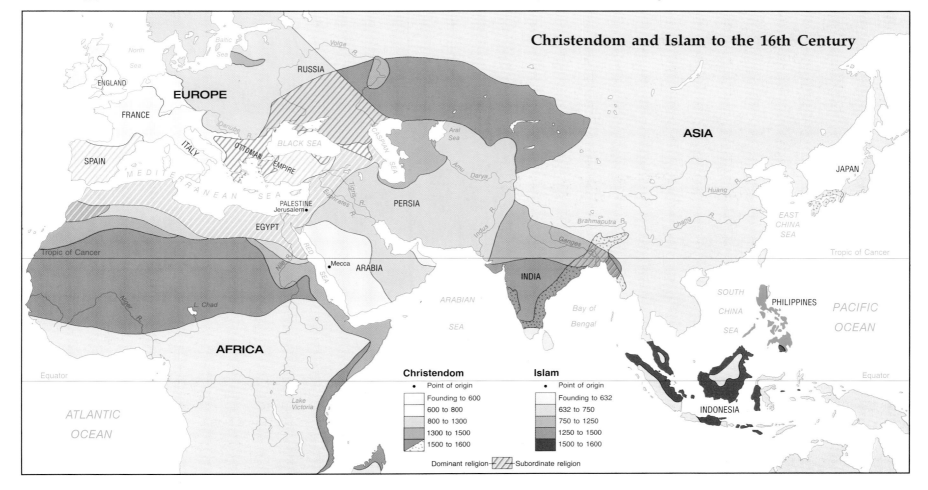

### Christendom and Islam to the 16th Century

| Christendom | Islam |
|---|---|
| • Point of origin | • Point of origin |
| Founding to 600 | Founding to 632 |
| 600 to 800 | 632 to 750 |
| 800 to 1300 | 750 to 1250 |
| 1300 to 1500 | 1250 to 1500 |
| 1500 to 1600 | 1500 to 1600 |

Dominant religion —— //// —— Subordinate religion

the mind is the healing "Diagram of the Supreme Moving Power" (*T'ai-chi T'u*), wherein, according to the Way of Nature (*Tao*), contending opposites are shown to be historically, as well as organically and metaphysically, at one. To identify one's own way, therefore, with what is thought to be that alone of heaven is to be off center, according to this symbol, out of accord no less with heaven's way (*T'ien Tao*) than with the good of man. For as the philospher Tzŭ Chi of Nan-kuo once told his philosophical crony Tzŭ Yu: to insist with inflexibility upon *any* of one's mentally held beliefs or purposes against the sense of the world outside one's head is *Three in the Morning*.

"And so what then," Tzŭ Yu inquired, "might *Three in the Morning* be?"

"A keeper of monkeys," Tzŭ Chi replied, "once said with regard to their ration of chestnuts that each monkey was to have three in the morning and four at night. But at this the monkeys were very angry, so the keeper said they might have four in the morning and three at night, with which arrangement they were all well pleased. The actual number of chestnuts remained the same, but there was an adaptation to the likes and dislikes of those concerned. Such is the principle of putting oneself into subjective relation with externals."

"Wherefore," wrote the philosopher Ch'uang Tzŭ in comment on this conversation, "the true sage, regarding contraries as identical, adapts himself to the laws of Heaven. This is called following two courses at once.

"The knowledge of the men of old had a limit," Ch'uang Tzŭ continues. "It extended back to a period when matter did not exist. That was the extreme point to which their knowledge reached. The second period was that of matter, but of matter unconditioned. The third saw matter conditioned, but contraries were still

unknown. Where these appeared, Tao began to decline. And with the decline of Tao, individual bias arose."[98]

Likewise in contemporary India; with the mellowing of the understanding of those who in the footsteps of the Buddha had donned the yellow robe as the one way of release from delusion, there finally dawned the realization that to separate the idea of release from that of participation (*nirvāṇa* from *samsāra*) was to practice world splitting and therewith to confirm oneself in delusion.

Thus the Buddha had taught "(1) all life is sorrowful, (2) there is release from sorrow, (3) release from sorrow is *nirvāṇa*, and (4) the way to *nirvāṇa* is the Middle Way, the Eightfold Path of Right Views, Right Aspirations, Right Speech, Right Conduct, Right Livelihood, Right Effort, Right Mindfulness, and Right Rapture.

The response of those first interested had been to retreat from the world, either alone into the forest or together into monasteries, there to engage with effort in the cultivation of Right Views, Right Aspirations, and so forth, living on alms collected from those still attached to delusion. This is the way now known as the *Theravāda*, the "Doctrine (*vāda*) of the Elders (*thera*)," and as *Hīnayāna*, the "Little (*hīna*) Vehicle" or "Ferry" (*yāna*) to the Yonder Shore," in which only those prepared to quit the world are eligible to embark.

**220.** Scholars and their children contemplating the mystery of the complementarity of opposites. Painting on silk, seventeenth century. British Museum.

**221.** The beheading of 2700 Muslim inhabitants of the city of Acre (Palestine), men, women, and children, by Richard I the Lion-Heart of England, at the opening of the Third Crusade, A.D. 1191. Illustrations from a fourteenth century manuscript in the Bibliotheque Nationale, Archives Photographiques, Paris.

Any comparison of this Medieval orgy with a successful New Guinea head-hunt would be improper: firstly because, although justified as a religious exercise, the heads taken were not named and cherished in and for themselves. (A head without a name, as we have learned, is worthless. See above: 67.) And secondly, because the aim of the enterprise had not been the gathering of required heads, but the conquest of a city. Moreover, the occasion was marked by a breach of faith. The city had been for three years under siege, 1189–91. Saladin, the Muslim Conqueror in 1187 of the Christian-held city of Jerusalem, on learning of the surrender of Acre, arranged for an exchange of prisoners, together with his restoration of the relic, captured in Jerusalem, of the True Cross. But he then made the mistake of fulfilling his part of the bargain first.

With the realization during the period of the Kushana kings (first centuries A.D.), however, that since *nirvāṇa* and *saṃsāra* are equally void they are one and the same, a total transformation of the Buddhist attitude toward the universe occurred. Everything was now seen as radiant of its own buddha nature, so that a magnificent flowering of the arts transpired throughout Buddhist Asia. And in the ideal of the Buddhist saint there was also a transformation: no longer the *arhat*, the accomplished monk, but the *bodhisattva*—that one whose "being" (*sattva*) is "illumination" (*bodhi*)—became the model of the Way (*mārga*) known as the *Mahāyāna*, the big (*mahā*) vehicle or ferry (*yāna*), to the Yonder Shore, on which all are riding.

For the way here is not a retreat from the world (the sacrifice of all that is cherished) but a giving of oneself to the world in unqualified compassion (sacrifice of one's own release), the most widely venerated example of which supreme symbol of the Mahāyāna ideal is that mythic personification of inexhaustible compassion-without-attachment known in China as Kwan Yin, Japan as Kannon, Tibet as Chenrazi (there regarded as incarnate in the Dalai Lama), and in India (where the ideal originated) as Avalokitesvara—which is a name that has been interpreted both as "lord" (*īśvara*) "looking on (in mercy)" (*avalokita*) and as the "lord" (*īśvara*) "seen (within)" (*avalokita*). In the latter sense, as pointed out by W. Y. Evans-Wentz, he is "synonymous with *Christos* within."[99] And in the former sense, I would add, he corresponds to that one who, "though his state was divine. . . . emptied himself, to assume the condition of a slave" (Philippians 2:6–7).

For the legend associated with this figure is of his having arrived in meditation at the very point of attaining buddhahood and therewith release from *saṃsāra*, when he became aware of sounds all about him of grief. Whereupon, overcome with compassion for the countless myriads of suffering beings in this world, he renounced with a solemn vow his own attainment of extinction until, through the influence of his teaching, all beings should be brought to illumination. Within and through us all he is now operative inasmuch as we illuminate each other in

**222.** The Bodhisattva Avalokiteśvara-Padmapāni, "Bearing in hand (*pāni*) the Lotus (*padma*) of the World." Fresco detail. Ajanta, Cave I. c. A.D. 600–642. Photograph by Eliot Elisofon.

our social intercourse, appearing as a merchant to merchants, a warrior to warriors, to kings as a king, to beasts as a beast, a demon to demons, and to gods as a god.

To me it seems unquestionably evident, not only that Christ Jesus and the Bodhisattva ideal are of the same archetype, but also — given the simultaneity in development of the two legends at the western and eastern terms of the same Late Hellenistic culture province—that they represent together a single, historically defined development in what has long been recognized as a very old and widespread oriental tradition. The lines already quoted from the *Tao Te Ching:*

> *He who knows the white, yet*
> *cleaves to the black*
> *Becomes the standard by which all*
> *things are tested*

surely are of the same Gnosis.

Among the numerous transformations of the figure of the Bodhisattva, there is one in which he has a thousand arms with an open eye in the palm of each hand that looks very much like the open wound in each hand of the risen Christ—into which "doubting Thomas" (the same who was later to be martyred in Madras) was asked to put his finger (John 20:24–28). St. Paul's epistle to the Philippians, in which the Christological passage appears of the One who let go of equality with God, dates from c. A.D. 50–60 and is earlier, thus, by about a century, than the appearance of the *Mahāyāna.* Influences evidently were traveling both ways on that 2,500-mile military highway.

In the Hellenistic and then the Roman Near East the archetype or "elementary idea" of the one that is two (True God and True Man) became engaged in a complex local web of Egyptian, Greek, and Syrian mystery-cult mythologies, together with Jewish and Zoroastrian expectations of the end of the world (Mark 13; *The Dead Sea Scrolls*), to all of which, then, the shocking execution by crucifixion of a charismatic young Nazarene who seems to have identified himself with the dead and resurrected mystery-cult Savior (Σωτήρ), torn to pieces and reborn (Mark 14:18–28), contributed a memorable syncretizing emblem.

Volume IV of this atlas, *The Way of Man*, will be dedicated to a systematic survey of the separate and then variously conjoined mythologies, gnostic insights, and theologies of this whole magnificent symbolic unfolding of the human genius, from the period of young Svetaketu's illuminating division of the fig to the crisis of the Renaissance, when a fifth *Paideumatic* influence took charge of the European imagi-

nation, which has, within five centuries, not only transformed the planet, but also eliminated every ground for accepting the usual, orthodox, *historical* interpretations of a tendentious Levantine scripture that for some 2,000 years has passed in the Western world as the unassailable exposition of God's Truth; for there was no Garden of Eden antecedent to the Lower Paleolithic finds of c. 3 to 4 million years ago, no time when the Serpent could talk, no Fall, no Exile from such a Paradise with sword-bearing cherubim at its gate: the unequivocally documented history of the evolution of life and mankind on this planet has wiped that fairytale off the map. And if there was no Fall, what then of the need for Redemption? What god was offended and by whom? (Some especially touchy cave bear whose skull had been improperly enshrined?) What devil then took mankind in pawn, so that we all had to be redeemed? And there was no Universal Flood, no Noah's Ark, no Tower of Babel, no scattering of the peoples, after Babel, over the planet, no Seven Plagues of Egypt, no drowning of any pharaoh and his army in the Red Sea, and no stopping of the sun and moon so that Joshua, God's special friend, might finish off in a battle the residents of a neighborhood he was invading. It is not the sun that moves in the sky, but the earth that revolves on its axis, and if this spinning had been suddenly stopped, every man, woman, and child, and every dog, elephant, and giraffe, would have been sent flying in trajectories east at a speed of some 1,500 feet a second, like Aunt Sarah through the windshield when her Cadillac hit the tree.

So let's be serious!

Mythology is not history, and history is not myth. Mythologies are products of the human imagination, which in turn is grounded in the energies that animate the organs of the human body, and since these have not significantly changed since the appearance of Cro-Magnon Man, c. 40,000 B.C., there can be recognized in the mythologies and associated ceremonials of all mankind certain themes and images that are constant. These are the "archetypes" of Jung, the "elementary ideas" of Bastian. They are not denotative of historical events, but symbolic of powers, potentials, and requirements of the psyche, or to use an earlier term, the soul.

Histories, on the contrary, are chronicles of social events in the field of space and time, which, according to place and time, greatly differ. The mythological images by way of which the universal archetypes or elementary ideas are given local form necessarily derive from the separate social histories and natural environments of the greatly various peoples served by these myths, and these, therefore, vary greatly differ. They are the local "masks"

(*personae*) of Jung and the "ethnic, or folk ideas" (*Völkergedanken*) of Bastian.

In traditions like those of the Greeks, the Romans, the Hindus, and the Buddhists, where the masking of "folk ideas," or "personae," have been generally recognized for what they are ("He whom you call Indra, we call Zeus!"), the universal inward, psychological, or spiritual guidance of the imagery is readily realized, whereas when an unremitting emphasis on the local form or forms, over and against and above all others, becomes the cardinal dogma (as in Judaism, Christianity, and Islam), such a calcification of the local masking follows that archetypes become locked to personae, elementary ideas become ethnic, and all the passion that might have been turned to illumination is short-circuited into inflating programs for the world. There is no sense of humor, furthermore, with regard to one's own mythic forms. Mistaken for natural and historic facts, they are especially vulnerable to science. And where the light of day has dissolved them like dream, there is no supporting ground to one's life.

Which is a pity! Because the time has come when every one of the world's ethnic systems is dissolving, since there are no more locally fixed horizons within the bounds of which an ethnocentric bigotry can be honestly maintained. Dissolving, the ethnic ideas become transparent to the archetypes, those elementary ideas of which they are no more than the local masks. And the moment such an epiphany is recognized, the omnipresence of the god behind the masks of other masquerades than one's own can be readily recognized, and a carnival of mutual instruction and admiration celebrated.

In 1945 there was recovered from a cemetery near the Egyptian town of Nag Hammadi (not far from Luxor) a jar containing the texts of some fifty-odd religious discourses from the first four Christian centuries, among which there was a gospel attributed to St. Thomas; the same who had placed his finger in the mark of the nails in the hands of the risen Christ, had carried his words to Kanishka's India, and is buried beneath the cathedral in Madras. And here, he tells that when, one day, the disciples asked the Savior, "When will the Kingdom come?" Jesus answered: "It will not come by expectation; they will not say: 'See here,' or 'See there.' But the Kingdom of the Father is spread upon the earth and men do not see it" (Logion 113). "Whoever drinks from my mouth," he is also reported to have said, "shall become as I am and I myself will become he, and the hidden things shall be revealed to him" (Logion 108). And again: "When you make

**223.** Bartel Bruyn, The Annunciation. Oil on canvas. Cologne, sixteenth century. Rheinisches Landesmuseum, Bonn, West Germany.

Led by the Holy Spirit in the shape of a radiant white dove, the little Savior, already bearing his cross, comes flying to his intended mother on a beam of light that illuminates her face, while the angel, equipped with birdlike wings, utters the words of her realization: *Ave, gratia plena, Dominus tecum!* "Hail, full of grace, the Lord is with thee!" The cross will now be hers to bear, as well.

The angel Gabriel's wand, held in such a way that its relevance to the dove is obvious, carries on its tip the emblem of the Greek mystery-god Hermes, conductor of souls to the knowledge of immortal life: his winged wand of interlaced serpents, the caduceus. This artist, that is to say, is recognizing in the symbolic forms of the Classical and Christian traditions equivalent metaphors of a specific realization, of which as a Rhineland artist he will surely have learned (and perhaps gone on to experience) through the

writings of the great Rhineland mystics of two centuries earlier: Meister Eckhart (1260-1329), Jan van Ruysbroeck (1293-1381), Heinrich Suso (1296-1366), Johann Tauler (1300-1361), and the anonymous author of the *Theologia Germanica* (fourteenth century).

At the Virgin's knees, in the lower right of the painting, is a vase initialled IHS, which is the monogram generally taken to signify, *In Hoc Signo (vinces),* "In This Sign (thou shalt conquer)," words supposed to have been seen by Constantine written in the sky along with a cross on the eve of his epochal victory at Saya Rubra, October 28, 312, which marked the triumph in the Roman Empire of the Church over paganism. The initialled vase with its three sprays of flowers must, therefore, have been meant to represent the Roman Church, which through the miracle of the Virgin Motherhood of Mary is the earthly vessel of, 1) the red flower of the Incarnation, 2) the white of the Father Eternal, and 3) the lightly flowered spray of the Holy Spirit—matching thus the triad of Gabriel's wand.

**224.** Rembrandt van Rijn. Dr. Faustus in his Study Beholds in the Magic Mirror the Sign of the Macrocosm. Etching on oatmeal paper, first state, A.D. 1652. Museum of Fine Arts, Boston.

The sense of the mirrored reflection is, apparently, of Christ Crucified as the archetype of Life in Being. The initials INRI (reading from the bottom clockwise) refer to the inscription hung by Pilate to the Cross: *Jesus Nazarenus, Rex Judaecorum,* "Jesus the Nazaren, King of the Jews" (John 19:19). Arranged around the center of a radiant disk quartered by a symmetrical cross, they correspond exactly to the figure in Bruyn's "Annunciation" (opp., **223**), of Christ descending with his cross, led by the Holy Spirit in the likeness of a dove in a radiant disk. Moreover, on the occasion reported in the gospels of the Holy Spirit in the shape of a dove descending upon Jesus when he emerged, baptized, from the Jordan (Matt. 3:16; Mark 1:10; Luke 3:21-22; John 1:32), the same symbolic figure appears, which in that case must be read as a pictorial metaphor connoting the exaltation of the historical Nazaren, who, being empty of ego (the full sacrifice), was open to an experience from within, as well as from without, of himself and the world (microcosm and macrocosm) as of one substance with *the Will that is not of any "I" or "Thou," but of the Life that is all that lives,"* putting on bodies and putting them off, as a man casts off worn out clothes and puts on others that are new" (*Bhagavad Gita* 2:20).

The Virgin was also of this egoless disposition, as shown by her response to the angel, "Be it done unto me according to thy word" (Luke 1:28): hardly, however, Dr. Faustus, who was an actual necromancer of Martin Luther's times, a certain Magister Georgious Sabellius Faustus Junior (1480?-1540?), as he is said to have called himself, who was described by some of his contemporaries as an outrageous mountebank, but by others as an accomplished master renowned for his skill, not only in chiromancy, necromancy, physiognomy, visions in crystal, and other such arcane arts, but also in medicine. It was a Protestant pastor in Basel, Johann Gast (d. 1572), who invented the cock-and-bull story of his pact with the Devil who carried him off, which then became throughout Protestant Europe enormously popular as an argument against both medieval Catholicism and the novel sciences of the Renaissance.

As here represented by the Lutheran Rembrandt, the colorful master has by magic brought about what appears to him to be a revelation. However, like the young American Indian of the Winnebago tale recounted in Volume I.2: 304–305, who in his vision-quest would be satisfied with nothing short of a direct view of the Great Spirit and, when finally (as he thought) successful, had actually been (as he found to his shame) deceived by an inferior spirit, so also here: the master is represented with his ego still intact, gazing at a figure that is not a reflex of his own innermost being, but an external spirit reflected in a mirror held to him by a deceiving hand. The question is a crucial one, familiar to all dream intepreters and visionaries, of distinguishing authentic from deceptive revelations.

Christopher Marlow in his play *The Tragicall History of Dr. Faustus* (published 1604), followed to the end the Protestant pastor's plot, consigning Faust's soul to the Devil. But he turned the moral tale into a tragedy by representing his hero as a daring Renaissance experimenter, insatiable in his striving and thirst for knowledge, and Goethe, two centuries later, thinking that the end of such a career should not be damnation but salvation, represented the same hero in his own great drama, *Faust* (Part I, 1808; Part II, 1832), as the prototype of the ever-striving, outward-yearning, creative spirit of specifically European man;

the two one, you shall become sons of Man, and when you say: 'Mountain, be moved,' it will be moved'' (Logion 106).[100]

These are themes in accord with the Bodhisattva Way and do not require the biblical legend of Fall and Redemption to give them point. Indeed, on the contrary, once the meaning of the Kingdom as here given has been grasped, the historically impossible tale of the Garden, the Fall, and the Exile at the beginning of Time can be recognized as poetically metaphorical of the condition of the unilluminated mind, so engaged by the senses in the experiences here, in the field of space and time (the philosopher's *Principium individuationis*), good and evil, I and thou, male and female, man and god, that the radiance over all the earth of the paradise that is of the metaphysical unity of all things remains unseen.

And herein resides the irony of mythology—namely, that its poetic metaphors, through which transcendent revelations are delivered, become translated by what Nietzsche called the ''Socratic'' mind into prose, so that not only is the revelation lost, but an additional leaden weight of delusion is laid upon the mind.

The day that is now upon us out of the revelations of science, however, of this one planet with its one humanity of many folkways intermeshed, requires that the dominating prosaic idea of one god and/ or one society to be imposed over all the rest, be as soon as possible dissolved, chiefly by opening this piece of prose to the light of poetic insight. ''Man's last and highest leave taking,'' Meister Eckhart has said, ''is leaving God for G O D''[101]: leaving, that is to say, one's ethnic idea of the divinity for a breakthrough to transcendence—beyond names and forms, right and wrong, heaven and earth, and so on. *Alles Vergängliche ist nur ein Gleichnis.* ''Everything temporal,'' wrote Goethe, ''is but a metaphor.'' To which Nietzsche added, *Alles Unvergängliche is nur ein Gleichnis.* ''Everything eternal is but a metaphor''. Those, then, are the two sacrifices asked of each today; and with the voice of one's own god pianissimo for a change, one should be able to hear and respond to the choral symphony of the rest, in every part of the earth, celebrating that ''one'' that is (yet is not) two and the two that dwell, multiplied, within each of these ten thousand things.

representing Mephistopheles as a provider only of the implementation and information by which Faust's creative projects might be realized, a master merely of those means (the known laws of nature and the spirit) of which creative reason makes use in its passage through and beyond them. As set forth by Goethe in a notable statement:

''The Godhead is effective in the living and not in the dead, in the becoming and the changing, not in the become and the set fast; and therefore, accordingly, reason (*Vernunft*) is concerned only to strive toward the divine through the becoming and the living, and understanding (*Verstand*) only to make use of the become and set fast.''[60]

Rembrandt's etching provides an eloquent illustration to this matter, as well as an appropriate symbolic figure with which to conclude this Introduction; for it represents in a memorable way both the negative and the positive conditions of the Faustian heritage. Indeed, the disclosure of something very like Rembrandt's Sign of the Macrocosm through all the images of Man that have been mirrored in the mythologies of the world might be said to be the first aim of

the present work. As in Rembrandt's etching, however, the sign will appear as the product of a scholar's study, reflected *out there*, as in a magic mirror. For objectivity is the fixed rule of this school of the mind.

And yet, there flash throughout these chapters the irrepressible flames of a sense of outrage at the vast calamity that the becoming, changing, and striving of Faustian man toward what he has conceived to be the Divine has wrought upon what Jamake Highwater has termed the ''primal'' cultures of this planet. For again as in Rembrandt's etching, the sign of the presence of Godhood has been recognized only *out there*, in the fixed field of a Levantine theology (a mere *Völkergedanke*, ''Ethnic Idea,'' see above: 28, 111), and as a consequence, there has always followed right behind this ever-striving and daring benefactor of the world the visage (again as in Rembrandt's etching) of empty-eyed Death. The second aim, therefore, of this writing, beyond the first, or presentational, of the objective mythological mirror, is to break somehow the Mephistophelean spell that for the Western mind has held the radiant disk of the Holy Spirit ''out there,'' and release its homing Dove to her proper dwelling.

APPENDIX

# ENDNOTES

## TEXT

[1]Oswald Spengler, *Der Untergang des Abendlandes* (Munich: C.H. Beck'sche Verlagsbuchlandlung, 1930), vol. 2, pp. 3–4.

[2]Ibid., pp. 3–4.

[3]Jamake Highwater, *The Primal Mind* (New York: Harper & Row, 1981).

[4]Leo Frobenius, *Paideuma, Umrisse einer Kultur-und-Seelenlehre,* (Munich: C.H. Beck'sche Verlagbuchhandlung, 1921); second enlarged ed., published as vol. 4 of *Erlebte Erdteile*, 7 vols. (Frankfurt am Main: Frankfurter Societäts-Druckerei, 1925–1930).

[5]Natalie Curtis, *The Indians' Book: An Offering by the American Indians of Indian Lore, Musical and Narrative, to Form a Record of the Songs and Legends of Their Race* (New York: Harper and Brothers, 1907), p. 96.

[6]Cited by W.F. Otto, *Gesetz Urbild und Mythos* (Stuttgart: J.B. Metzler, 1951; reprinted, New York: Arno Press, 1978). p. 14.

[7]Loc. cit.

[8]Leo Frobenius, *Erlebte Erdteile*, op. cit., vol. 7, *Monumenta Terrarum*, pp. 213–226.

[9]Carl O. Sauer, *Agricultural Origins and Dispersals* (New York: American Geographical Society, 1952), reedited and published with additional chapters as, *Seeds, Spades, Hearths, and Herds* (Cambridge, Mass.: Massachusetts Institute of Technology Press, 1969), see especially pp. 12–25, and 40–42; also pp. 54–61.

[10]Ibid., pp. 24–25.

[11]Ibid., pp. 28–29.

[12]Ibid., p. 28.

[13]James Mellaart, *Earliest Civilizations of the Near East* (London: Thames and Hudson, 1965), p. 15, pp. 18–38.

[14]Sauer, op. cit., p. 19.

[15]Paul C. Mangelsdorf, Richard S. MacNeish, and Gordon R. Willey, "Origins of Agriculture in Middle America," in Robert Wauchope (ed.), *Handbook of Middle American Indians*, 13 vols. (Austin: University of Texas Press, 1964–1973), vol. 1, pp. 427–428, and 444.

[16]Sauer, op. cit., p. 40.

[17]Mangelsdorf, MacNeish, and Willey, op, cit., pp. 428–429.

[18]Sauer, op. cit., pp. 57–60.

[19]Carl O. Sauer, "Cultivated Plants of South and Central America," in Julian H. Steward (ed.), *Handbook of South American Indians*, 7 vols., Smithsonian Institution, Bureau of American Ethnology, Bulletin 143 (Washington, D.C.: United States Printing Office, 1944–1957), vol. 6, pp. 536–538.

[20]George Peter Murdock, *Africa: Its Peoples and their Culture History* (New York: McGraw-Hill Book Company, 1959), pp. 223–224.

[21]Frobenius, op. cit., pp. 208–209.

[22]Sauer, *Seeds, Spades, Hearths, and Herds*, op. cit., pp. 55–56.

[23]Plato, *Phaedo* 66E, translation by H.N. Fowler in *Plato*, 12 vols., Loeb 36, (Harvard University Press, 1914) pp. 402–403.

[24]Sauer, *Agricultural Origins and Dispersals* (New York: The American Geographical Society, 1952), p. 32.

[25]George F. Carter, "Pre-Columbian Chickens in America," in Carroll L. Riley, J. Charles Kelley, Campbell W. Pennington, Robert L. Rands (eds.), *Man Across the Sea* (Austin/London: University of Texas Press, 1971), citing Erland Nordanskiöld, "Deductions suggested by the geographical distribution of some post-Columbian words used by the Indians of South America," in *Comparative Ethnographic Studies*, (Göteburg, 1922), vol. 5, pp. 1–46.

[26]Carter, loc. cit.

[27]Frobenius, *Paideuma*, in *Erlebte Erdteile*, op. cit., vol. 4, pp. 241–242.

[28]Ibid., p. 252.

[29]Ananda K. Coomaraswamy, "A Figure of Speech or a Figure of Thought?" in Roger Lipsey (ed.), *Coomaraswamy, Bollingen 89, 2 vols. (Princeton, N.J.: Princeton University Press, 1977), vol. 1, p. 40.*

[30]James George Frazer, *The Golden Bough*, 1-vol. ed. (New York: The Macmillan Company, 1922) p. 386.

[31]Frobenius, op. cit., p. 255.

[32]Natalie Curtis, op, cit., p. 255.

[33]Colin Turnbull, *The Forest People, A Study of the Pygmies of the Congo* (New York: Simon & Schuster, Touchstone, 1962).

[34]Spengler, op. cit., vol. 2, pp. 4–5.

[35]*Chândogya Upanishad* 6.8.7. Translations of all Sanskrit texts by Joseph Campbell.

[36]*Mahā-parinibbāna* Sutta 61.

[37]E. de Jonghe, "Histoyre du Méchique" (History of Mexico), Manuscrit français inedit du XVI siècle, *Journal de la Société des Américanistes de Paris*, Nouvelle Serie, tome 2, no. 1 (1905), pp. 28–29.

[38]For the reading "clung to," see *The Jerusalem Bible* (Garden City, New York: Doubleday and Company, 1966), p. 339, note 2f.

[39]Selected and edited by Edna Kenton, *The Jesuit Relations and Allied Documents: Travels and Explorations of the Jesuit Missionaries in North America (1610–1791)*, with an introduction by Reuben Gold Thwaites (New York: Albert and Charles Boni, 1925), pp. 126–129. This valuable book of 497 pages, plus index, is a one-volume selection from the 73 volumes of *The Jesuit Relations and Allied Documents* that were published, 1896 to 1901, by the Burrows Brothers Company of Cleveland, Ohio, along with a page-for-page English translation of the original French, Latin, Italian texts.

[40]Friedrich Nietzsche, *Die Geburt der Tragödie; oder Griechenthum und Pessimusmus* (Leipzig: E.W. Fritzch, 1886), passages from the ends of Sections 1 and 16, translation by the author.

[41]Swami Chidatmananda (publisher), *Life of Sri Ramakrishna* (Calcutta: Advaita Ashrama, 8th impression, 1964), p. 144.

[42]Melanie Klein, *The Psycho-Analysis of Children*, translation by A. Strachey (London: The Hogarth Press, 3rd ed., 1949), chap. 3, pp. 187–188.

[43]*Webster's Third New International Dictionary* (Springfield, Mass.: G. & C. Merriam Co., 1981), p. 327, entry "cannibal."

[44]Frederick J. Dockstader, *Indian Art in America* (Greenwich, Conn.: New York Graphics Society, 1961), comment to fig. 47.

[45]Eduard Seler, *Codex Vaticanus No. 3773*, First Half (English Edition: Berlin/London, 1902–1903), p. 181.

[46]Frazer, op. cit., p. 494.

[47]*Bhagavad Gītā* 4:23–24.

[48]*Acts of John* 94–97, abridged. Translation (slightly modified) from Montague Rhodes James, *The Apocryphal New Testament* (Oxford: The Clarendon Press, 1955), pp. 253–254.

[49]See, for example, R.B. Smith and W. Watson (eds.), *Early South East Asia* (New York/Kuala Lumpur: Oxford University Press, 1979), pp. 16–17.

[50]Chester F. Gorman, "Hoabinhian: A pebble-tool complex with early plant associations in Southeast Asia," *Science*, no. 163 (1969), pp. 671–673.

[51]Gorman, loc. cit., and "The Hoabinhian and After: subsistence patterns in Southeast Asia during the late Pleistocene and early Recent periods," *World Archaeology*, 2 (1971), pp. 300–320.

[52]Wilhelm G. Solheim II, "A Look at 'L'Art Prébouddhique de la Chine et de l'Asie du Sud-Est et son Influence en Océanie' Forty Years After," *Asian Perspectives*, vol. 22, no. 2 (1982), p. 196.

[53]Loc. cit.

[54]Donn T. Bayard, "Excavations at Non Nok Tha, Northeastern Thailand, 1968: An Interim Report," *Asian Perspectives*, vol. 13 (1972).

[55]Bayard, *Studies in Prehistoric Anthropology*, no. 4, *Non Nok Tha: The 1968 excavation. Procedure, stratigraphy and a summary of the evidence* (Dunedin, New Zealand: University of Otago, 1971); also, C.F.W. Higham and B.F. Leach, "An Early Center of Bovine Husbandry in Southeast Asia," *Science*, no. 172 (1971), pp. 54–56.

[56]B. Bronson and M.C. Han, "A Thermoluminescence Series from Thailand," *Antiquity*, no. 46, pp. 322–326.

[57]Solheim, op. cit., p. 194.

[58]Ibid., p. 196.

[59]Leo Frobenius, *Das Unbekannte Afrika* (Munich: Oskar Beck, 1923), pp. 100–101.

[60]Herodotus, *The Persian Wars*, book 4, paragraph 103, translation by George Rawlinson, *The Greek Historians* (New York: Random House, 1942), vol. 2, pp. 262–263.

[61]Paul Wirz, *Die Marind-Amin von Holländisch-Süd-New-Guinea*, 2 vols. (Hamburg: L. Friedrichsen & Co., 1922, 1925), vol. 1, part 1, pp. 37–38.

[62]Ibid., vol. 1, part 1, pp. 37–62.

[63]Ibid., vol 1, part 2, pp. 10–11.

[64]Robinson Jeffers, "The Roan Stallion" (1924), in *The Selected Poetry of Robinson Jeffers* (New York: Random House, 1951), pp. 153–154.

[65]Nietzche, op. cit., Section 3.

[66]Ibid., Section 9.

[67]Wirz, op. cit., vol. 2, part 3, p. 1.

[68]Ibid., vol. 2, part 3, pp. 44.

[69]See Frazer, op. cit., pp. 48–60.

[70]Uno Holmberg, "Siberian Mythology," in *The Mythology of All Races*, vol. 4 (Boston: Marshall Jones and Company, 1927), part 2, p. 287.

[71]"The Epitome of the Great Symbol" (*Phyag-chen gyi zin-bris bzhug-so*), 108–118, as translated by W.Y. Evans-Wentz, *Tibetan Yoga and Secret Doctrines* (London: Humphrey Milford, Oxford University Press, 1935), pp. 145–148, with Evans-Wentz's commentary in his notes, 1, 2, 3, pp. 146–147.

[72]Quoted by Ananda K. Coomaraswamy from J. Evola, *Rivolta contra ilmondo moderno* (Milan, 1934), p. 374, n. 12.

[73]Ananda K. Coomaraswamy in Roger Lipsey (ed.), *Coomaraswamy*, 2 vols., op. cit. vol. 1, pp. 286–287.

[74]Vaman Shivram Apte, *Sanskrit-English Dictionary* (Poona: Shiralcar and Co., 1890), p. 801, col. 1.

[75]Walter F. Otto, *Die Götter Griechenlands* (Frankfurt am Main: Verlag G. Schulte-Bulmke, 1947), p. 17.

[76]This doctrine of the "Real Presence" was confirmed as dogma at the Fourth Lateran Council, 1215.

[77]James G. Frazer, *The Golden Bough*, 12-vol. ed. (London: St. Martin's Press,1911–1915).

[78]Brihadāranyaka Upanishad 1.4.6 and 7 (abridged).

[79]Chādogya Upanishad 6.1.1.–6.12.3 (greatly abridged).

[80]*Tao Te Ching* 28, translation by Arthur Waley, *The Way and Its Power* (London: George Allen and Unwin, Ltd., 1934), p. 178.

[81]These are quoted from F.M. Cornford, *Greek Religious Thought from Homer to the Age of Alexander* (London/Toronto: J.M. Dent and Sons, Ltd., 1934), pp. 78–84.

[82]Eduard Meyer, *Geschichte des Alterums*, (Stuttgart/Berlin: J.G. Cotta, 1925–1939) vol. 3, p. 97, n. 2.

[83]*Yasna* 30:2; translation by L.H. Mills *The Zend-Avesta*, pt. 3, *Sacred Books of the East*, vol. 31 (Oxford: The Clarendon Press, 1887), p. 29.

[84]*Vendidad* 4.47–49; translation by James Darmstetter, *The Zend-Avesta*, pt. 1, *Sacred Books of the East*, vol. 4. (Oxford: The Clarendon Press, 1880), pp. 46–47.

[85]*Yasna* 30:9, op. cit.

[86]Sigmund Freud, *Moses and Monotheism* (New York: Alfred A. Knopf, 1939).

[87]Rock Edict XII, in Vincent A. Smith, *The Edicts of Asoka* (Broad Campden: Essex House Press, 1909) p. 20.

[88]*The Periplus of the Erythraen Sea*, translation from the Greek by Wilfred H. Schoff (New York: Longmans, Green and Co., 1912).

[89]E.J. Rapson (ed.), *Ancient India*, vol. 1 of *The Cambridge History of India* (New York: The Macmillan Co., 1922), pp. 431–432.

[90]Plutarch, *Praecepta gerendae reipublicae* (Moralia, 821, D) cited by E.J. Rapson, "The Successors of Alexander the Great," in Rapson (ed), op. cit., p. 551.

[91]*The Questions of King Milinda:* translation by T.W. Rhys Davids, *Sacred Books of the East*, vols. 35 and 36 (Oxford: The Clarendon Press, 1890, 1894), vol. 35, pp. 6–7.

[92]D.C. Sircar, "Inscriptions in Sanskrit and Dravidian Languages," *Ancient India*, no. 9 (1953), p. 216.

[93]*Sutta-nipātā 5.7.8.*

[94]*Vajracchedika-sūtra* 32. Translation by F. Max Muller in *Sacred Books of the East*, vol. 49, *Buddist Mahāyāna Sūtras* (Oxford: The Clarendon Press, 1894), p. 144.

[95]Nietzsche, op. cit., end of Section 7.

[96]For a discussion of the importance of these two texts in Jewish thought, see Dr. J.H. Hertz, C.H., Late Chief Rabbi of the British Empire, *The Pentateuch and Haftorahs*, Hebrew text, English translation, and commentary (London: Soncino Press, 2nd ed., 1961), p. 922.

[97]Th. W. Juynboll, "Law (Muhammadan), " in James Hastings (ed.), *Encyclopedia of Religion and Ethics*, 13 vols. (New York: Charles Scribner's Sons,1928), vol. 7, p. 881.

[98]Ch'uang Tzŭ, Book 2, "Essay on the Uniformity of All Things," pt. 1, sec. 2, "The Adjustment of Controversies," translation by Lionel Giles, *Musings of a Chinese Mystic: Selections from the Philosophy of Ch'uan Tzŭ* (London: John Murray, 1906), pp. 46–47. The passage also appears in *Sacred Books of the East*, vol. 39, op. cit. (1891), "The Texts of Taoism," pt. 1, pp. 184–186, translation by James Legge.

[99]Evans-Wentz, op. cit., p. 233, n. 2.

[100]Guillaumont, H.-Ch Puech, G. Quispel. W. Till and Yassal 'abd al Masih, *The Gospel According to Thomas* (Leiden: E.J. Brill; New York: Harper and Brothers, 1959), pp. 52–57.

[101]Eckhart, "Sermons and Collations," no. 96, "Riddance,' in Franz Pfeiffer, translation by D. deB. Evans, *Meister Eckhart*, 2 vols. (London: John M. Watkins, 1947), vol. 1, p. 289.

## CAPTIONS

[1]Edgar Wind, *Pagan Mysteries in the Renaissance*, revised and enlarged edition (Harmondsworth, U.K.: Penguin in association with Faber, 1967), p. 125.

[2]Carter, loc. cit.

[3]Krohn, *In Borneo Jungles* (Indianapolis: Bobbs Merrill Co., 1977), p. 155.

[4]Julian H. Steward and Alfred Metraux, "Tribes of the Peruvian and Ecuadorian Montana," in Julian H. Steward (ed.), *Handbook of South American Indians*, 7 vols., Smithsonian Institution, Bureau of American Ethnology, Bulletin 143 (Washington, D.C.: Government Printing Office, 1948), vol. 3, p. 625.

[5]*A Voyage to the Pacific Ocean. Undertaken by the Command of His Majesty, for Making Discoveries in the Northern Hemisphere. To Determine the Position and Extent of the West Side of North America: its Distance from Asia: and the Practicability of a Northern Passage to Europe. Performed under the Direction of Captains Cook, Clerke, and Gore. In his Majesty's ships Resolution and Discovery. In the Years 1776, 1777, 1778, 1779 and 1780. In 3 vols. Vols. 1 and 2 written by Captain James Cook, F.R.S., vol. 3 by Captain James King LL.D. and F.R.S. Published by the Order of the Lords Commissioners of the Admiralty, London: 1784.* The episode of the plucked eye appears in vol. 2, p. 44.

[6]Samuel A.B. Mercer, *The Pyramid Texts in Translation and Commentary*, 4 vols. (New York, London, Toronto: Longmans, Green and Co., 1952), vol. 1 Utterances 39, 301, 451a, and 29; on pages 27, 100, 24–25, slightly abridged.

[7]Kathleen M. Kenyon, *Archaeology in the Holy Land* (New York: Praeger Paperbacks, 1960), pp. 190–191.

[8]Samuel K. Lothrop, "The Archaeology of Panama," in *Handbook of South American Indians*, op. cit., vol. 4, p. 147.

[9]Robert H. Lowie, "The Tropical Forest: An Introduction," in *Handbook of South American Indians*, op. cit., vol. 3, p. 24.

[10]Julian H. Steward, "The Witotoan Tribes," in *Handbook of South American Indians*, op. cit., vol. 3, p. 750, and Pl. 81.

[11]Carl O. Sauer, *Agricultural Origins and Dispersals* (New York: The American Geographical Society, 1952), p. 30, citing E. Dahr, "Stude in über Hunde aus primitiven Steinzeitkulturen in Nordeuropa," *Lunds University. Arsskrift*, N.S. sec. 2, vol. 32, no. 4, 1937; also Freda Kretschmar, *Hundstammsvater und Kerberos*, 2 vols. (Stuttgart, 1938).

[12]Jill Leslie Furst, *Codex Vinobonensis Mexicanus I: A Commentary* (Institute for Mesoamerican Studies, State University of New York at Albany, pub. no. 4, 1978), pp. 22, 165, and 190, Fig. 61.

[13]Ibid., p. 318.

[14]Michael D. Coe, *The Maya* (London/New York: Thames & Hudson, 1966, enlarged and revised edition, 1980), p. 130, citing Bishop Fray Diego de Landa in *Memoirs of the Peabody Museum of Archaeology and Ethnology* (Cambridge, Mass.: Harvard University Press, 1952).

[15]Sylvanus Griswald Morley, *The Ancient Maya* (Palo Alto, Cal.: Stanford University Press, 1946), pp. 236–237.

[16]Morley, loc. cit.

[17]J. Erik S. Thompson, *Maya History and Religion* (Norman: University of Oklahoma Press, 1970), p. 236.

[18]Karl Kerényi, *Dionysos*, translation by Ralph Manheim, Bollingen 65.2 (Princeton, N.J.: Princeton University Press, 1976) p. 21.

[19]Euripides, *The Bacchae* 12–20, translation by William Arrowsmith, in David Green and Richard Lattimore (eds.), *The Complete Greek Tragedy*, 4 vols. (The University of Chicago Press, 1958, 1959), pp. 543–544.

[20]Hesiod, *Theogeny* 22–34.

[21]Following Gafurius, *Practica Musica* (1496), in Edgar Wind, op. cit., p. 268.

[22]Euripides, loc. cit.

[23]Kerényi, op. cit., pp. 110–114, citing and quoting Athenagoras, *Libellus pro Christianis* 20; Orpheus, fr. 58 and 145, in O. Kern (ed.), *Orphicorum fragmenta;* Ovid, *Metamorphoses* VI. 117; the Homeric Hymn to Demeter 469; and Euripides, *Helen* 1307.

[24]Jill Leslie Furst, op. cit., p. 2.

[25]Eduard Seler, *Codex Borgia* (Berlin, 1904), vol. 2, p. 96, fig. 67. *Codex Borgia* now is in the Apostolic Vatican Library.

[26]Bernardino de Sahagún, *Historia de las cosas de la Nueva Espana*, 3 vols. (Mexico, 1829) book 7, chap. 2; as summarized by Eduard Seler, *Codex Vaticannus No. 3773* (Berlin/London: 1902, 1903), p. 183.

[27]Stith Thompson, *Motif Index of Folk Literature*, 6 vols. (Bloomington: Indiana University Studies, 1932–1936), item D671.

[28]*Florentine Codex: General History of the Things of New Spain*, translation by Arthur J.O. Anderson and Charles E. Dibble, monographs of The School of American Research, no. 14 (Santa Fe: The School of American Research and the University of Utah, 1951–1970), as quoted by Richard Fraser Townsend, *State and Cosmos in the Art of Tenochtitlan*, "Studies in Pre-Columbian Art and Archaeology," no. 20 (Washington, D.C.: Dumbarton Oaks, 1979), p. 47.

[29]See Rato Khyongla Nawang Losang (Joseph Campbell, ed.), *My Life and Lives* (New York, E.P. Dutton, 1977), chap. 8, pp. 75–87.

[30]Seler, op. cit., vol. 1, p. 132.

[31]Marija Gimbutas, *The Goddesses and Gods of Old Europe* (New York: Thames and Hudson, 1974; revised ed. Berkeley/Los Angeles: University of California Press, 1982), p. 211.

[32]Harrison, op. cit., pp. 120, 126.

[33]Frazer, *op. cit.*, pp. 469–471.

[34]Robert Gardner, *Gardens of War* (New York: Random House, 1968), p. 45.

[35]Wirz, op. cit., vol. 1, pt. 1, p. 46.

[36]Ibid., p. 60.

[37]Ibid., pp. 61–62.

[38]Ibid., vol. 1, pt. 3, p. 49.

[39]George Catlin, *The North American Indians, Being Letters and Notes on Their Manners, Customs, and Conditions, Written During Eight Years Travel Amongst the Wildest Tribes of Indians in North America, 1832–1839*, 2 vols. (Philadelphia: Leary, Stuart, 1913), vol. 1, p. 46.

[40]My description follows Sir Charles Leonard Wooley, *Ur of the Chaldees* (London: Ernest Benn, Ltd., 1929), pp. 44–56, and *Ur: The First Phases* (London/New York: Penguin, 1946), pp. 19–23. The primary source is Wooley, *Publications of the Joint Expedition of the British Museum and of the Museum of the University of Pennsylvania to Mesopotamia*, vol. 2, *Ur Excavations: The Royal Cemetery* (London: Oxford University Press, 1934).

[41]Wooley, *Ur: The First Phases*, op. cit., p. 20.

[42]Loc. cit.

[43]Frazer, *The Golden Bough*, 1-vol. ed., op. cit., pp. 279–280.

[44]Loc. cit.

[45]H. de Genouillac, *Textes religieux sumerians du Louvre* (Paris: Paul Geuther, 1930), text no. 5374, p. 191, as cited and translated by Stephen Herbert Langdon, *Semitic Mythology*, in John Arnott MacCulloch (ed.), *The Mythology of All Races*, 13 vols. (Boston: Marshall Jones Company, 1916–1932), vol. 5, p. 345.

[46]S.N. Kramer, *Sumerian Mythology* (Philadelphia: The American Philosopical Society, 1944), p. 88, abridged.

[47]Bernard Goldman, *The Sacred Portal: A Primary Symbol in Ancient Judaic Art* (Detroit: Wayne State University Press, 1966), p. 56.

[48]Aeschylus, *Prometheus Bound*, 11. 540–544. Translation by David Greene, in David Greene and Richard Lattimore (eds.), *The Complete Greek Tragedies*, 4 vols. (University of Chicago Press, 1959), vol. 1, p. 330.

[49]Ibid., 11. 937–939, vol. 1, p. 345.

[50]Anglicization of Chinese terms follows Herbert A. Giles, James Legge, etc., *Chinese/English Dictionary* (London: B. Quaritch; Shanghai [etc.]: Kelly and Walsh, 1892).

[51]Chung Yung 1. 1., translation by James Legge, in Legge (ed.), Ssu-Shū, *The Four Books* (Shanghai: The Chinese Book Co., 1933), p. 349.

[52]Ibid., 22., pp. 398–399.

[53]These captions follow The Cambridge History of India, vol. 1, E.J. Rapson (ed.), *Ancient India* (New York: The Macmillan Co., 1922), pp. 465–466, and 588.

[54]Theodore Gaster, *Dead Sea Scriptures* (New York: Anchor/Doubleday, 1976), pp. 386–387.

[55]M. Aurel Stein, *Ruins of Desert Cathay*, 2 vols. (London: Macmillan and Co., Ltd., 1912), vol. 1, pp. 452–477.

[56]Ibid., vol. 1, pp. 457, 469, and 476–477.

[57]*Jataka* 1.64. Translation from Henry Clarke Warren, *Buddhism in Translations* (Cambridge, Mass.: Harvard University Pres, 1922), p. 66.

[58]Loc. cit.

[59]Translation following Abdullah Yusuf Ali, *The Holy Qur-an: Text, Translation and Commentary*, 2 vols. (New York: Hafner Publishing Company, 1946), vol. 1, pp. 14–15.

[60]Johann Peter Eckermann, *Gesprache mit Goethe in den letzten Jahren seines Lebens, 1823–1832* (Berlin: Deutches Verlagshans Bong & Co., 1916), vol. 1, p. 251 (Feb. 13, 1829). Translation by Charles Francis Atkinson, in Oswald Spengler, *The Decline of the West*, 2 vols. (New York: Alfred A. Knopf, 1926), vol. 1, p. 49, note 1.

## A NOTE ON THE INDEXES

*References to pages, captions, maps, and map captions*

In the Place Name Index and the Subject Index, references to pages are page numbers, e.g.,

Kodiak (Alaska), 17

which means that a reference to Kodiak is to be found on page 187. In both indexes, commas, rather than dashes, are used to indicate separate mentions of a topic in adjacent pages, e.g.,

66, 67

References to captions consist of a boldface caption number (or range of caption numbers), followed by a hyphen and a page number. For example,

**223**-112

**86–87**-47

References to maps consist of a boldface capital "M" and map number (or range of map numbers) followed by a hyphen and a page number, e.g.,

**M8**-54

**M14–15**-107

Map captions are referred to similarly, but with an additional letter "C," e.g.,

**MC4**-16

# SUBJECT INDEX

# PLACE NAME INDEX

# CREDITS AND ACKNOWLEDGEMENTS

## PICTURES

*Key:*

**ACSAA** = Color Slide Project, University of Michigan, Ann Arbor; **AMNH** = American Museum of Natural History, New York; **AW** = Achille Weider, Zurich; **BAM** = Baghdad Museum; **BM** = British Museum, London; **BMFA** = Boston Museum of Fine Arts; **BMH** = Bishop Museum, Honolulu; **BN** = Bibliotheque Nationale, Paris; **BPK** = Bildarchiv Preussischer Kulturbesitz, Berlin; **CL** = Carl Lumholtz, *Through Central Borneo*, (New York: Scribners, 1920); **CRPH** = Cultural Relics Publishing House, Beijing; **CUL** = Columbia University, New York, The Libraries; **FI** = Frobenius Institute, Frankfurt; **FSC** = Film Study Center, Harvard, Cambridge; **JC** = Joseph Campbell; **JV** = Jean Vertut, Issy-les-Moulineaux, France; **LB** = Lee Boltin, Croton-On-Hudson, New York; **LM** = Lorna Marshall, Cambridge, Mass; **MAI** = Museum of the American Indian, New York; **MCSA** = Ministry of Culture and Science, Athens; **MG** = Musée Guimet, Paris; **MH** = Musée de l'Homme, Paris; **MMA** = Metropolitan Museum of Art, New York; **MV** = Museum für Völkerkunde, Munich; **MVB** = Museum für Völkerkunde, Berlin; **NYPL** = New York Public Library; **PM** = Peabody Museum, Cambridge, Mass; **PMC** = Paul Mellon Collection, Upperville, Virginia; **PW** = Paul Wirz, *Die Marind-Anim von Holländisch-Süd-Neu-Guinea*, (Hamburg: L. Friederichsen & Co., 1922-25); **SGM** = S.G. Morley, *The Ancient Maya*, (Stanford University Press, 1946); **SI** = Smithsonian Institution, Washington, D.C.; **UMP** = University Museum, Philadelphia; **VE** = Victor Englebert, Cali, Colombia.

**COVER:** Pinacoteca Gallery, Ferrara, Italy.

## PROLOGUE

**1** MG; **2** Uffizi, Florence; **3** FI; **4** Steven Fuller, Yellowstone, Wyoming; **5–6** New York Botanical Garden; **7** BMFA; **8** National Palace Museum, Taipei; **9** Egyptian National Museum, Cairo; **10** Egyptian Government Tourist Office; **11** CL; **12–13** AMNH; **14** Cranbrook Institute of Science, Bloomfield Hills, Mich.; **15** CL; **16** VE; **17** Michel Huet/Agence Hoa-Qui, Paris; **18** PW; **19–21** AMNH; **22** SI; **23** FI; **24** CL; **25** Jacques Jangoux/Peter Arnold, New York; **26** Norman Myres/Bruce Coleman Agency, New York; **27** BMH; **28** Jericho Excavation Fund, London; **29** PM; **30** LM; **31** Australian Information Service; **32–33** BMH; **34** AMNH; **35** Burt Glinn/Magnum; **36** Michel Huet/Agence Hoa Qui; **37** NYPL; **38** FI; **39** UMP; **40** VE; **41** AMNH; **42** Kern Institute, Leiden University, The Netherlands; **43** Robert Walter; **44** BM; **45** NYPL; **46** BMFA; **47–48** MAI; **49** Otto E. Nelson/The Asia Society, New York: Mr. & Mrs. John D. Rockefeller III Collection; **50** BM; **51** Stovall Museum, University of Oklahoma; **52** MAI; **53–54** University of Chicago Press; **55** AMNH; **56** SGM; **57** Peter T. Furst/*Maya Handschrift Der Landesbibliothek Dresden*, (Akademie-Verlag Berlin, GmbH); **58** E.A. Wallis Budge, *Osiris and the Egyptian Resurrection* (New York: G.P. Putnam's Sons, 1911); **59** SGM; **60** BBC/Radio Times Hulton; **61** JV; **62** LM; **63** N.R. Farbman/Time Inc.; **64** Eliot Elisofon/Museum of African Art/SI; **65** AMNH; **66** MG; **67** Sakamoto Photo Research Lab, Tokyo; **68** ACSAA

## THE SACRIFICE: THE PRIME SYMBOL: PMC

**69** CUL; **70** Pinacoteca Gallery, Ferrara, Italy; **71–72** FI; **73** Carnegie Institution, Washington D.C. **74** PM; **75** JC; **76** SGM; **77** MVB; **78** SGM; **79** NYPL; **80** LB; **81** AMNH; **82** Museum of Culture and Science, Heracleion, Crete; **83** Art Resources, New York; **84** BN; **85** Caecilia Moessner, Munich; **86** German Archaeological Institute, Rome; **87** del Museo Archaeologico Nazionale, Ferrara, Italy; **88** Victoria and Albert Museum, London; **89** Peter T. Furst/by permission of the Akademische Druck-und Verlagsanstalt, Graz; **90–91** MAI; **92** CUL; **93** NYPL; **94** G. Popper, London; **95** National Gallery, London; **96** CUL; **97** NYPL; **98** LB; **99** MV; **100** AMNH; **101** LB; **102** UMP; **103** Prof. Wm. G. Solheim, University of Hawaii, Honolulu; **104–107** UMP; **108** FSC; **109** Württemberg Museum, Stuttgart; **110–111** Marija Gimbutas, Los Angeles; **112** AMNH; **113** MCSA; **114** Marija Gimbutas, Los Angeles; **115** Michael Holford, London; **116** FSC; **117** JC; **118** FSC; **119** Kunsthistorisches Museum, Vienna; **120** Staatliche Antikensammlungen und Glyptothek, Munich; **121** BM; **122–154** PW; **155** AW; **156** JV; **157** MAI; **158** Edward S. Curtis/Philadelphia Museum of Art; **159** National Collection of Fine Arts, Washington, D.C.; **160** Victoria Museum, Harare, Zimbabwe; **161** MH; **162** San Francisco Museum of Fine Arts; **163** NYPL; **164** Photo Researchers, New York; **165** Hirmer Verlag, Munich; **166–167** BM; **168** UMP; **169** BAM; **170** JC; **171** UMP; **172–173** BM; **174** BAM; **175** UMP; **176** BAM; **177–179** BM; **180–181** UMP; **182** Institute of Archaeology, Hebrew University, Jerusalem; **183** Ny Carlsberg Glyptotek, Copenhagen; **184** American Institute of Indian Studies, Ramnegar, Varanesi, U.P.; **185** BMFA/Gift of Robert Treat Paine, Jr.; **186–187** German Archaeological Institute, Berlin; **188** BM; **189** The Louvre, Paris; **190** Library of the Jewish Theological Seminary, New York; **191** National Archaeological Museum, Naples; **192** BM; **193–195** CRPH; **196** Israel Museum, Jerusalem; **197** Museum of the Jewish Diaspora, Tel Aviv; **198–199** Government Museum, Mathura, U.P.; **200** Staatliche Museum, Berlin; **201** BM; **202** Museum of Archaeology, Mathura, U.P.; **203** Field Museum of Natural History, Chicago; **204–205** National Museum, New Delhi; **206** BPK; **207** M. Aurel Stein, *The Ruins of Desert Cathay*, (London: Macmillan & Co; 1912); **208–214** BPK; **215** CRPH; **216** Hiroki Fujita, Nara; **217** Benrido Company, Kyoto; **218** Sandak, Stamford, Conn.; **219** Dumbarton Oaks Center for Byzantine Studies, Washington, D.C.; **220–221** BM; **222** ACSAA; **223** Rheinisches Landesmuseum, Bonn; **224** MMA

## MAPS

**Maps 1, 2, 3, 4.** Based in part on information adapted from Carl O. Sauer, *Seeds, Spades, Hearths & Herds: The Domestication of Animals and Foodstuffs*, 2nd. ed. (Cambridge: M.I.T. Press, 1969; used with permission of the American Geographical Society); Carl O. Sauer, *Agricultural Origins and Dispersals* (New York: American Geographical Society, 1952); D.B. Grigg, *The Agricultural Systems of the World* (New York: Cambridge University Press, 1974); A. Sherratt, ed., *The Cambridge Encyclopedia of Archaeology* (New York: Crown Publishers Inc./Cambridge University Press, 1980; used with permission of Scepter Books, Inc.); R. van Chi-Bonnardel, *The Atlas of Africa* (The Free Press/Macmillan Publishing Co., Inc., 1973; used with permission of Editions Jeune Afrique); J.F. Ajayi and M. Crowder et al., eds., *Historical Atlas of Africa* (New York: Cambridge University Press, 1985); Stuart Struever, ed., *Prehistoric Agriculture* (Garden City, NY: The Ameican Museum of Natural History, 1971); P. Vidal-Naquet, ed., *The Harper Atlas of World History* (New York: Harper & Row, 1987); Geoffrey Barraclough, ed., *The Times Atlas of World History* (London: Times Books Ltd., 1978); *Cultivated Plants and their Wild Relatives* by P.M. Zukovski. 1962, CAB International, Wallingford, Oxfordshire, UK; F.E. Zeuner, *A History of Domesticated Animals* (New York: Harper & Row, 1963).

**Map 5.** Based in part on information adapted from C.L. Riley et al., *Man across the Sea* (Austin: University of Texas Press, 1971).

**Map 8.** Based in part on information adapted from P.S. Bellwood, *Man's Conquest of the Pacific* (New York: Oxford University Press, 1978; used with permission of Collins Publishing, New Zealand), and D. Newton, *New Guinea Art in the Collection of the Museum of Primitive Art* (Greenwich, Conn.: New York Graphic Society/The Museum of Primitive Art, 1967).

**Map 9.** Based in part on information adapted from David and Ruth Whitehouse, *Archaeological Atlas of the World* (London: Thames and Hudson, Ltd., 1975); J. Hughes and C. Flon, eds., *The World Atlas of Archaeology* (Boston: G.K. Hall & Co., 1985); and A. Sherratt, ed., *The Cambridge Encyclopedia of Archaeology* (New York: Crown Publishers Inc./Cambridge University Press, 1980; used with permission of Scepter Books, Inc.).

**Map 11.** Based in part on information adapted from Michael Grant, *Atlas of Ancient History* (Moonachie, N.J.: Dorset Press/Marboro Books, 1983); G. Duby, *Atlas Historique Larousse* (Paris: Librairie Larousse, 1978); A. Cottrell, ed., *The Encyclopedia of Ancient Civilizations* (New York: Mayflower Books, 1980); H. Erichstier et al., *Westermann Grosser Atlas zur Weltgeschichte* (Braunschweig, F.R.G.: Westermann Schulbuchverlag GmbH, 1985); P. Vidal-Naquet, ed., *The Harper Atlas of World History* (Harper & Row: 1987); and H. Ginsburg and H. Fullard, eds., *Aldine University Atlas* (Chicago: Aldine Publishing Co./George Philip & son Ltd., 1969).

**Map 12.** Based in part on information adapted from J.P. O'Neill and M.E.D. Laing, eds., *Along the Ancient Silk Routes* (New York: The Metropolitan Museum of Art, 1982); *Shepherd's Historical Atlas* by R.W. Shepherd, Barnes & Noble, Inc., Totowa, N.J.; J. Hughes and C. Flon, eds., *The World Atlas of Archaeology* (Boston: G.K. Hall & Co., 1985); and A. Sherratt, ed., *The Cambridge Encyclopedia of Archaeology* (New York: Crown Publishers, Inc./Cambridge University Press, 1980).

**Map 13.** Based in part on information adapted from Peter C. Swann, *Chinese Monumental Art* (Minneapolis: Viking Press, 1963); and J.P. O'Neill and M.E.D. Laing, eds., *Along the Ancient Silk Routes* (New York: The Metropolitan Musuem of Art, 1982).

**Map 14.** Based in part on information adapted from Francis Robinson, *Atlas of the Islamic World Since 1500* (New York: Facts on File, Inc./Equinox (Oxford) Ltd., 1982); Georges Duby, *Atlas Historique Larousse* (Paris: Librairie Larousse, 1978); R.I. Moore, *Rand McNally Historical Atlas of the World* (Chicago: Rand McNally and Co., 1981); *Shepherd's Historical Atlas* by R.W. Shepherd, Barnes & Noble, Inc., Totowa, N.J.; and H. Chadwick and G.R. Evans, eds., *Atlas of the Christian Church* (New York: Facts on File, Inc./Equinox (Oxford) Ltd., 1987).

HISTORICAL ATLAS OF
WORLD MYTHOLOGY

Editorial Director: *Robert Walter*

Designer: *Jos. Trautwein/Bentwood Studio*

Art/Photo Editor: *Rosemary O'Connell*

Associate Editors: *Hugh Haggerty*
*Antony Van Couvering*

Indexer: *Linda Buskus/Northwind Editorial Services*

Maps: *Cartographic Services Center of R.R. Donnelley & Sons Company*

Map Design: *Sidney P. Marland III*

Map Research, Compilation, and Project Coordination: *Luis Freile*

Map Drafting and Production: *Dan Etter*

Type Composition: *Typographic Art, Inc.*

Printing and binding: *Royal Smeets Offset, B.V., The Netherlands*